The Campus History Series

California State University, Dominguez Hills

On the Cover: Members of a dance repertory class led by Prof. Carol Tobbs pose on Claire Falkenstein's sculpture ***The Forum*** in the California State University, Dominguez Hills Sculpture Garden around 1985–1986. (Courtesy of University Archives, California State University, Dominguez Hills.)

The Campus History Series

CALIFORNIA STATE UNIVERSITY, DOMINGUEZ HILLS

GREGORY L. WILLIAMS

ARCADIA PUBLISHING

ISBN 978-0-7385-8005-0

Published by Arcadia Publishing
Charleston SC, Chicago IL, Portsmouth NH, San Francisco CA

Printed in the United States of America

Library of Congress Catalog Card Number: 2009935199

For all general information contact Arcadia Publishing at:
Telephone 843-853-2070
Fax 843-853-0044
E-mail sales@arcadiapublishing.com
For customer service and orders:
Toll-Free 1-888-313-2665

Visit us on the Internet at www.arcadiapublishing.com

For Anna, Class of 2012, 2016, and beyond.

CONTENTS

ACKNOWLEDGMENTS

The opportunity to write and compile this 50th-anniversary history of California State University, Dominguez Hills has been a great privilege. I'd like to thank university president Mildred García and university advancement vice president Greg Saks for the opportunity to complete this project. Special thanks go to the photographers who spent their professional lives on campus documenting CSU Dominguez Hills. Many of the early photographs are the work of Cliff Brown, and many more were taken by Gary Kuwahara, whose artful images, vision, and years of service in documenting this campus deserve applause.

I'd also like to thank archivist Tom Philo for his assistance and guidance during the production of the book. Thanks are also due to library dean Sandra Parham, wise historian and emeritus professor of history Judson Grenier, and former university president Donald R. Gerth for sharing their knowledge and enthusiasm for the history of this campus. Additional thanks go to Kathy Zimmerer, Tom Marinello, Bill DeLuca, Irene Vasquez, Guy Witherspoon, Lui Amador, Mel Miranda, Joanna Dunklee, Stewart Baker, Danelle Moon, Amy Bentley-Smith, Joanie Harmon, Brenda Knepper, and many other members of the university community. More thanks go to former university archivists, founding history faculty, and librarians who have helped make the Archives and Special Collections at the CSU Dominguez Hills library an important resource for the study of this campus and California.

Sources for this book come predominately from the University Archives collections (archives.csudh.edu), including university news releases, presidential records, student newspapers, yearbooks, and issues of *Inside Dominguez Hills*. Harry Nethery's history of the first 10 years of Dominguez Hills was also helpful. Most importantly, Jud Grenier's *The Rainbow Years*, a history of the first 25 years of the university, is essential in the study of the university. Photographs in this volume come from the University Archives and other campus sources except where noted. There are limitations to relying on university-produced photographs instead of individual snapshots, and this has led to a lack of images in some instances.

Finally, the story of CSU Dominguez Hills deserves a telling beyond this photograph history. The campus presents an amazing case study on how a university forms, matures, and thrives.

INTRODUCTION

The land encompassing California State University, Dominguez Hills has a vast and fascinating history that connects the diverse students on campus to a unique and equally diverse past. Dominguez Hills is named for the family that received the first land grant in California. The Rancho San Pedro was granted to Juan Jose Dominguez, a retired Spanish soldier, in 1784 by King Carlos III. The original grant covered 75,000 acres and included current-day San Pedro, Palos Verdes, Torrance, Redondo Beach, Lomita, Gardena, Harbor City, Wilmington, Carson, Compton, and parts of Long Beach and Paramount. Manuel Dominguez inherited the lands of the rancho in the 1820s and fought to consolidate the family's hold on the lands despite losing the Palos Verdes Peninsula to the Sepulveda family in the 1830s. He and his wife, Maria Engracia Cota, raised several children on the rancho and were prominent in the political, social, and religious life of Los Angeles and California. After Manuel's death in 1882, the land was divided among his six daughters, three of whom married into the Carson, Del Amo, and Watson families. While some of the lands were sold to develop the ports of Long Beach and Los Angeles and the cities of Wilmington, Torrance, and Compton, the sisters maintained control over much of the property by operating land management companies. Some of the land companies still exist today, operated by Carson and Watson descendants.

The need for a campus in the South Bay region of Los Angeles County became apparent in the late 1950s in light of a rising population influenced by the growth of families of World War II veterans and also by the emerging aerospace and defense industries. The California State Legislature acted to locate a college somewhere between the Los Angeles International Airport and San Pedro. At the same time, there was a great deal of higher education planning in California, which resulted in the 1960 Master Plan for Higher Education and the establishment of the California State Colleges (CSC) system. This interest in a coordinated, statewide higher education system had its influence on those planning the college that was initially called South Bay State College.

The first president, Leo F. Cain, was hired to establish the college in 1962. Between 1962 and 1966, Cain hired a stable of administrators and faculty while waiting for the CSC Board of Trustees to establish a final location for the campus. Cain, wanting to avoid a college that looked too institutionalized, hired the firm of A. Quincy Jones to create a campus physical master plan. At this time, the college was renamed California State College, Palos Verdes. The academic plan called upon many traditional liberal arts and sciences programs but also included new and experimental aspects. Students would be required to take two majors, one a traditional program, the other an interdisciplinary major. The original plans also called for establishment of a "small college" with experimental interdisciplinary programs that students would complete in three years. Faculty members were hired on the basis that they would be teaching at a liberal arts and sciences college in the somewhat remote coastal community of Palos Verdes.

After several years of wrangling over where the college would be located, classes at CSC Palos Verdes began in 1965 in a California Federal Bank building in Rolling Hills Estates, near Torrance. The 1965–1966 schedule of classes consisted of one page offering about 10 classes per semester. Between 40 and 50 students were taught by 11 faculty members, although each administrator also taught classes. Meanwhile, after the original Palos Verdes site had been ruled out because of land costs, the college's planning committee considered another 40 sites for the campus location. In the spring of 1965, the process was narrowed to three sites: San Pedro, Torrance, and Dominguez Hills. After the Watts Riots in Los Angeles in the summer of 1965, Gov. Edmund "Pat" Brown visited the area and determined that the Dominguez Hills site in the soon-to-be city of Carson would have the added advantage of attracting diverse students from a variety of communities. CSC Palos Verdes became CSC Dominguez Hills in 1966 and was moved into an apartment-like quad building constructed for the college's use in 100 days by developer Ray Watt. The temporary location, known as the Watt Campus, stood across the street from 346 acres of cattle-grazing land dotted with oil wells on a wide hill that would become the permanent campus. By 1967, the campus produced its first graduating class, consisting of four students.

Years of planning, however, came face to face with the reality of the new campus site and the expanded population it was meant to serve. The college planners and faculty, as well as the greater society, adjusted and listened to more voices. Rather than having a student body consisting of strictly suburban students, the college became accessible to students from more urban areas. With the inclusion of a diverse population of students, the campus curriculum began to expand by adding professional programs. Slowly the campus moved across the street to its innovative Small College. By 1973, the campus core, including the Educational Resources Center/Library, Natural Sciences and Mathematics, and Social and Behavior Sciences buildings, had opened.

President Cain retired in 1976. By that time, enrollment exceeded 6,800 students. Dr. Donald R. Gerth was hired as the second university president. During Gerth's eight years at the helm, several more campus buildings were completed, including Humanities and Fine Arts, the University Theatre, the gymnasium, and student housing. In addition, the college expanded its curriculum to include several additional areas of study, including health studies. In 1977, the college was awarded university status, and its name became California State University, Dominguez Hills.

In 1984, Dr. Richard Butwell was named president, and following his death in 1986, he was succeeded by Dr. John Brownell. In 1989, Dr. Robert Detweiler was named president, and he served until 1998. Herbert Carter served as interim president until Dr. James Lyons took over in 1999. Lyons served until 2007, when Dr. Mildred García became president. These administrators, along with faculty and staff, have fought to keep the university available to all interested students, committed the university to working with local employers, and worked with the community to bring about successful partnerships.

In 1984, the university hosted the cycling portion of the Los Angeles Olympics. A large outdoor velodrome was constructed. In 2003, the campus continued its sporting traditions by welcoming the Home Depot Center, an athletics and entertainment destination for fans of soccer, tennis, track and field, and cycle racing. The Home Depot Center is headquarters for two Major League Soccer teams, including the L.A. Galaxy and its star, David Beckham. The 27,000-seat stadium is also used for concerts and for commencement ceremonies.

The university has always highlighted its committed faculty and small classes to a diverse student population, many of whom are the first in their families to attend a university. In the words of Pres. Mildred García, the university is committed to "serving students who are hungry to learn and who are seizing the opportunity for intellectual empowerment and economic independence."

One

CAMPUS BEGINNINGS

THE 1960S

In the short history of our own college, change and uncertainty have been almost a way of life. . . . Within our first year of operation the college not only changed its location, but its name. . . . We found ourselves at the end of this first year closely bound together in the enterprise of higher education; more aware than ever that our institution should not become just another 'knowledge factory'; that, rather it should be a testament to man's perennial struggle to make a better world for himself, his children and his children's children.

—Pres. Leo Cain in the 1965–1966 yearbook.

At times, CSU Dominguez Hills has seemed caught in a maze of unyielding circumstance and social change. First it was a suburban college housed in a bank building in Rolling Hills Estate, then an urban college in an apartment complex, and finally a university in a beautiful setting in Carson with modern buildings. First there was a homogeneous set of students from the South Bay suburbs, and then there were those from throughout Los Angeles, bringing to campus students of African American, Hispanic, Asian, and European heritage. And at first there were college-age students, and then students of all ages and abilities. The university's tradition of welcoming diverse and non-traditional students began in the 1960s.

As 125 students moved onto the Dominguez Hills Watt Campus in 1966, the site was not yet ideal. Oil well fires occasionally took place across the street on what was to become the permanent campus. Rarely were classes full. Only one of 56 classes had more than the state average of 20 students, according to a state audit. Nevertheless, education took place. The interests and activities of students ranged from automobiles and camping to protesting tuition, the Vietnam War, and local police actions. By the end of the decade, groups of African American and Hispanic students had formed organizations to lobby for a more diverse faculty and curriculum. While the 1960s ended in some discord, the lack of an entrenched bureaucracy and the presence of a young faculty resulted in minimal campus unrest at CSC Dominguez Hills.

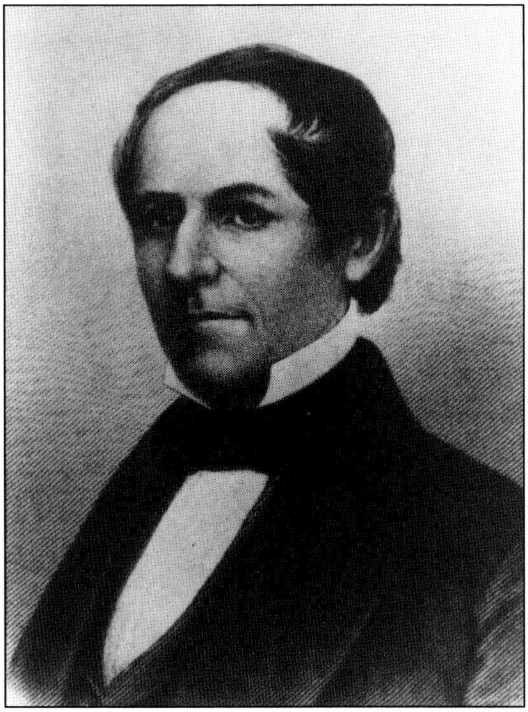

The land surrounding and including CSU Dominguez Hills is part of the original 75,000-acre Rancho San Pedro, granted to Juan Jose Dominguez by King Carlos III of Spain in 1784. Manuel Dominguez (pictured here) inherited the rancho in the 1820s. While California was controlled by Mexico and later by the United States, Manuel consolidated his hold on the lands, developed a rancho headquarters, and served in many civic capacities in Los Angeles.

The daughters of Manuel Dominguez inherited the remaining lands of the Rancho San Pedro in the late 19th century. Three of the sisters are pictured below (left side first row) in 1910, when the Los Angeles International Aviation Meet was held on Dominguez lands. This aviation event was the first international meet held in the United States and planted the seed for the aerospace industry in Southern California.

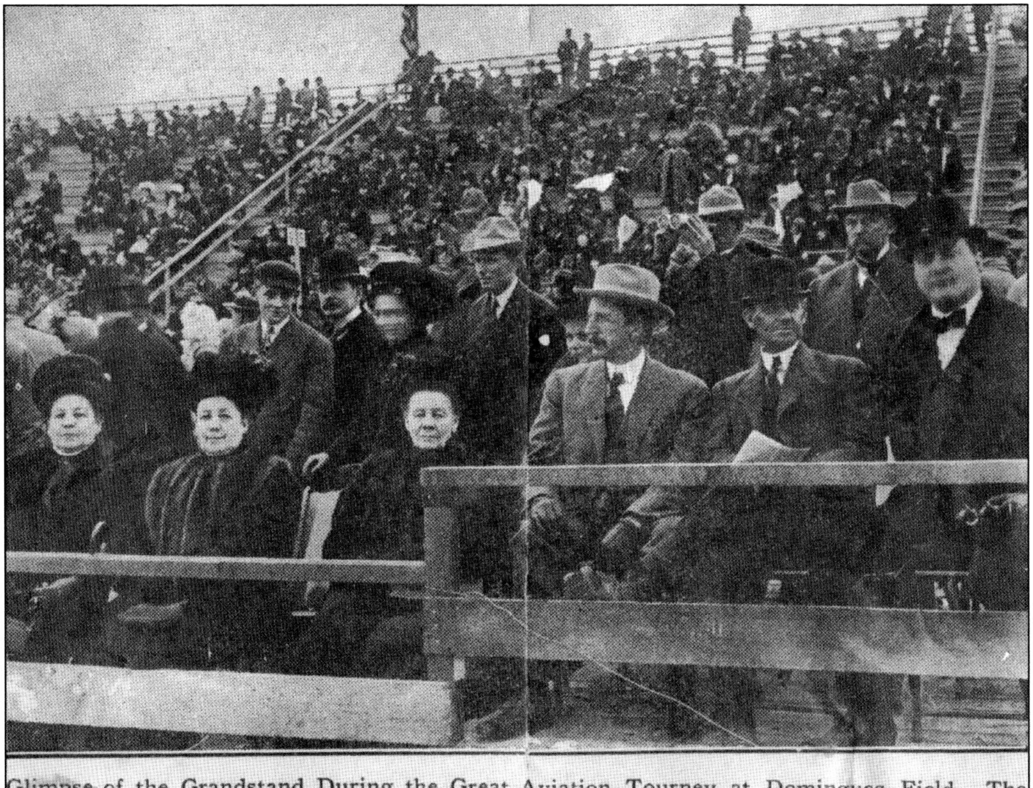

Glimpse of the Grandstand During the Great Aviation Tourney at Dominguez Field. The Three Ladies at the Lower Left Are Three Sisters, Daughters of Manuel Dominguez

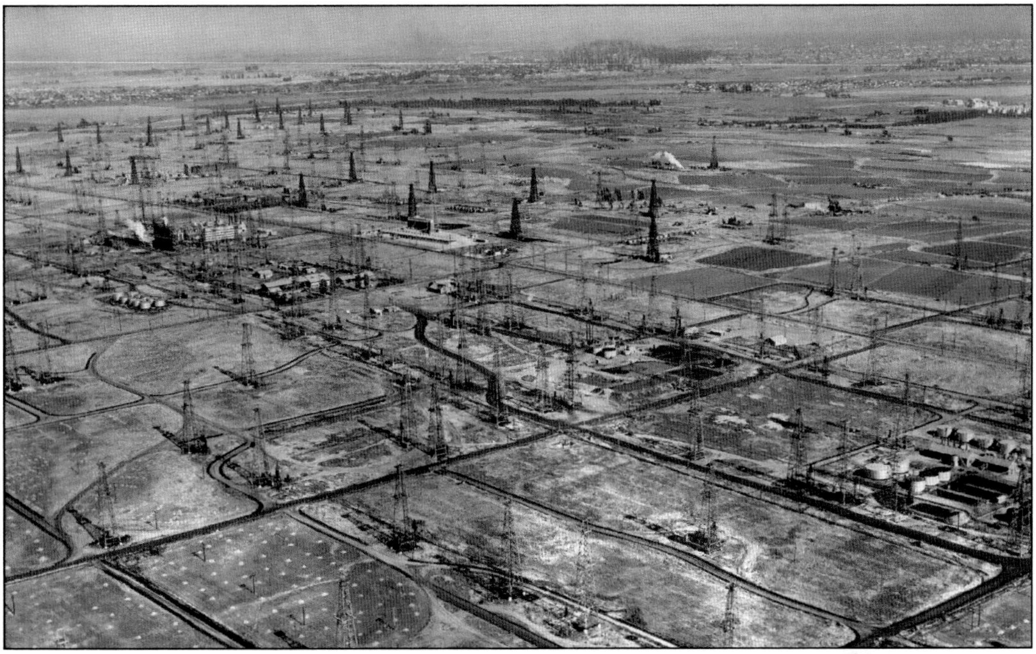

After World War I, oil drilling and oil refineries spread throughout South Bay Los Angeles. Among the many areas dotted with oil derricks was Dominguez Hills. The area brought considerable wealth to the Dominguez heirs through the 1940s. The oil fields were still in evidence when the college arrived at Dominguez Hills in 1966.

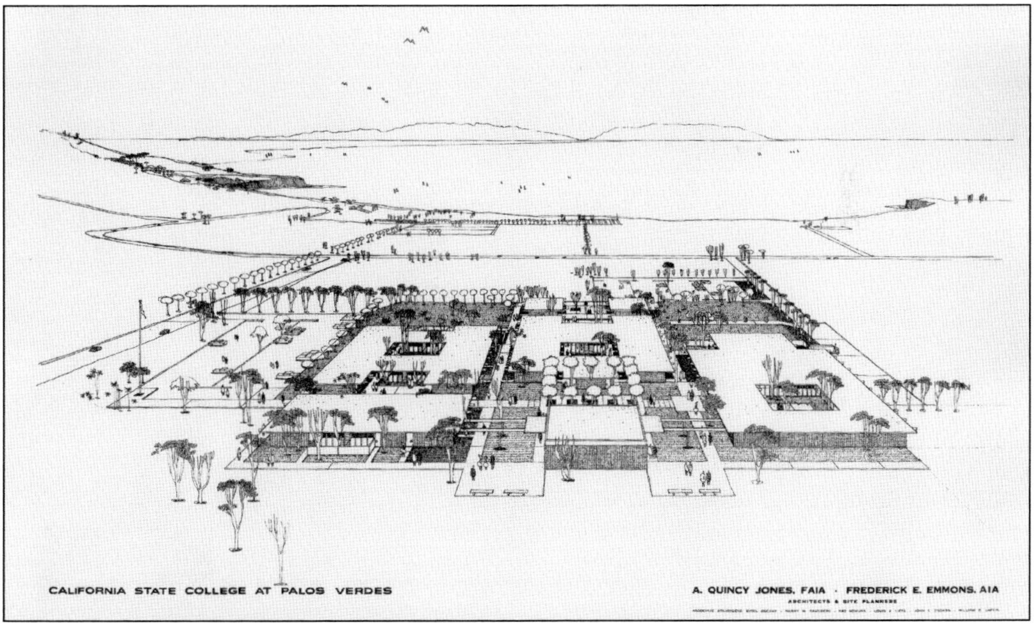

Reacting to calls for a state college along the coastal area of southern Los Angeles County, the California legislature established South Bay State College in 1960. After considerable debate about location, Palos Verdes was chosen. The college was named CSC Palos Verdes in 1962. This view of the campus envisioned by architect A. Quincy Jones and the eventual campus at Dominguez Hills share a similar layout, minus the ocean views.

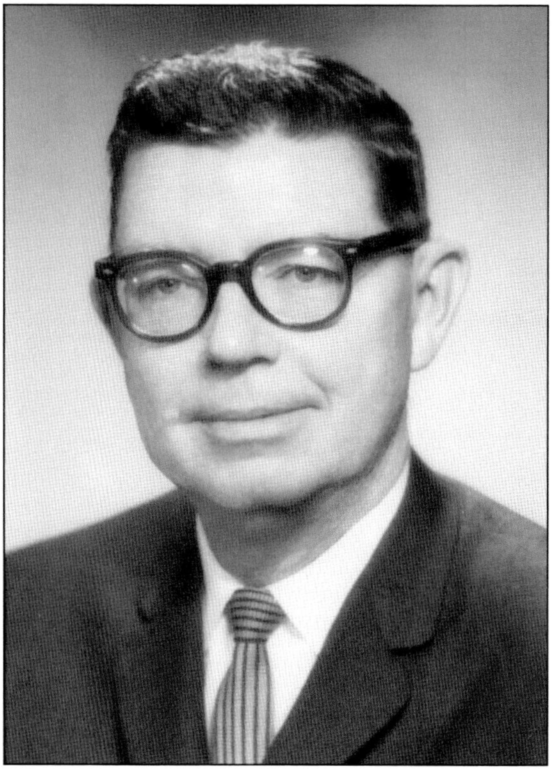

Leo Cain was appointed president of South Bay State College in 1962 and guided the establishment of the college through two name changes, 40-plus potential sites, political attempts to shut down the college, and the institution's architectural and curriculum development. Previously Cain had taught at San Francisco State College, where he'd created courses for teachers of gifted and disadvantaged children.

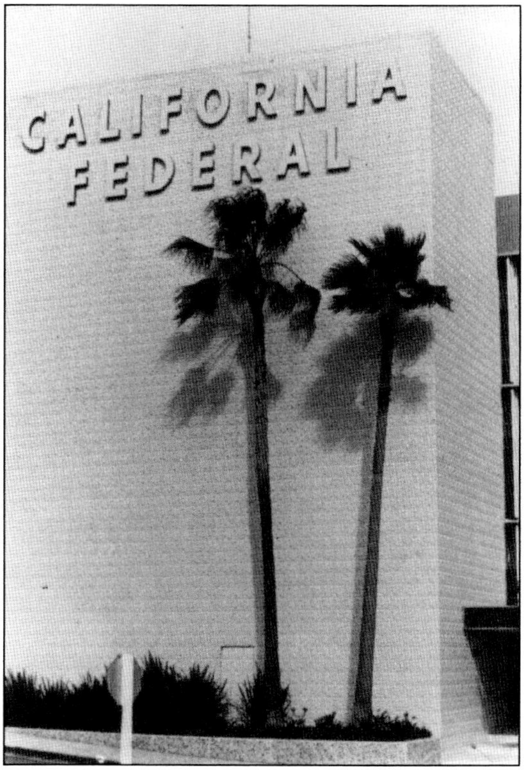

California State College, Palos Verdes opened its doors in the fall of 1965 at the California Federal Bank in Rolling Hills Estates until a permanent campus was found. Classes were held on the second floor of the bank during the 1965–1966 academic year. Between 40 and 50 freshmen and juniors enrolled and were taught by 11 faculty members. Ping-pong tables were provided for extracurricular activity.

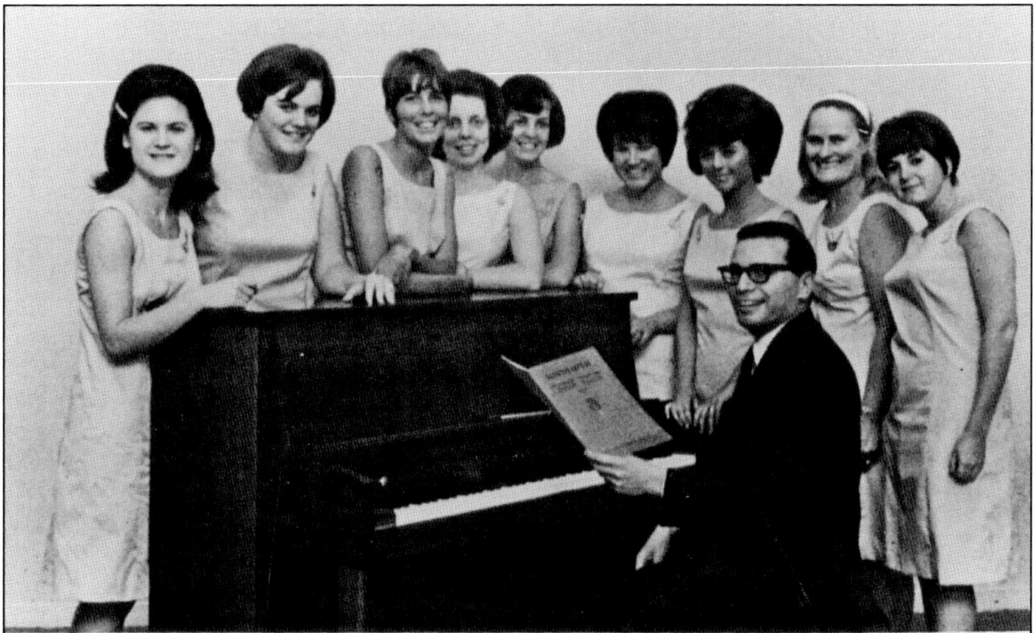

WOMEN'S CHORALE L-R Irene Peterlin, Jill Kennedy, Maryann Ivons, Judy Moyer, Janelle Cohen, Martha Austin, Judy Wurtz, Mr. Bialosky, Amy Hoffman, Dana Carpenter

Nearly all of the women of California State College, Palos Verdes joined the Woman's Chorale. Conducted by music professor Marshall Bialosky (seated), the chorale performed for a Christmas gathering at the college and throughout Palos Verdes. The chorale continued to perform for a few more years after moving to the Dominguez Hills campus.

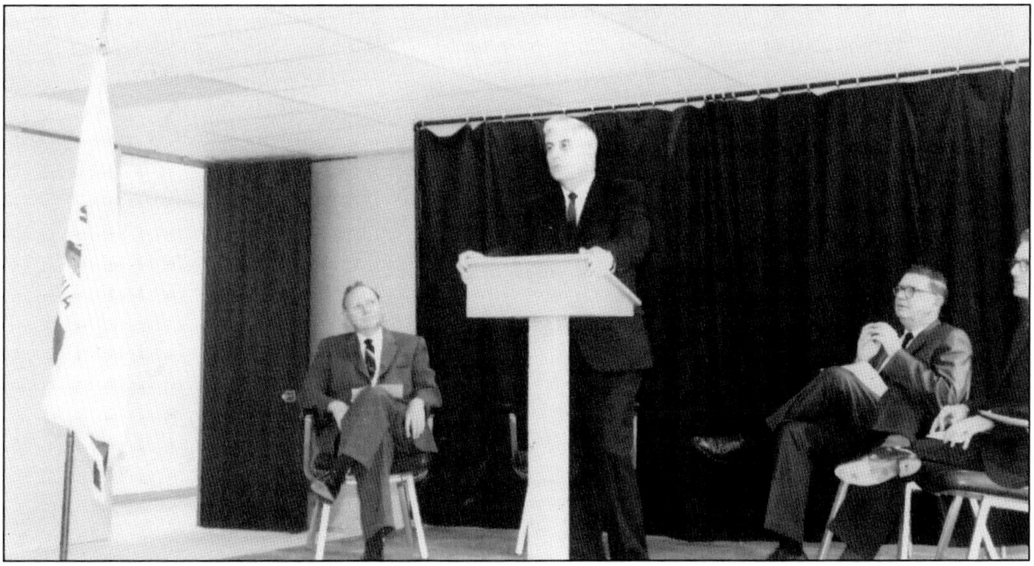

In May 1966, with no students to graduate, the honors convocation was held in an improvised auditorium at the bank building. CSC chancellor Glenn Dumke attended and said, "the possibility of attending a brand-new college is a tremendous experience." Awards were given for student publications, academic achievement, outstanding freshmen, and outstanding community service (for the landlord—the bank). A week later, the CSC Palos Verdes name was history.

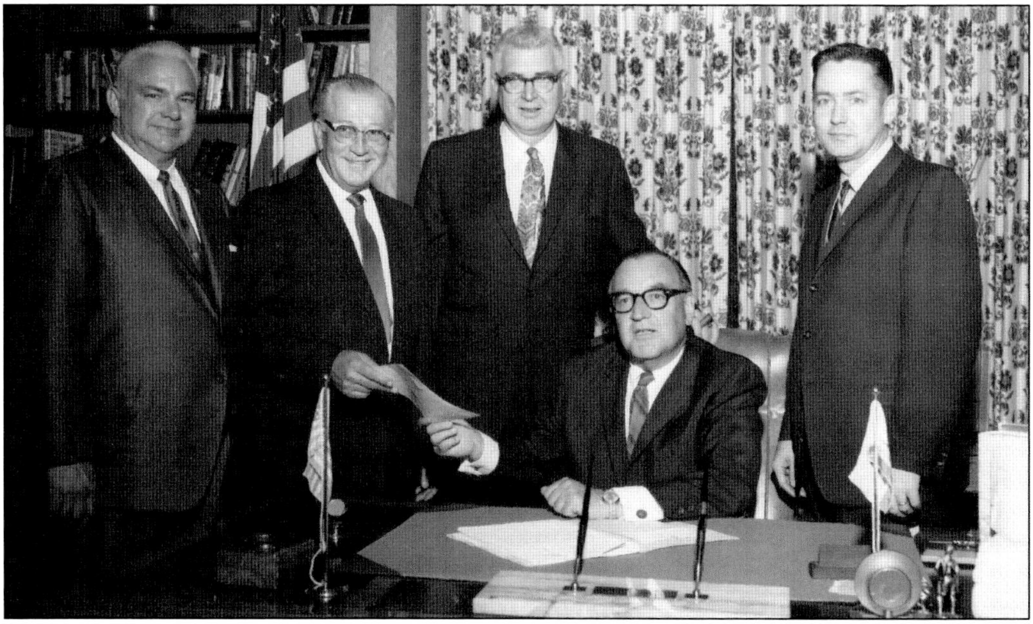

The plan to purchase land in Palos Verdes was abandoned because of increasing land costs. By mid-1965, the Dominguez Hills area was among the many contenders for the campus, and after the Watts Riots in South Los Angeles, that choice was reinforced. In March 1966, Gov. Edmund "Pat" Brown authorized the purchase of 346 acres of land at Dominguez Hills. The land was purchased for nearly $11 million.

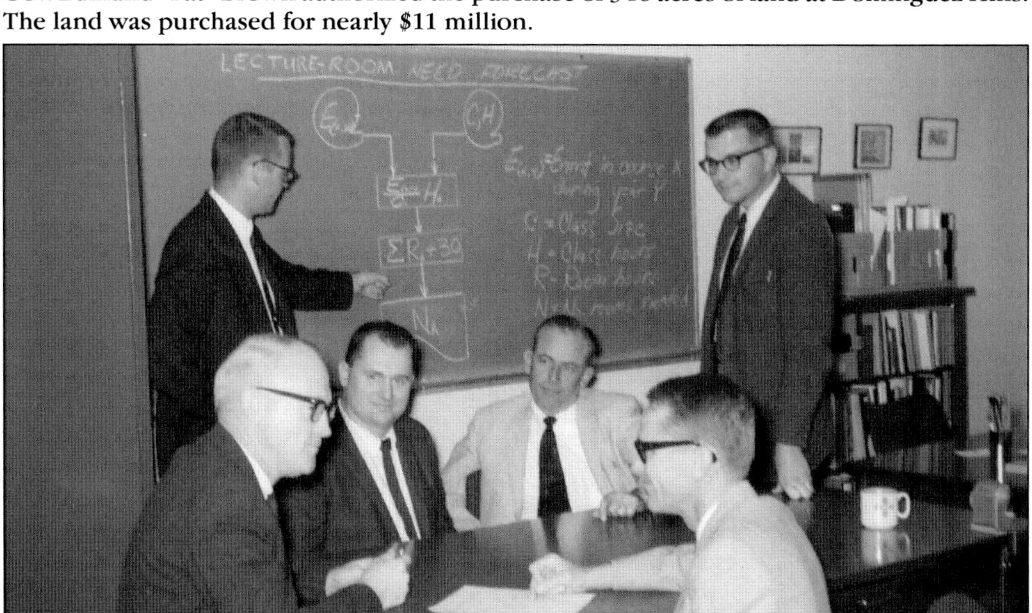

At a facilities planning meeting in 1965, CSC Palos Verdes deans and faculty met with a computer project specialist to develop an information and communication system. From left to right are (standing) programmer Don Dougherty and building program manager Tom Bullock; (seated) Vice Pres. Lyle E. Gibson, assistant mathematics professor John Gardner, dean of College Services and Facilities Planning Harry Nethery, and computers director Don Mild (in foreground).

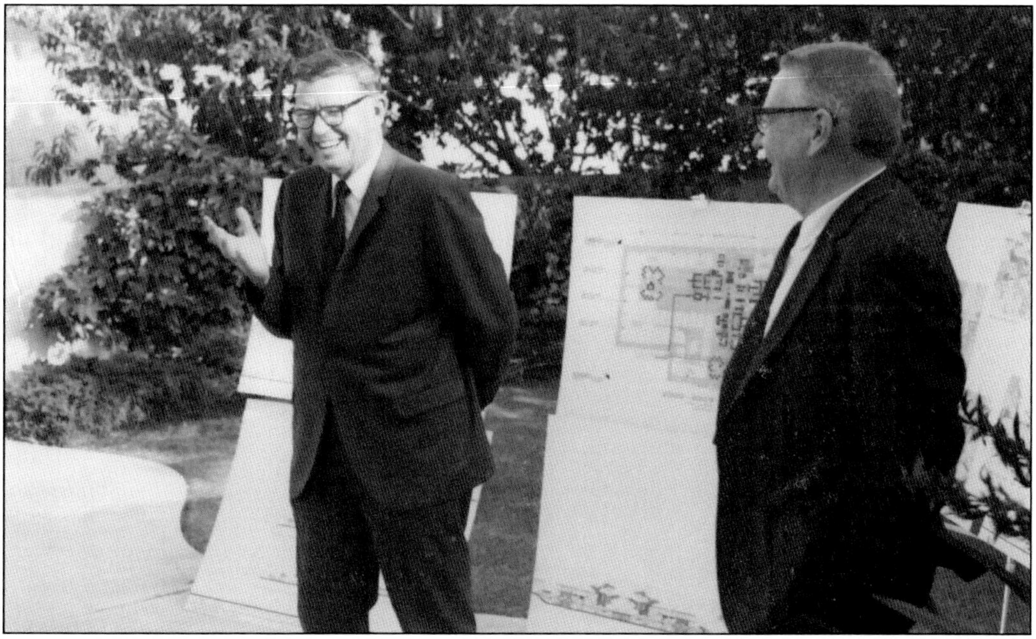

College president Leo Cain (left) and campus architect A. Quincy Jones present the physical master plan for the campus in 1965. Cain wanted a contemporary and cohesive campus. Jones set out to eliminate the oil fields and views of heavy industry. The campus plan arose from a concept to encourage students to cross academic disciplines and the physical spaces that represent those disciplines.

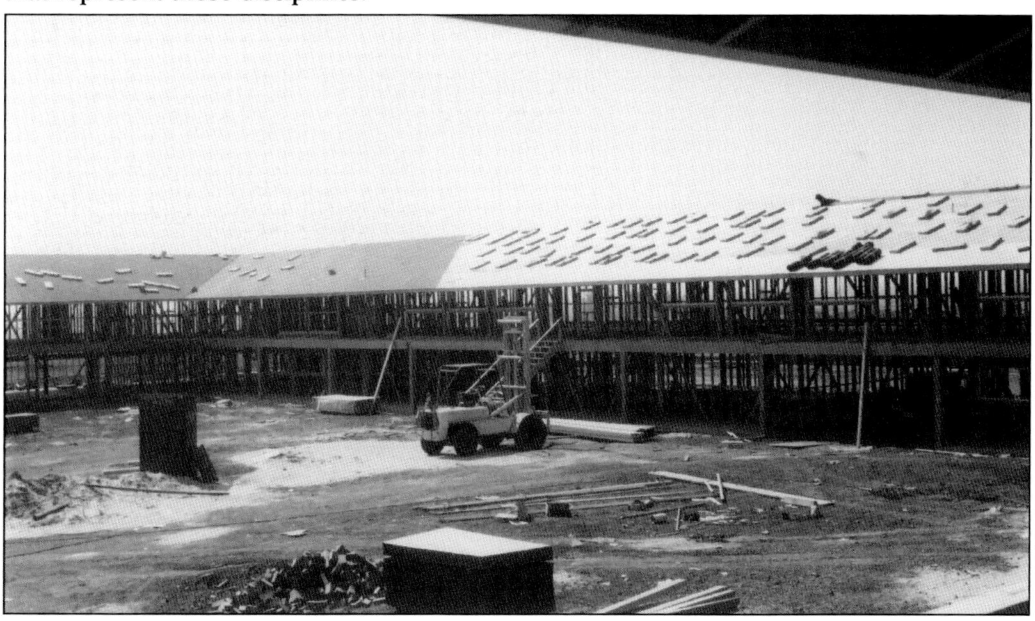

Built by Ray A. Watt of Gardena, the temporary campus across from the permanent site took less than four months to complete. The two-story, apartment-like building was constructed on a "crash program," according to President Cain. The 64,000-square-foot building could accommodate up to 600 students. Administrators were given a day to name the new college. It became the only CSC campus to include a family name in its title.

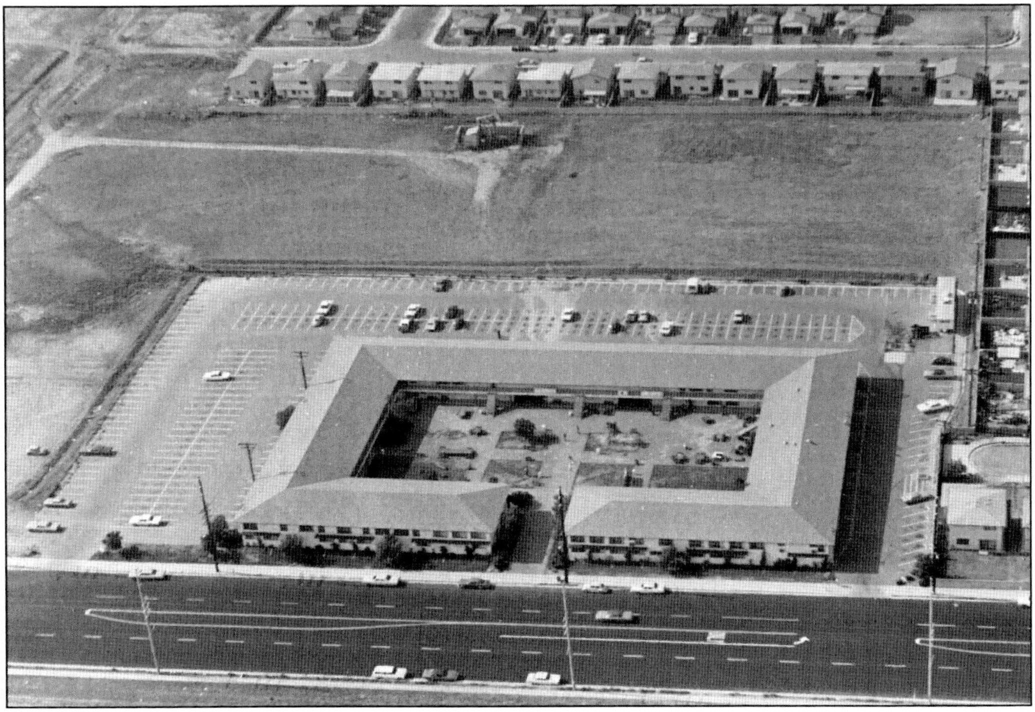

With negotiations to purchase the permanent campus still incomplete, faculty, staff, and administrators moved into the Watt Campus on August 26, 1966. Later that week, the college officially became California State College, Dominguez Hills. Registration for what the *Los Angeles Times* called a "space-age institution of learning" began on September 19. Classes began three days later. The first extracurricular event was a dance called the "Hootenanny Under the Stars."

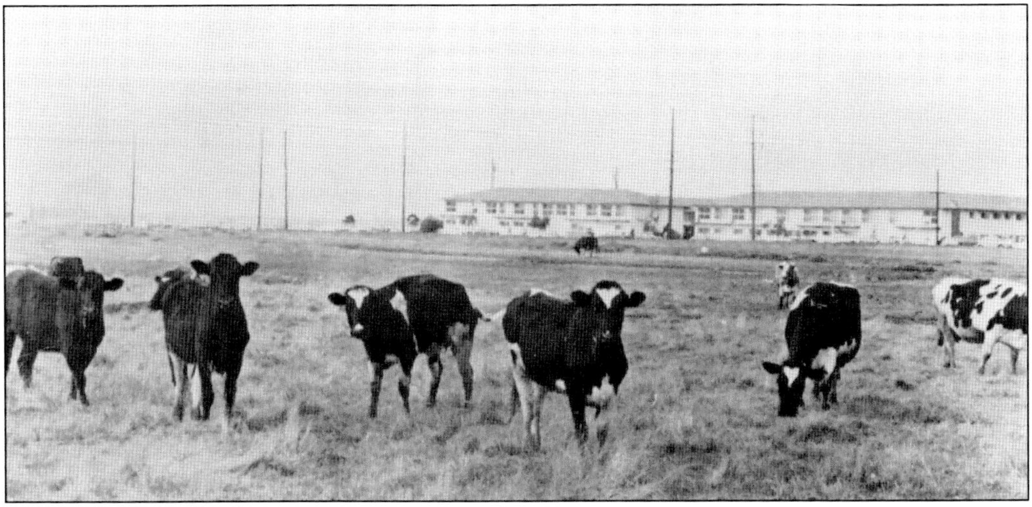

The most prevalent inhabitants of the future college site were cattle. Biology professor Lois Chi remembered in 1991, "I used to say there were more cows than there were students." Larry McClelland, an employee, noted that "cowboys would round-up cattle and take them down to where the mobile home park is now." The student newspaper and *Los Angeles Times* worried about the spirit of the Dominguez cowboy as his eviction neared.

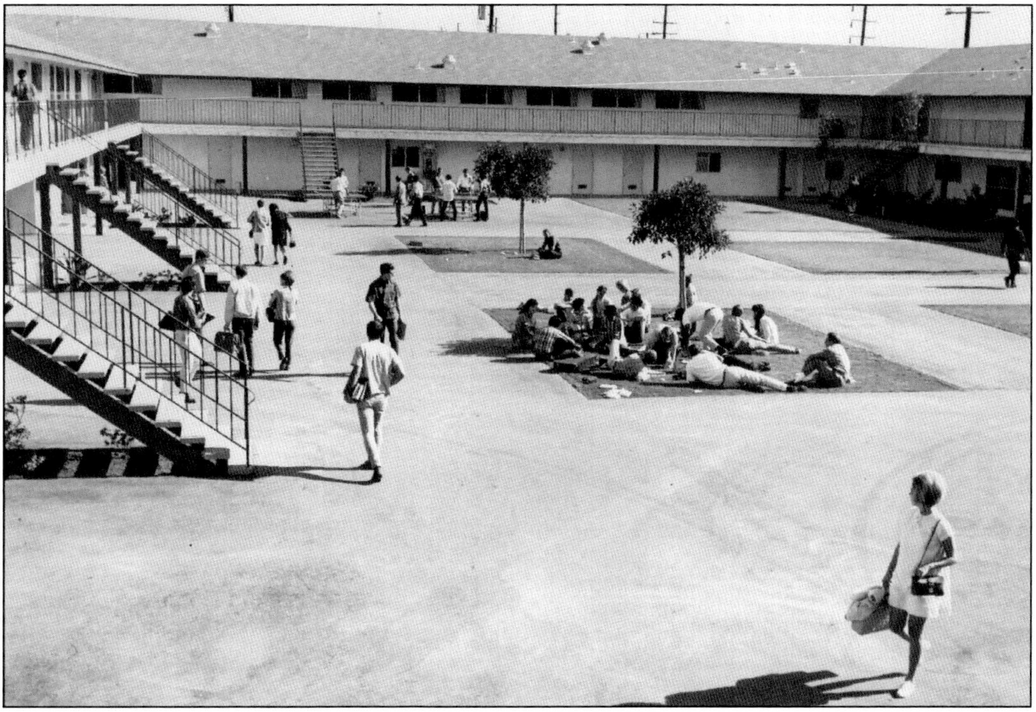

"It was a nice, close environment," said Larry McClelland. "The campus looked more like a motel than a university, two stories centered around a courtyard. I literally knew all the students, and you could look out the window and see what everyone was up to." One student columnist quipped: "The vending machines are just down the hall. . . . Check out time is 5:30. The only thing missing is room service."

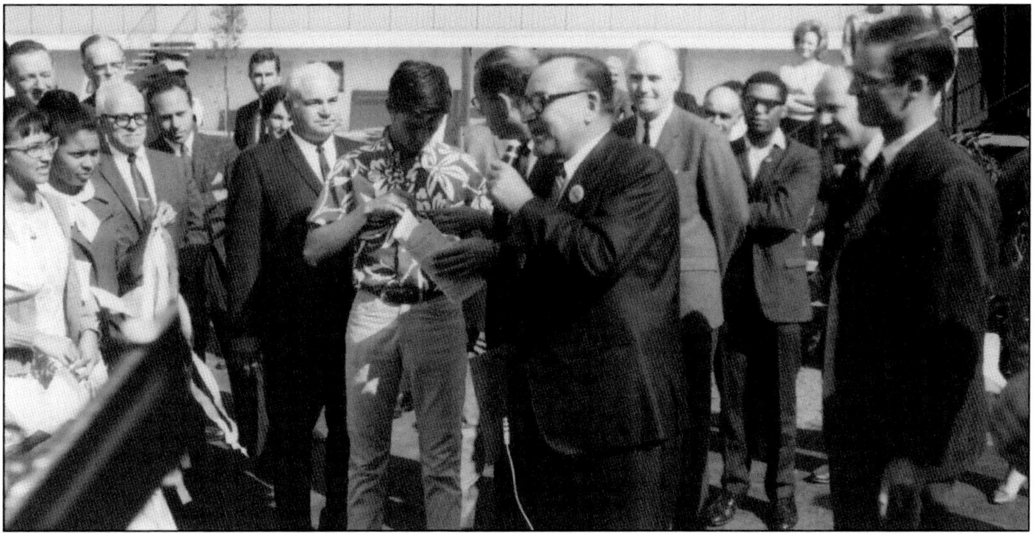

Visiting "the baby of the State College system," as he called it, Gov. Pat Brown stated a week before the 1966 gubernatorial election that "the state's investment in education benefits not only students, but everyone in the state." He also said that students should vote for him because his rival favored charging tuition. Ronald Reagan won the election. Class fees were introduced to the CSC system within the year.

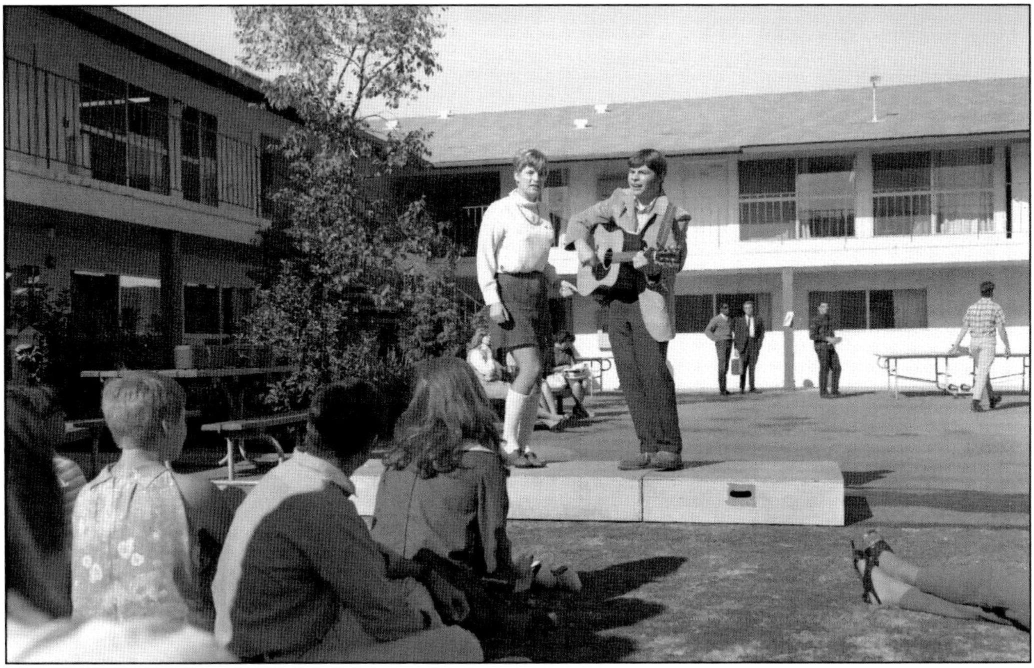

As students listen, Ron Griffin (right) joins a female student in a folk duet on a temporary platform in the Watt Campus courtyard during the 1968–1969 academic year.

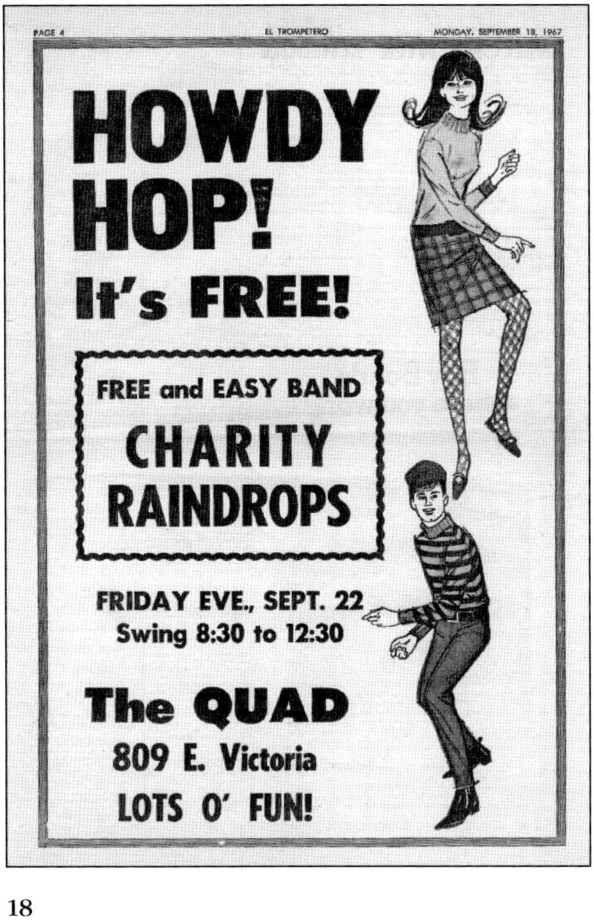

Each new academic year, students were greeted with a dance and social event. In September 1967, the Howdy Hop dance took place on the quad at the Watt Campus.

The Students Interested in Black America Club was formed during the 1967–1968 academic year in response to students who saw the need for a black student organization on campus. The club gathered food and clothing donations for charities in Mississippi and presented speakers for Black History Week. It was a prelude to the Black Student Union, which formed during the next academic year.

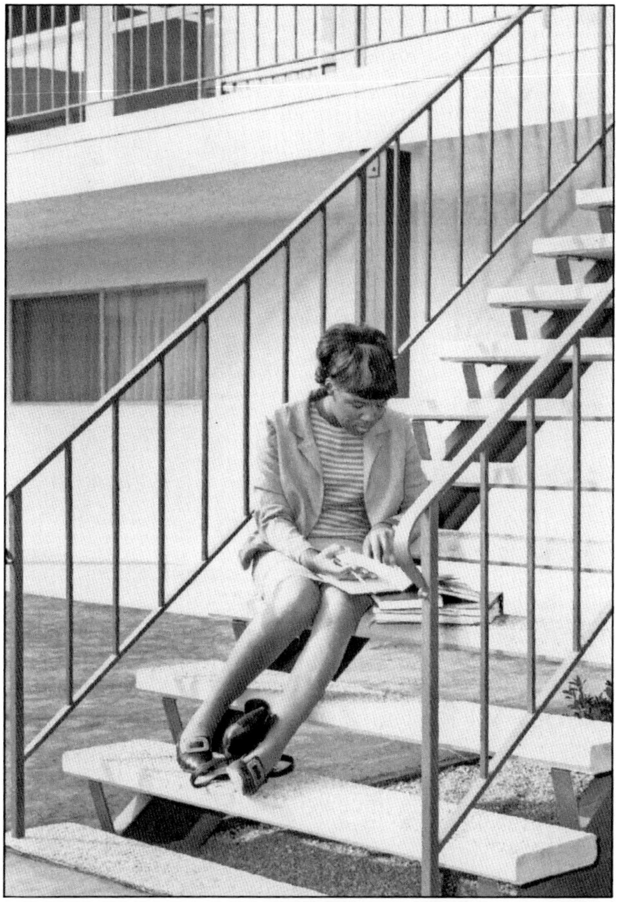

The tradition of hard-fought ping-pong matches that started at CSC Palos Verdes continued on at CSC Dominguez Hills. The student recreational programs grew to include hiking, flag football, horseshoes, horseback riding, basketball, bowling, golf, and ice skating. In an address in 1967, President Cain noted, "Even the athletic program, although limited to ping-pong and volleyball, has reflected some of the spirit of the student body."

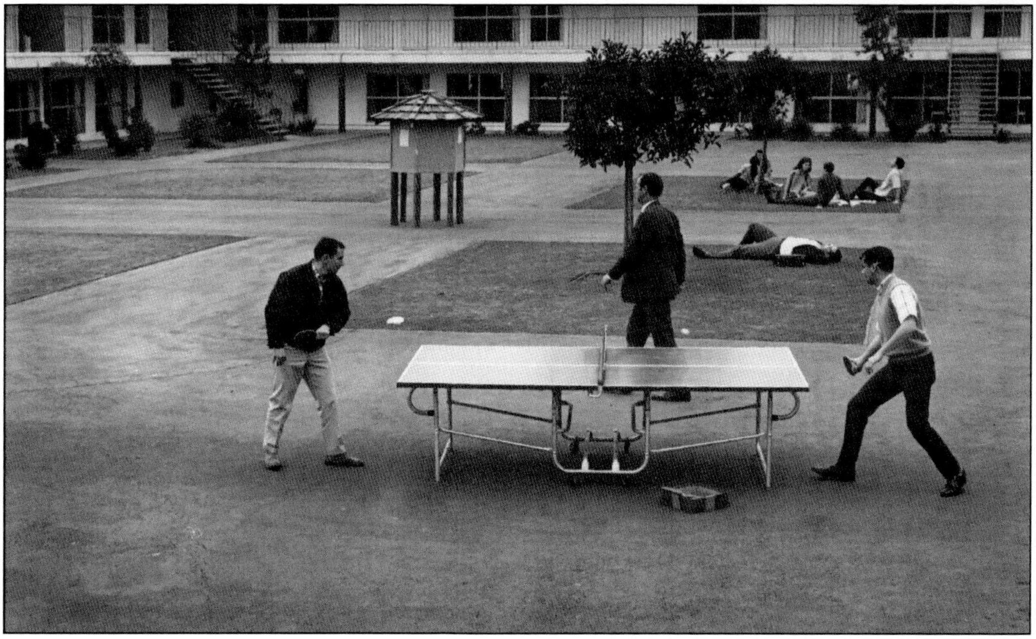

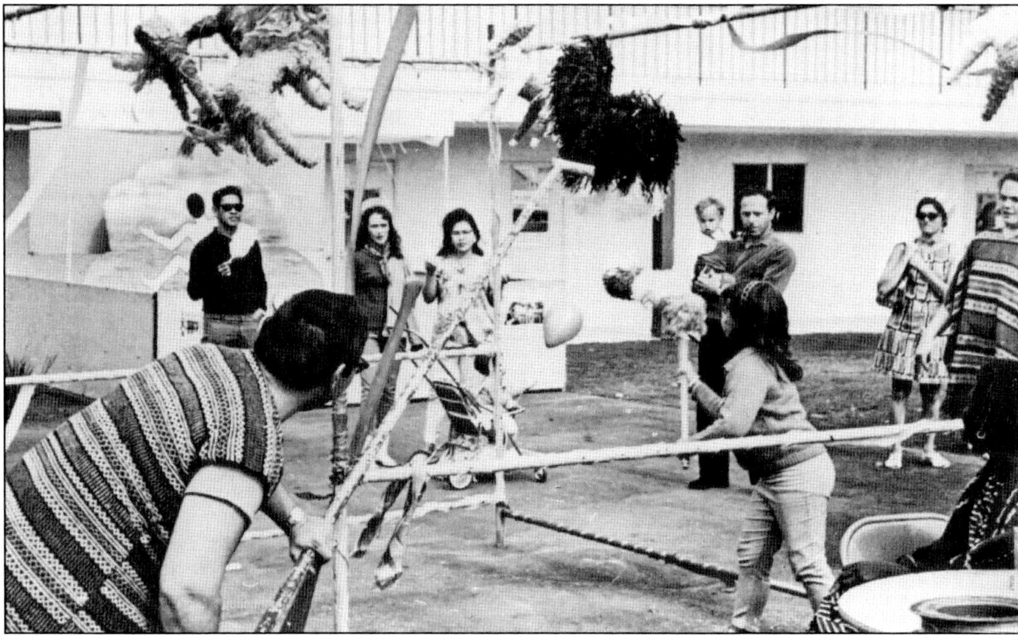

The Festival de los Gitanos, sponsored by the Circulo Hispanico Club, was held on May 27, 1967, in the courtyard of the Watt Campus. Activities included folk singing and a piñata event. *Gitanos*, the Spanish name for gypsies, was the first nickname adopted by students for the college. Adopting the term gitanos had more to do with the travails of locating a permanent campus than the need for a mascot for the college sports teams.

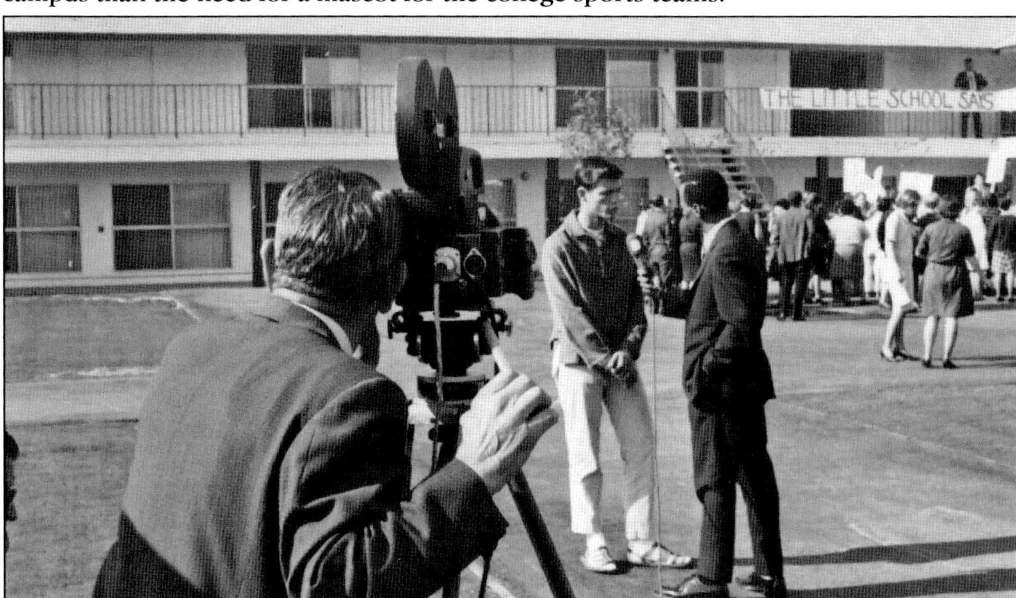

A local newsman interviews student leader Mark Johnson about the tuition protests at CSC Dominguez Hills in January 1967. Upon taking office, Gov. Ronald Reagan proposed cuts in education and a tuition charge of $200 for state colleges. There was also some talk about closing down the college. Prior to this proposal, students were assessed fees for incidentals but not tuition. Students and faculty feared access to education would be affected.

The first commencement at CSC Dominguez Hills was held on June 9, 1967. The commencement address was given by Louis Heilbron, the first chairman of the CSC Board of Trustees. The graduating class consisted of four students who received bachelor of arts degrees. They were, from left to right, William Hart, Pamela Striplin, Othille Moritz, and Sharon Chambers.

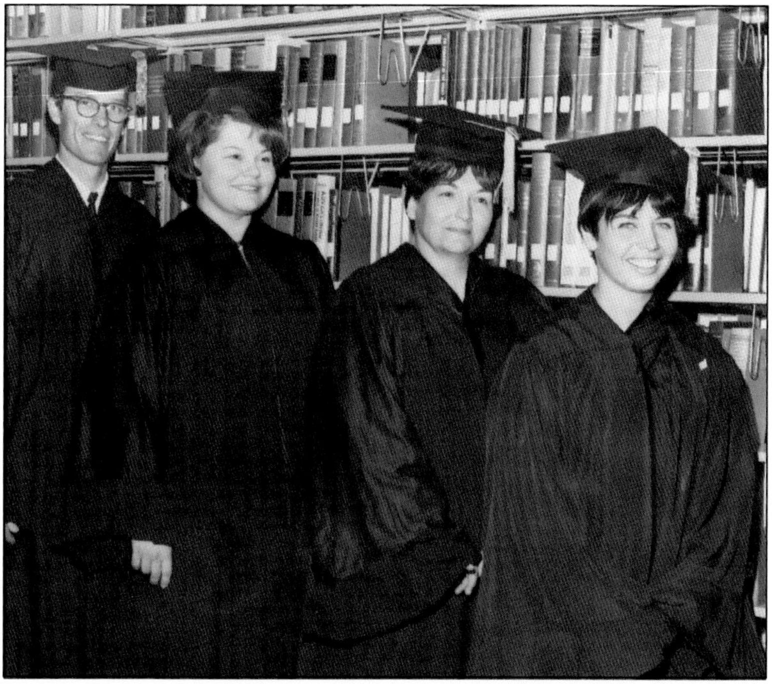

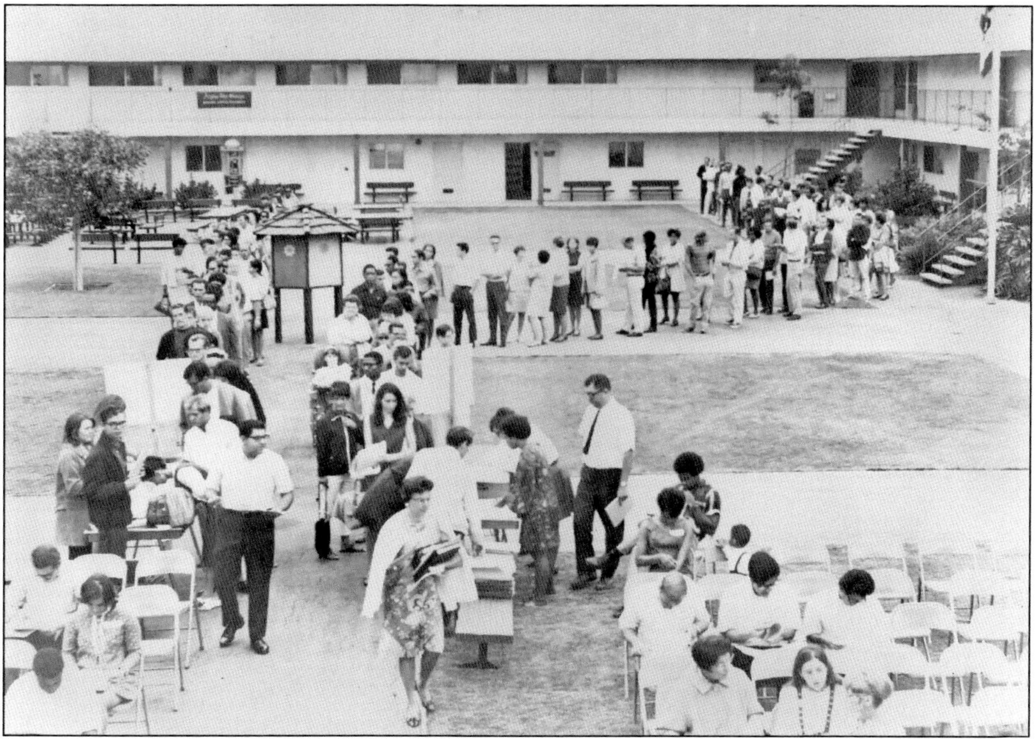

Students assemble for orientation in the Watt Campus courtyard in 1968. The student body grew despite warnings from an April 1967 *Los Angeles Times* article that said "oil well fires are a regular feature of extracurricular life" and that the "campus had a sweeping view of junk yards and tract housing."

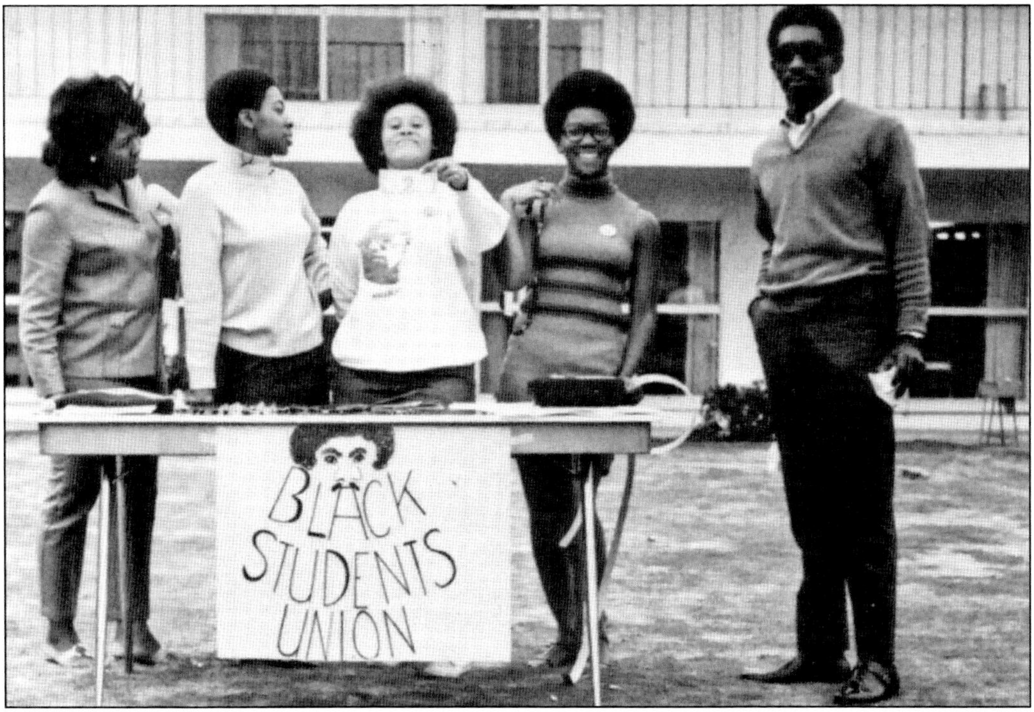

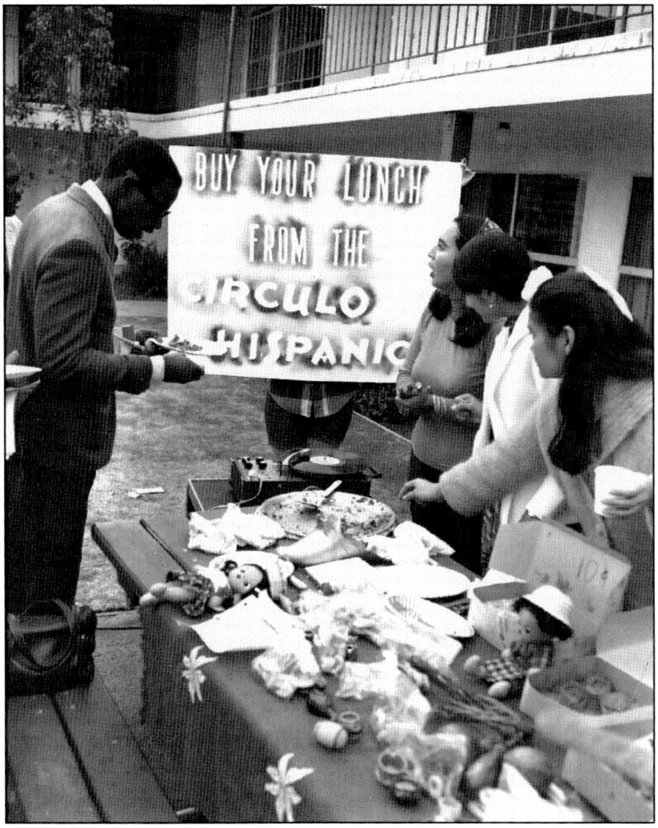

Pictured above are Black Student Union members on Club Day. The Black Student Union, founded in 1968, sponsored dances and focused its efforts on developing an African American studies major and the recruitment of minority professors. They also called a strike to protest police actions at a local junior high. In 1969, the *Los Angeles Times* wrote that 40 of the 100 black students at Dominguez Hills were members of the Black Student Union.

Circulo Hispanico was the first club on campus to promote interest in the Spanish language and Mexican culture. Raising funds with potlucks and other activities, the club held monthly lectures or field trips. Members of the club are pictured here during Club Day 1968.

Herman Loether (coordinator of the psychology, sociology, and anthropology departments) talks up the Sociology Club with students on Club Day 1968. The sign hanging over the second floor railing encourages students to join the Ramblers Hiking Club.

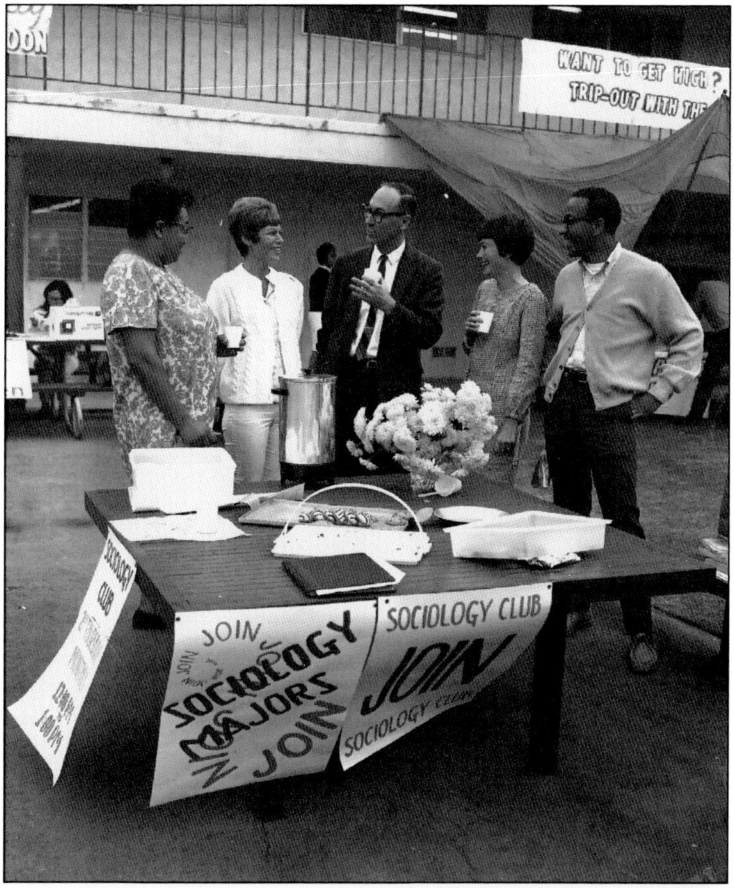

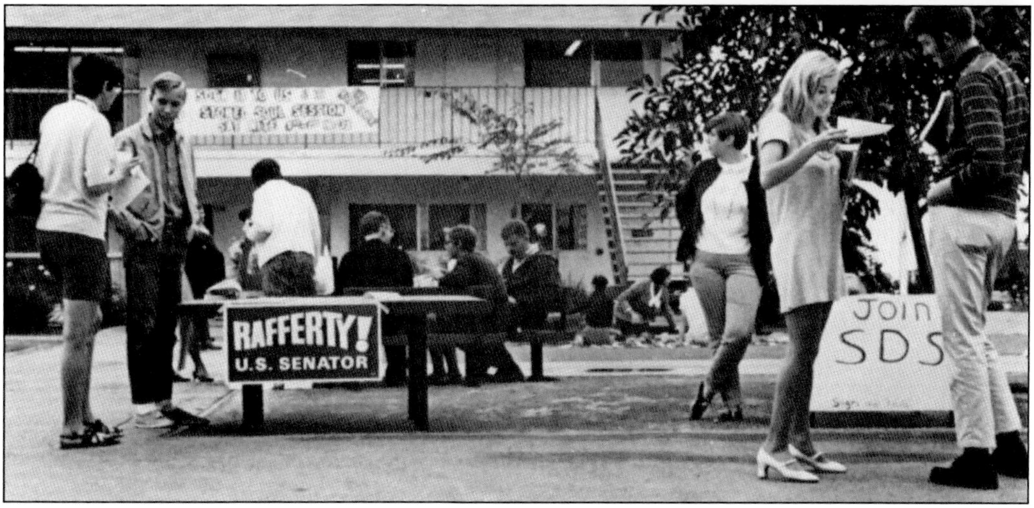

The 1968 national election campaign heated up at the Watt Campus during Club Day. The college chapter of the Students for a Democratic Society is pictured here with a table alongside that of Republican Max Rafferty supporters. Rafferty, the state superintendent of public instruction, who came to prominence trying to ban a textbook seen as too diverse, ran a losing U.S. Senate campaign.

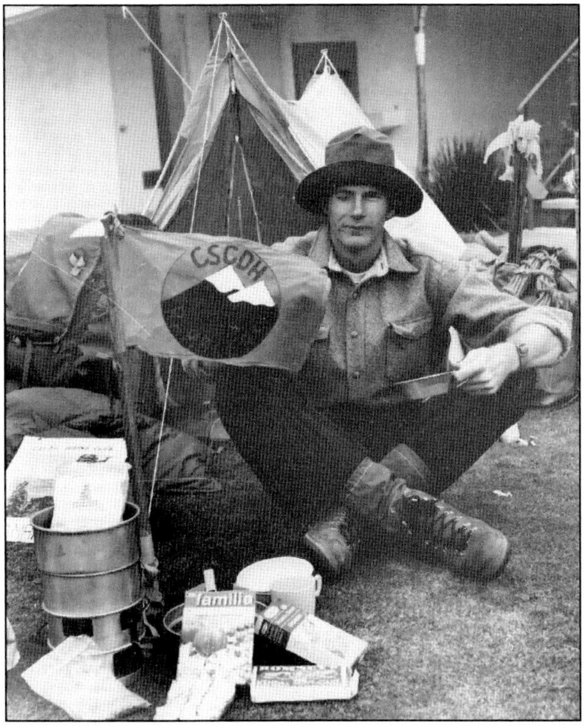

During the first few years at the Watt Campus, the Ramblers, a campus outdoors camping and hiking club led by student Mike Tipton, was quite popular and had outings to sites such as the San Gabriel Mountains, Joshua Tree, and Manzanita Springs. The Ramblers' Club Day display was complete with tent, hiking boots, and freeze-dried food.

This is the first graduation class of the CSC Dominguez Hills Teacher Education program. Pictured in 1968 are, from left to right, (first row) Ruth Martinson (director, Teacher Education), Marian Rosser (secretary), Virginia Finnegan, and Gayle Uyeno; (second row) Lucienne Bowes, Barbara Wood, Gaye Hollins, and Pamela Striplin.

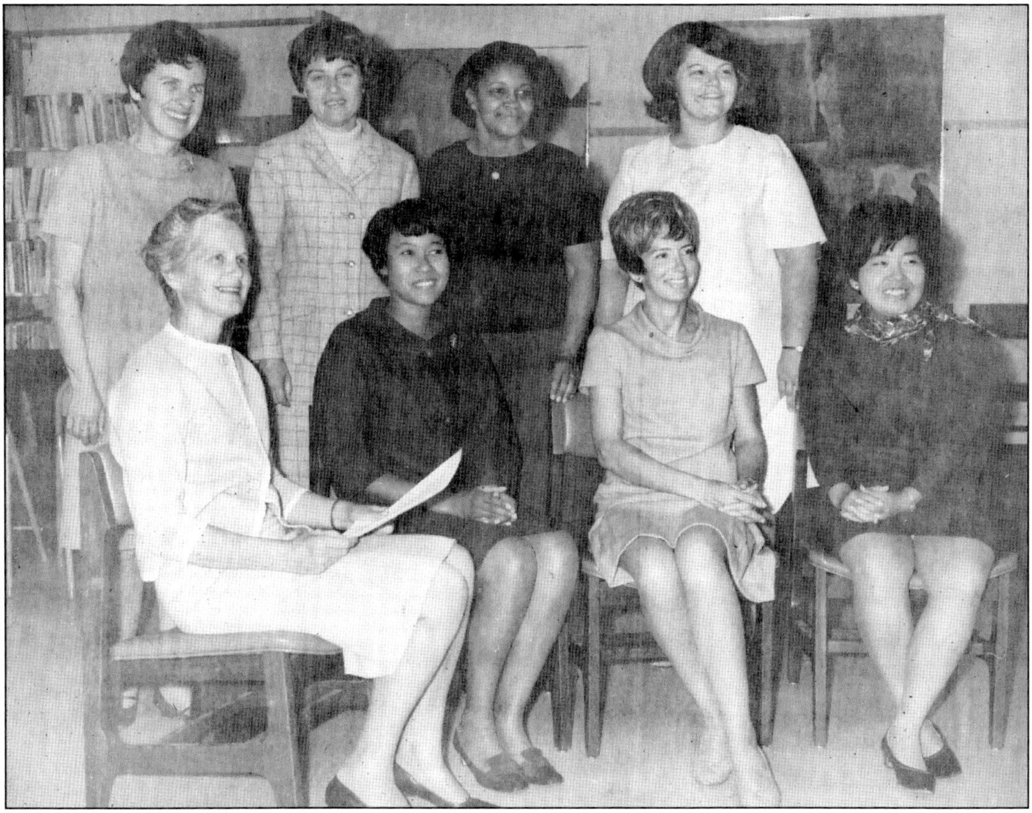

Gayle Jones (right) recruits for the Alpha Phi Omega fraternity during the Watt Campus Club Day open house. The college chapter of this national service fraternity also sponsored several campus events, including a fund-raising dance, during the 1968–1969 academic year. Though not located in residences or houses, campus fraternities and sororities have a long history of assisting various community organizations.

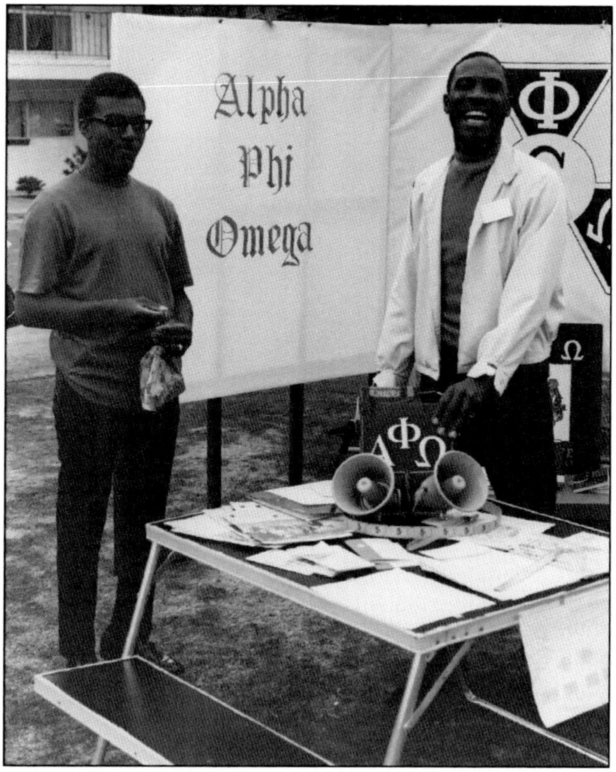

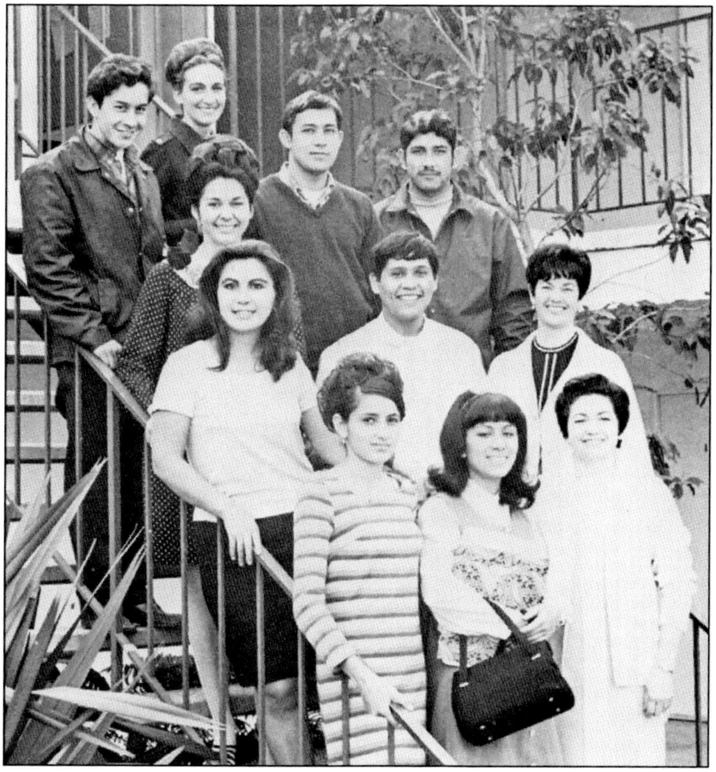

The organization United Mexican American Students (UMAS) was formed in October 1968. Students in the group visited area high schools to discuss the opportunities at CSC Dominguez Hills. The school yearbook stated that "the final goal of UMAS is to create an educational environment where there is no need for UMAS."

In The Library,

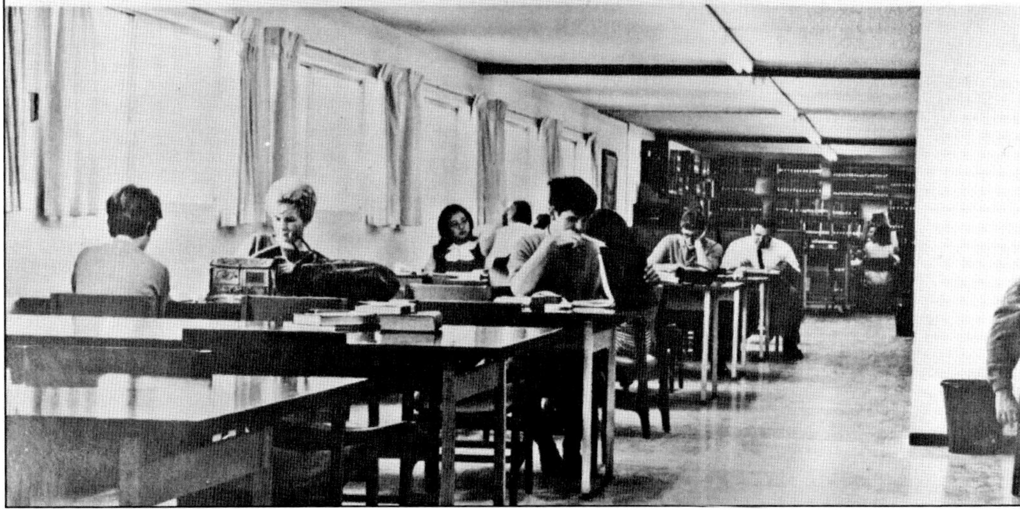

Upon arriving at the new campus, President Cain said he was glad he did not have to move any of the 50,000 volumes into the Watt Campus Library. Planning a library for the college had been a major undertaking long before the campus had a home. Teaming up with the library of the new CSC San Bernardino, the campus librarian ordered, cataloged, and created a collection at several off-campus sites.

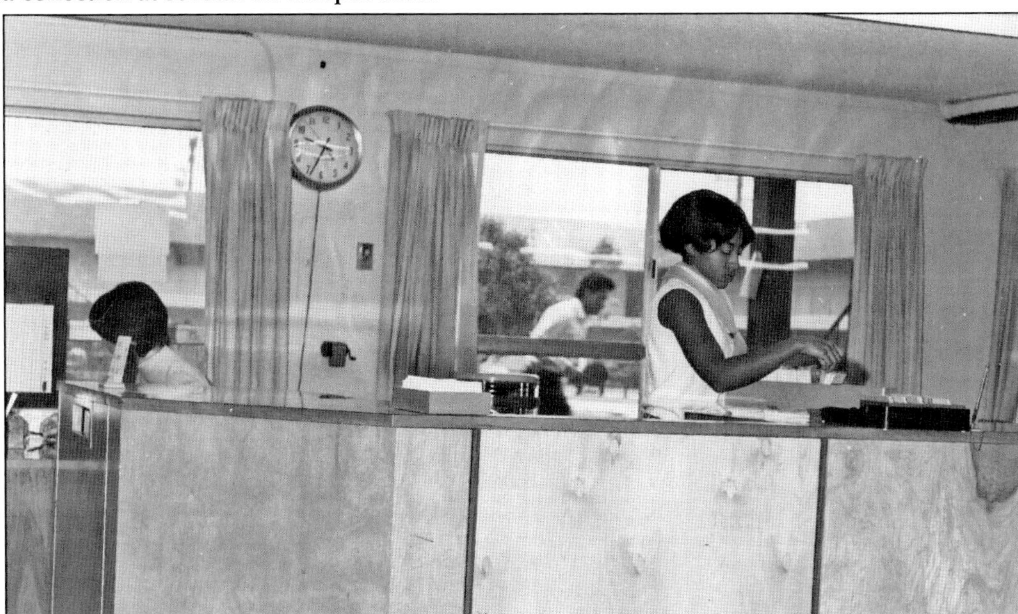

The circulation desk at the Watt Campus Library served as the main checkpoint for library patrons. Speaking at Dominguez Hills' first commencement in 1967, former CSC Board of Trustees chairman Louis Heilbron explained that the ratio of students to library books at Dominguez Hills was 333 to one, whereas at other state colleges it was 30 books to one student.

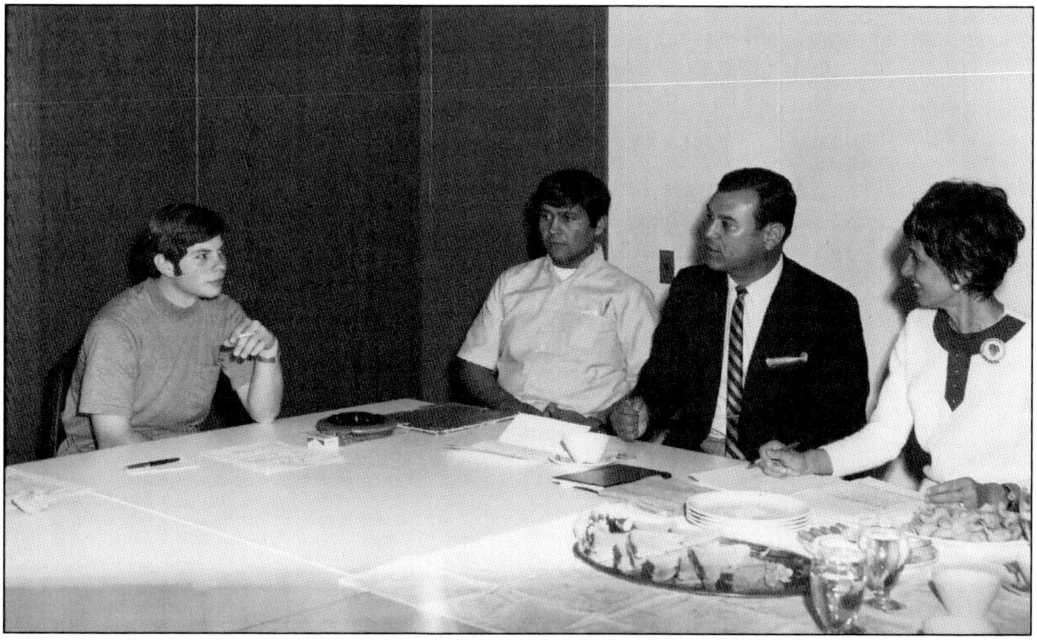

Led by Dr. Porfirio Sanchez, director of Mexican American studies, CSC Dominguez Hills held a two-day institute on the recruitment and retention of Chicano students in 1970. In the previous year, Mexican American students had lobbied for the campus to reflect the population of surrounding communities, hire Mexican American counselors, and add additional Mexican American professors.

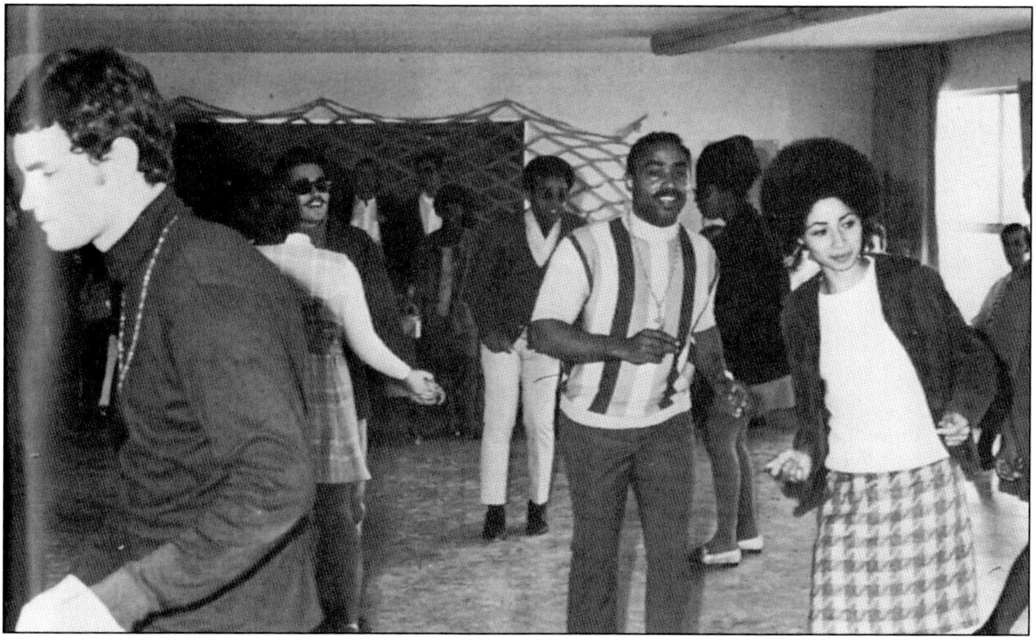

Smartly dressed students enjoy a Black Student Union–sponsored dance in the Upstairs Theater on the Watt Campus during the 1968–1969 academic year. The student yearbook described the event as "movin' and groovin'." A banner during Club Day stated that on a particular Saturday night there would be a "Sock It to Us, Stoned Soul Session" dance.

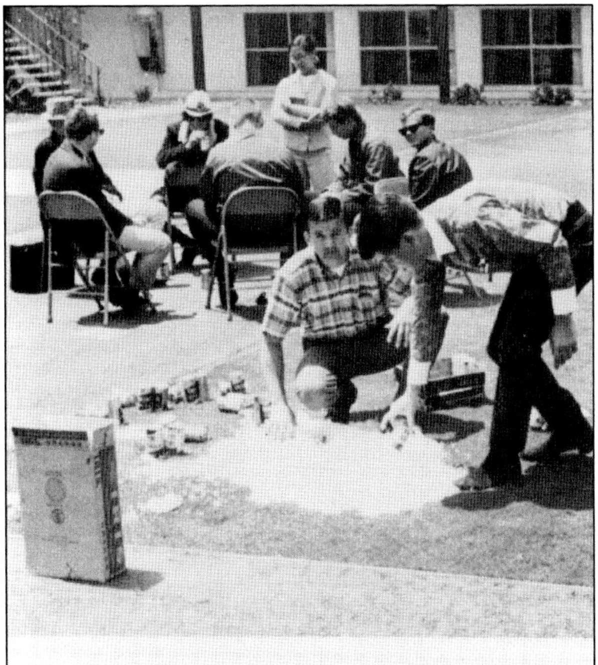

Action at the "Love-in." Quick, hide the beer!

During the campaign for student government president in 1967, candidate Ric Thomas conceived of the idea of having a campus love-in. According to the *Los Angeles Times*, students were invited to bring flowers, lunches, and the things they loved (teddy bears, strawberries, and a grandchild were brought). Students pinned carnations on administrators and faculty as they shared their lunches. Thomas was elected class president.

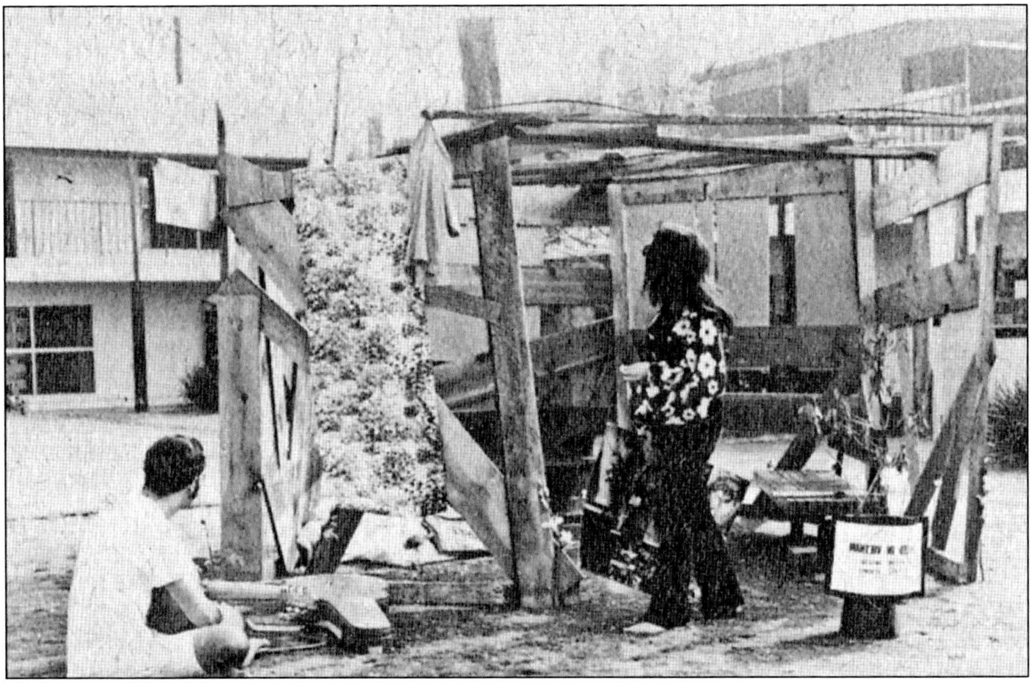

The Temple of Peace, a sort of love shack, stood for two days in 1969 on campus as a statement against the Vietnam War. The student body president, his wife, a student actor, and another person slid under big blankets inside the temple and proclaimed their determination "to symbolize the disparity between life as it could be and life as it is." Administrators watched for any penal code violations.

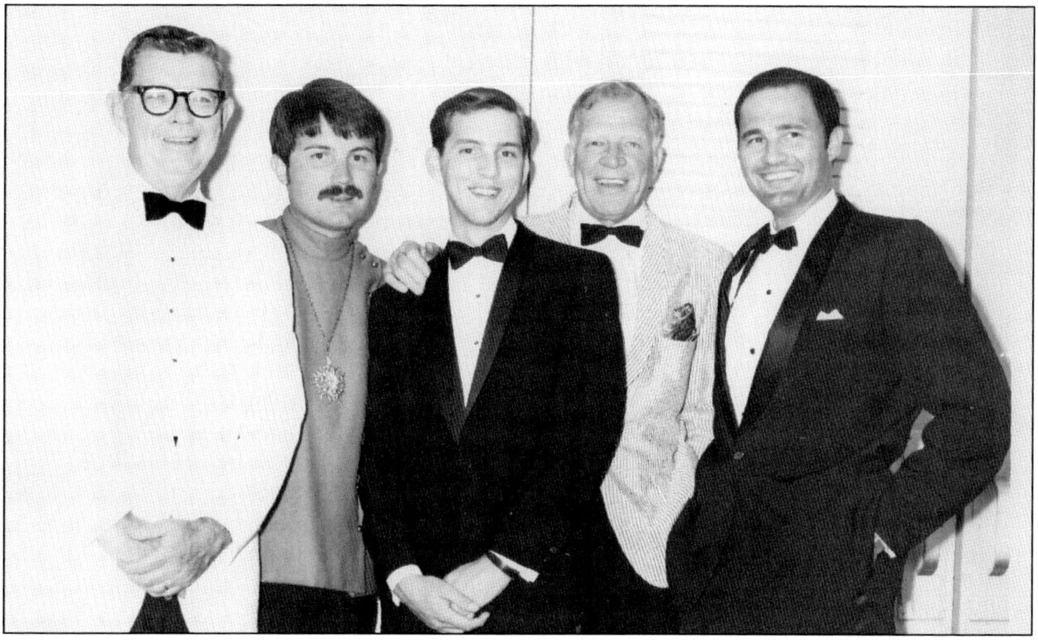

The gentlemen of Dominguez Hills decked out in black ties and a Nehru jacket for the 1968 spring formal. Donald P. Loker (second from right), a member of the Campus Advisory Board, donated $1,000 to fund a student union. Student unions could not be funded by the state. Nearly 25 years later, the Donald P. and Katherine B. Loker Student Union opened its doors.

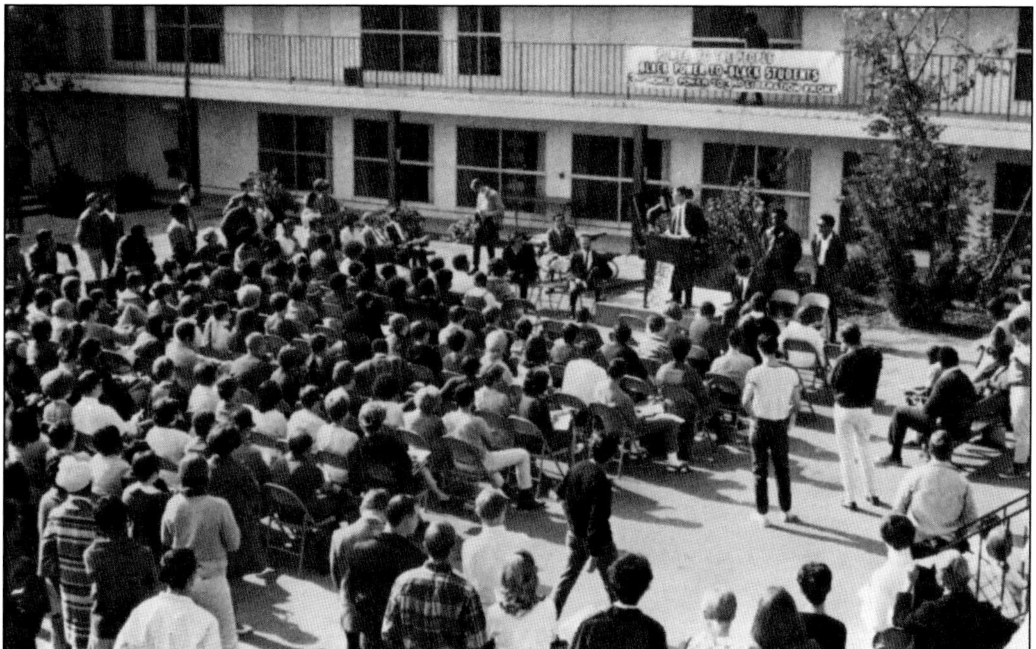

A campus-wide convocation was called to discuss recent disruptions and strikes at San Francisco State University and general higher education reform. In 1969, there were also convocations on a police action at a local middle school and a Vietnam War moratorium protest.

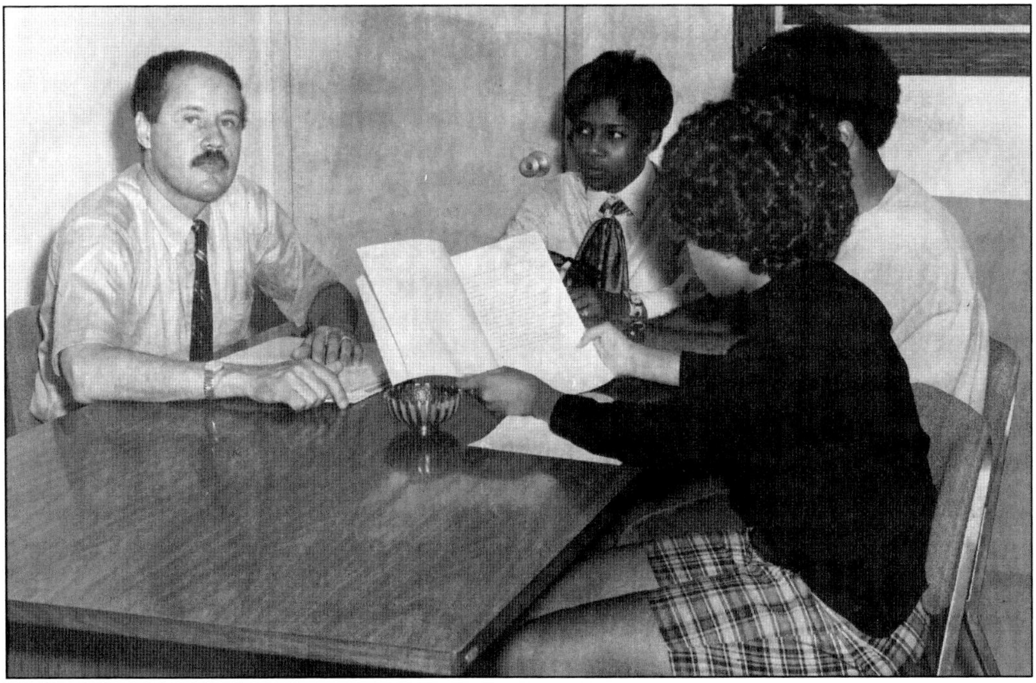

Clockwise from left, John Smith, director of the Educational Opportunity Program (EOP), sits with students Denise McGruder, Dwight Harris, and Shirley Griggs in 1969. The EOP program has operated for 40 years and is focused on students who may not meet university admission criteria but show the potential to succeed in higher education.

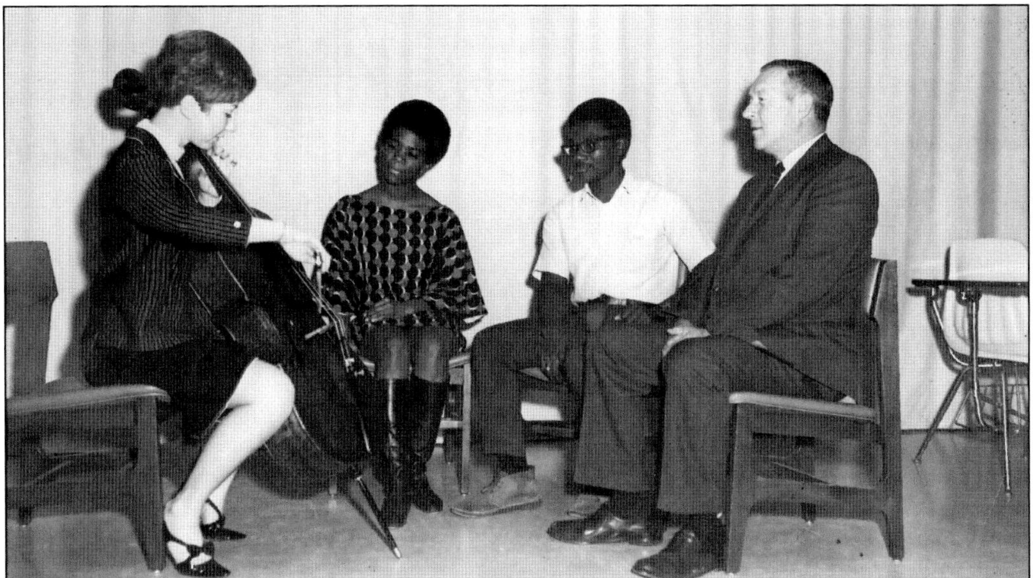

Music professor Frances Steiner plays cello for an appreciative audience, including student Ron Wilson and dean of humanities Marvin Laser (right). Professor Steiner later became one of the first female conductors of a municipal orchestra. She served as the conductor of the Carson–Dominguez Hills Symphony for over three decades. She was the first woman to conduct at the Los Angeles Music Center.

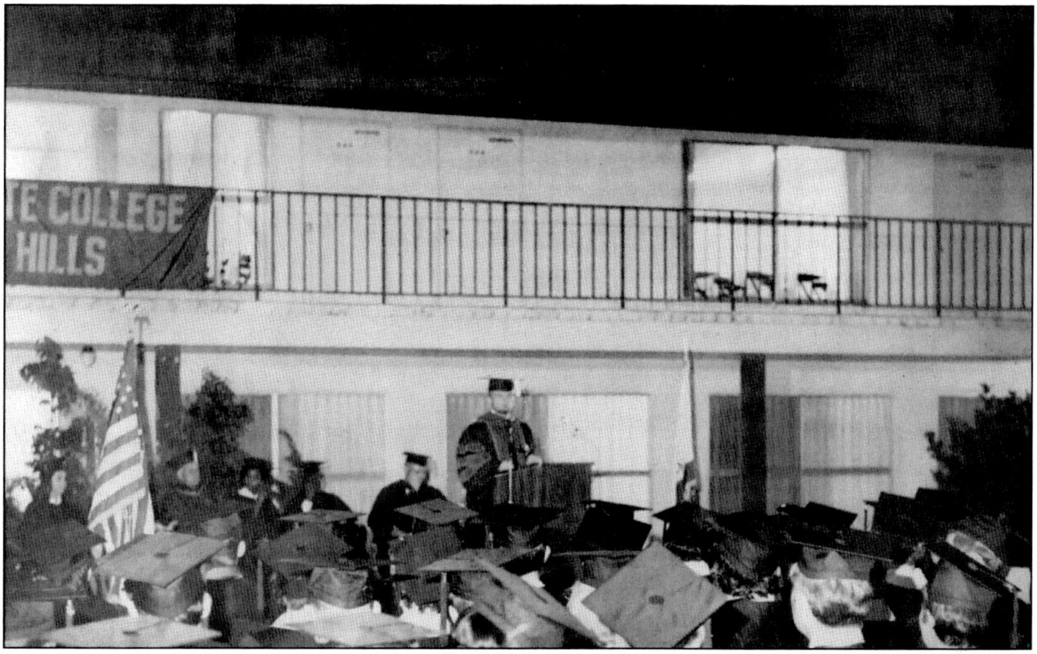

History professor Judson Grenier, in his role as chair of the CSC Dominguez Hills Academic Senate, addresses graduates at the last commencement held in the Watt Campus quad on June 14, 1969. About 85 students graduated in the class of 1969.

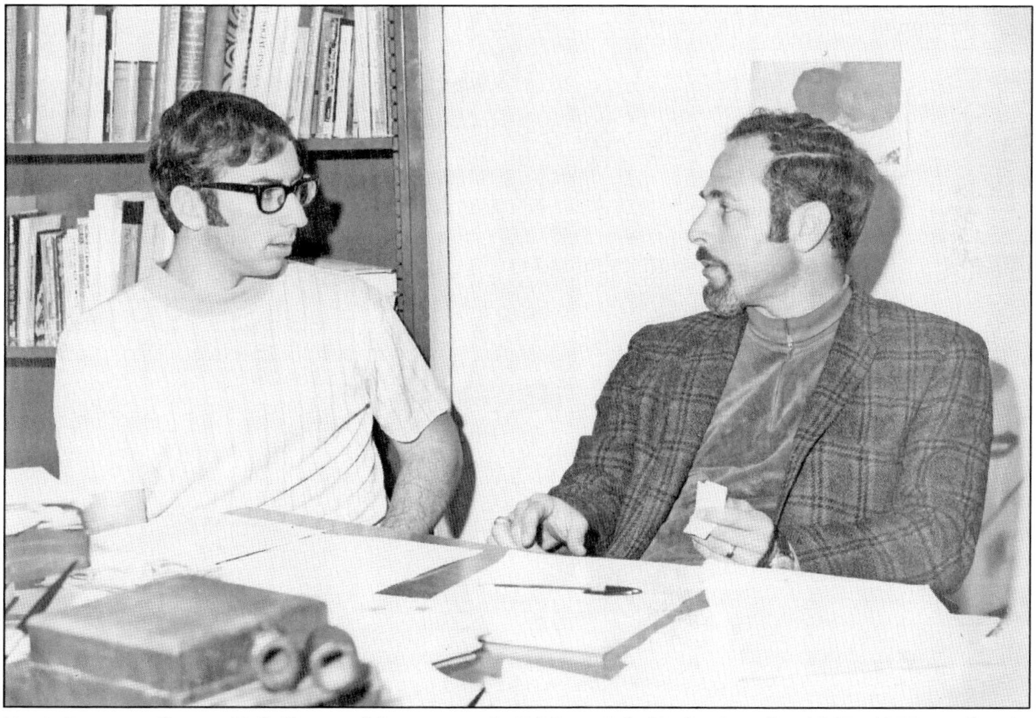

Sociology professor Hal Charnofsky counsels Ed Segal (left) during the 1969–1970 academic year. Charnofsky was a founding member of the sociology department and helped launch the master of arts degree program in marriage, family, and child counseling.

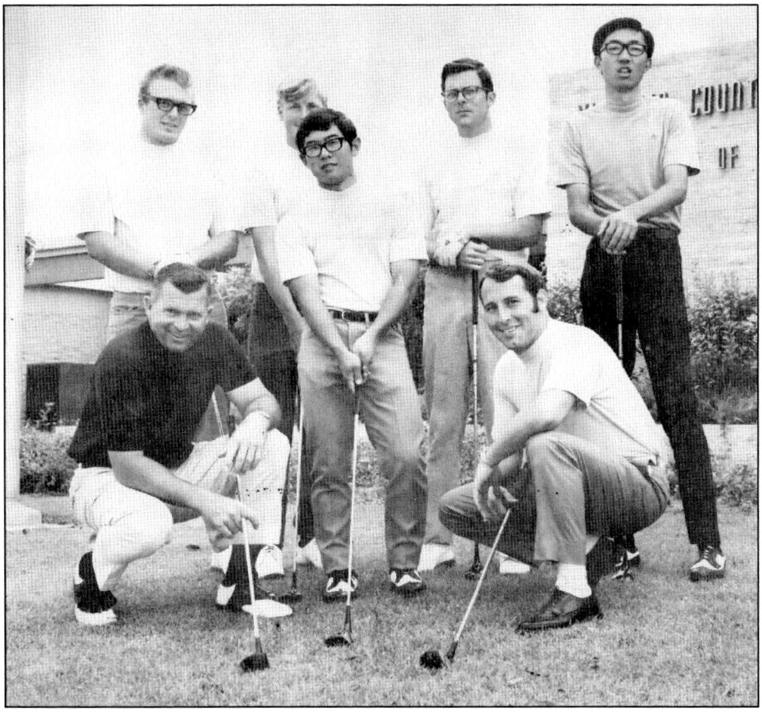

The first intercollegiate team at Dominguez Hills was the 1969 golf team. Kneeling in the dark shirt is John Johnson, coach and first athletic director. Also pictured are future baseball coach Bob Bafia (standing at left) and future tennis coach Mike Ego (standing at right). After 40 years, Johnson still leads the golf team at age 88. "Teaching and coaching keeps you around young people, and that keeps you young," said Johnson in 2009.

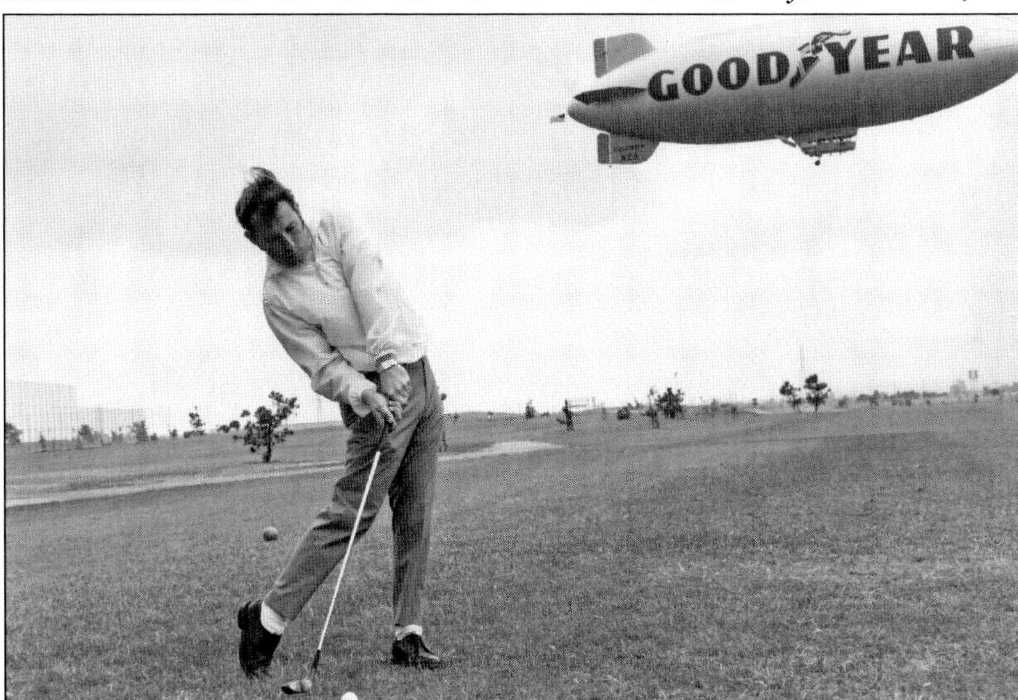

Ron Hollis strikes the ball during a 1969 golf tournament on the Links at Victoria Park in Carson near CSU Dominguez Hills. In the background is longtime campus neighbor, the Goodyear Blimp. The airstrip is less than a mile from campus and home to the *Spirit of America* blimp.

After the golf team, the tennis team arrived on campus. The 1969 men's tennis team consisted of, from left to right, (standing) Tom Milligan, unidentified, Leonard Thompson, and coach William Nupp; (kneeling) Bob Mirabal, Rob King, and Chris Tsuji.

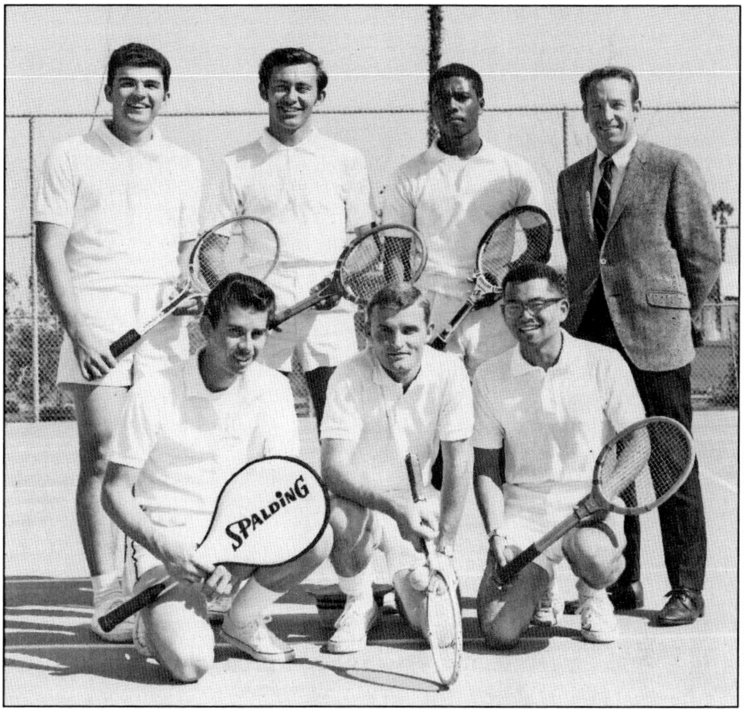

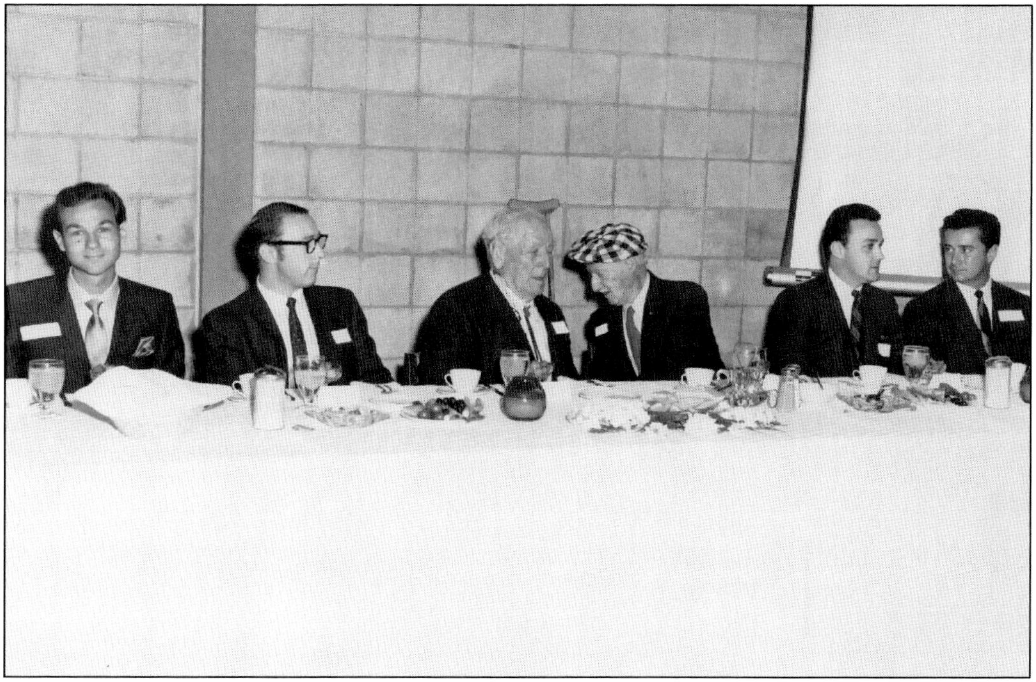

A group of students decided to celebrate the 60th anniversary of the 1910 air meet at Dominguez Field to raise funds for a student union. The attempt lost $3,000, but before plans were cancelled, a lunch with early aviators was held in the Small College. The stars of the movie *Wings* (the first Academy Award for Best Picture in 1927) were also in attendance, as well as Carson booster and television personality Regis Philbin (far right).

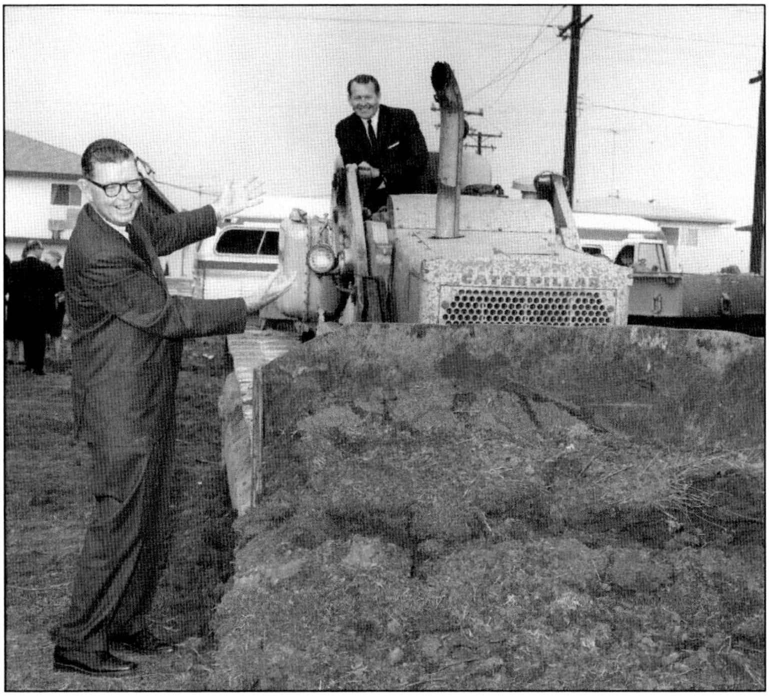

President Cain and Lt. Gov. Robert Finch broke ground for the permanent campus with the help of a bulldozer on December 5, 1967. A 40-piece band, 150 students and guests, and various California State College officials joined in the festivities. The *Los Angeles Times* noted that soon the long-fought-over project would turn "the sprawling cow pasture . . . into a 20,000-student liberal arts college."

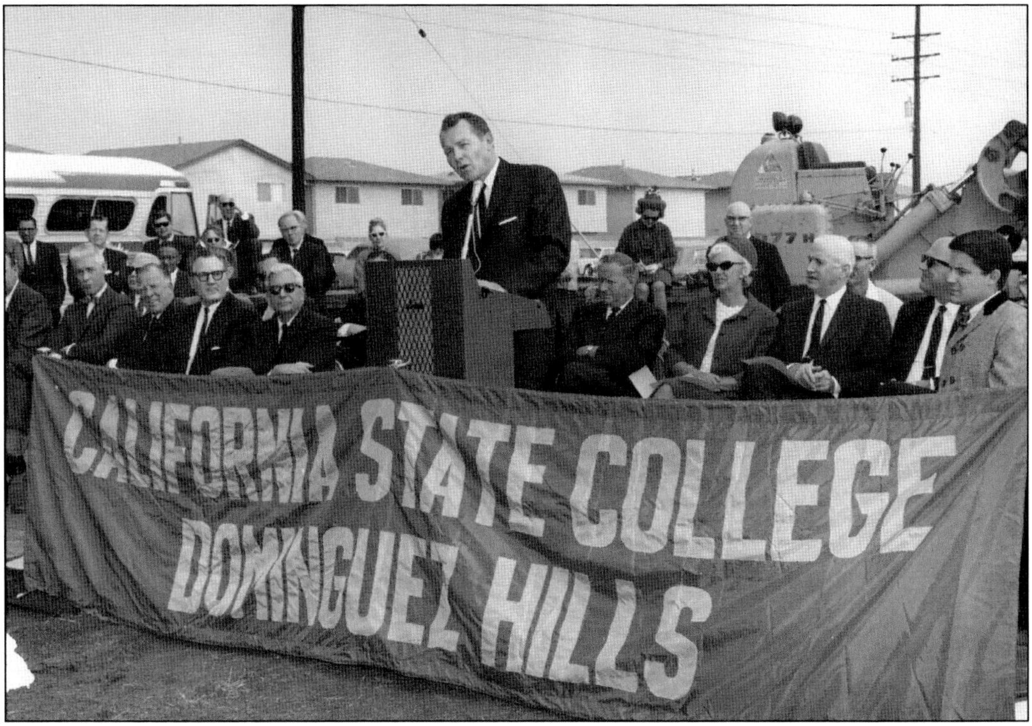

During the keynote speech at the ground-breaking, Lt. Gov. Robert Finch (a year away from being appointed a cabinet member in the Nixon administration) pointedly commenting on 1960s campus unrest, stated, "Certain arrogant and cowardly groups on campuses have provided insight into the totalitarian mind at work."

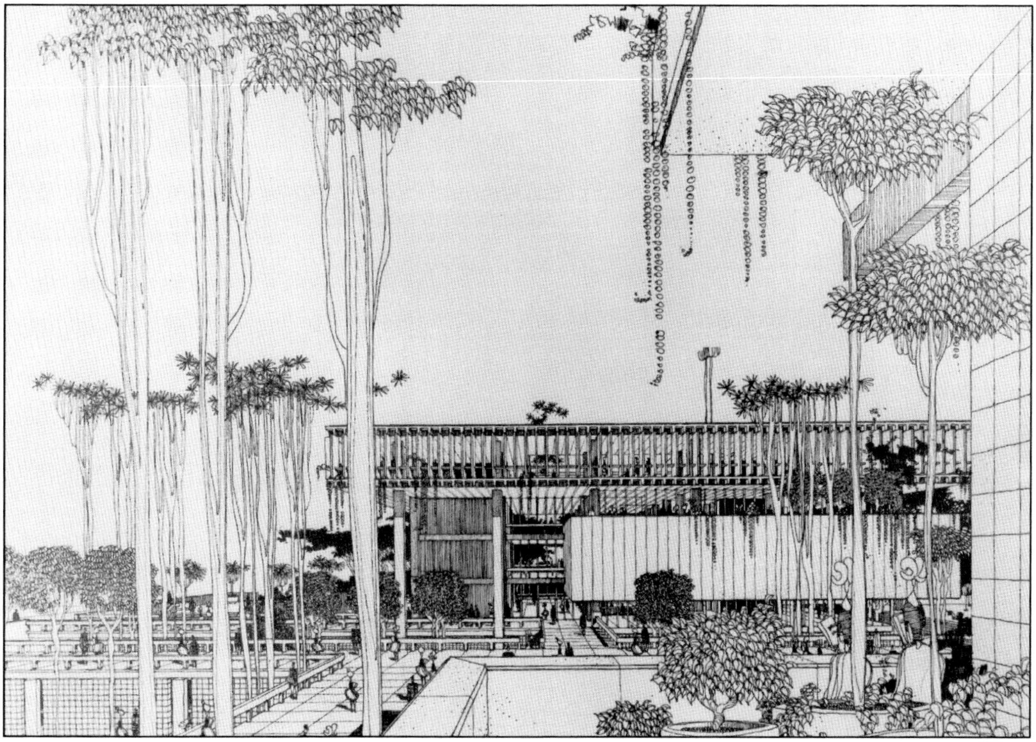

The five-story Educational Resources Center building, now known as the Leo Cain Library, was architect A. Quincy Jones's theme building in the heart of the campus academic core. The physical outline of the campus plan consisted of clusters of academic buildings surrounding a campus mall and other open spaces.

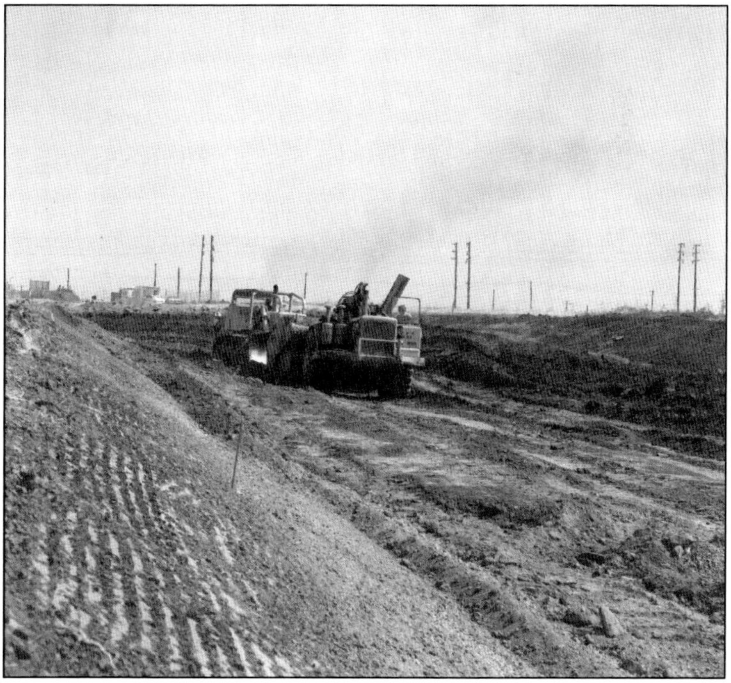

Campus architect A. Quincy Jones's concept of split-level buildings that connect with each other to provide garden courts is in evidence in this photograph, which shows early grading at the campus. Jones intended to provide the campus with "variety and surprises" and draw attention away from nearby refineries and manufacturing plants.

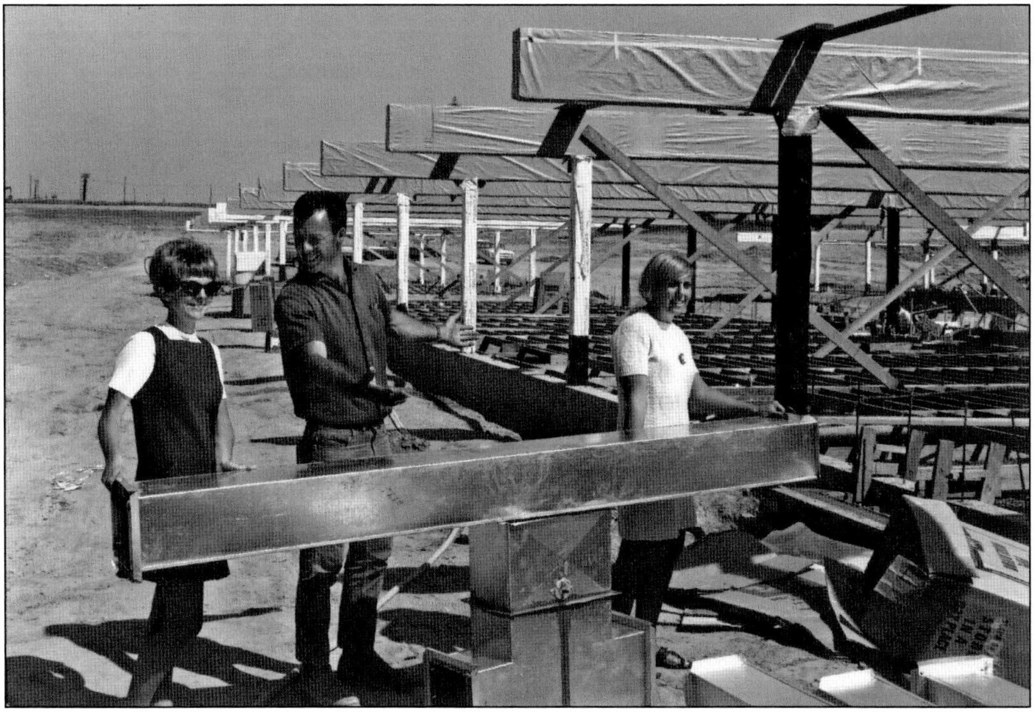

Students Patti Landuaer (left) and Irene Skrejans inspect a ventilation duct with a construction worker during the building of the Small College in 1968. The set of small buildings were the first structures on the permanent CSC Dominguez Hills location. The campus would become the "Taj Mahal of higher education," an administrator told the *Los Angeles Times*.

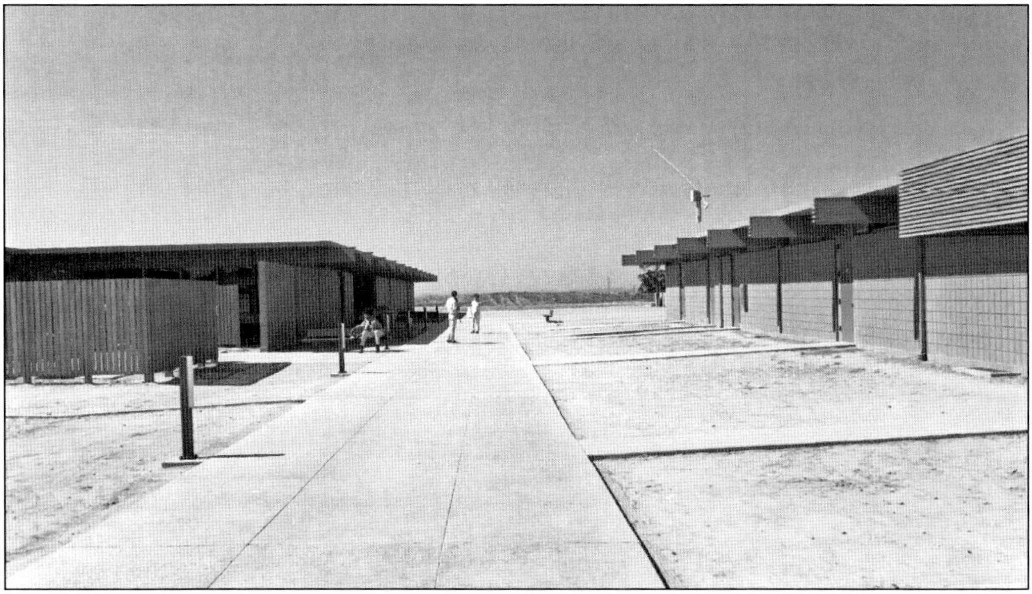

The Small College appears new and without foliage. The cluster of buildings that made up the Small College opened in the fall of 1968. With the growth of student enrollment, the buildings were used for classrooms, administration offices, a theater, a food service facility, and as part of the library.

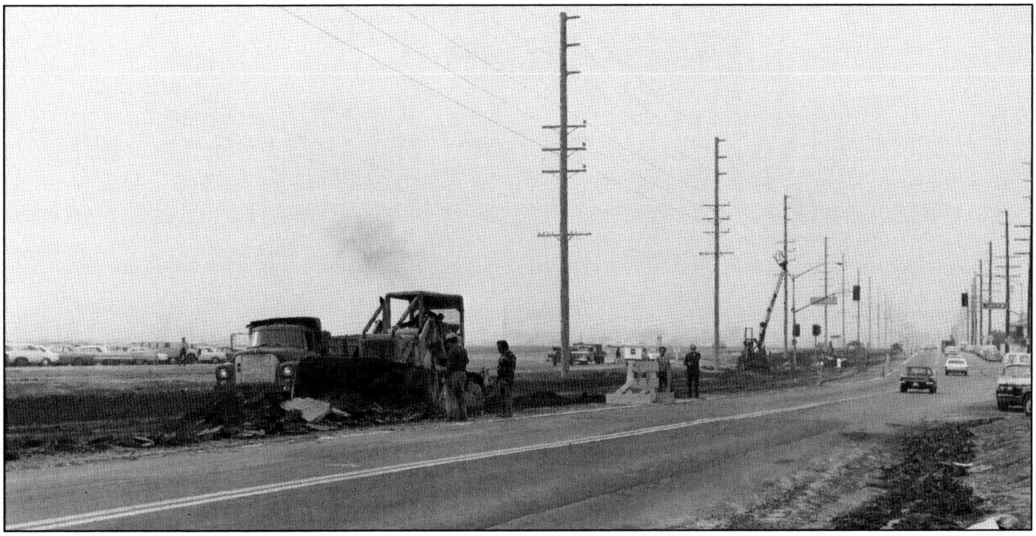

Construction on the transformation of Victoria Street from a rural two-lane road into a four-lane artery was undertaken in late 1969. With the growth of the campus and student body, the county spent nearly $230,000 on the road along the front of the campus.

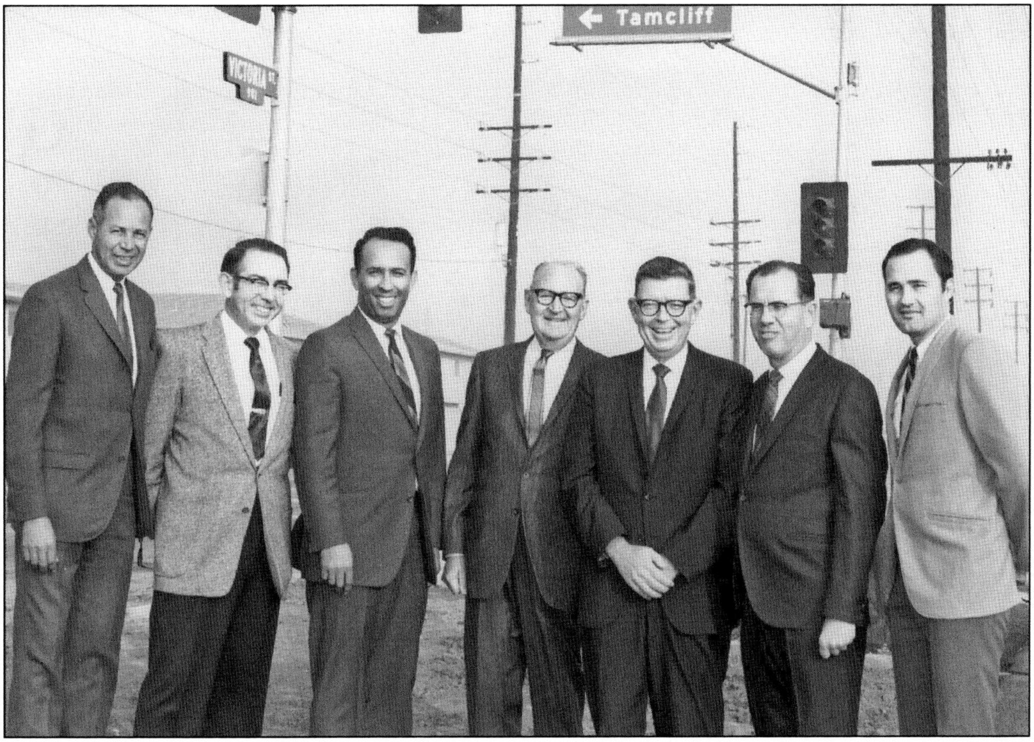

The City of Carson incorporated in 1968. The city's relationship with the campus has always been integral to the infrastructure, governance, and cultural events of both entities. Longtime campus booster and future Carson mayor Gil Smith (third from left) stands with President Cain (third from right), Supervisor Kenneth Hahn (second from right), Robert Bersi (far right), and others during a ceremony to celebrate the paving of Tamcliff Avenue, a road that runs through the campus.

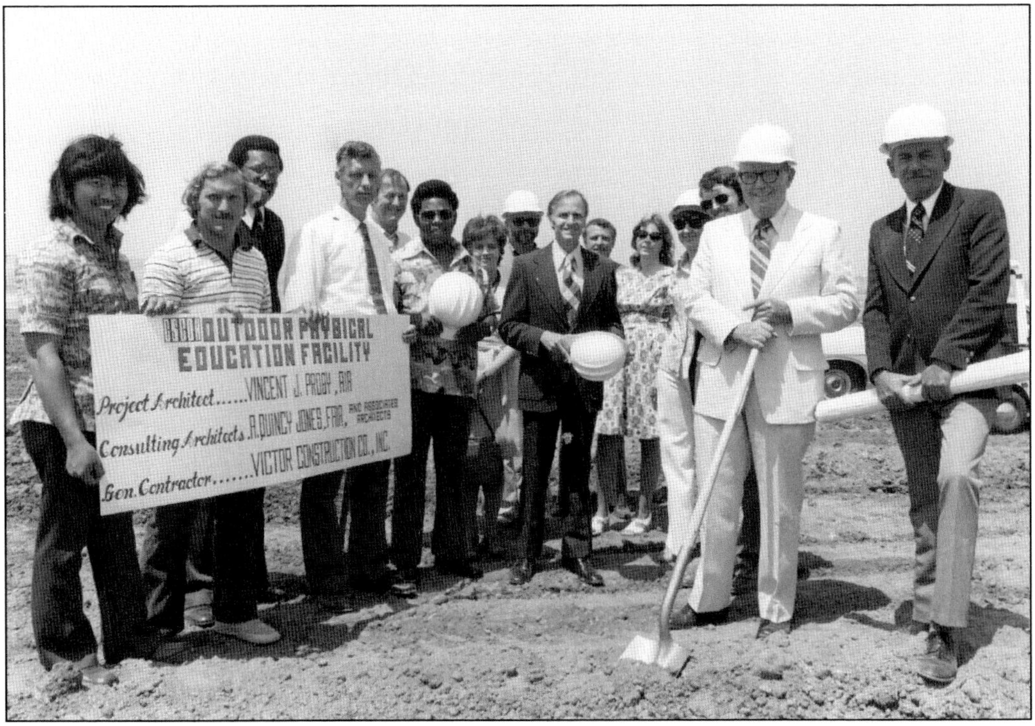

Some of the initial construction on the new campus was not for buildings but for tennis courts and baseball fields. The Outdoor Physical Education Facility was built in 1969. At the ground-breaking, President Cain (holding the shovel) and Harry Nethery (at right, in charge of planning the campus) lead the proceedings.

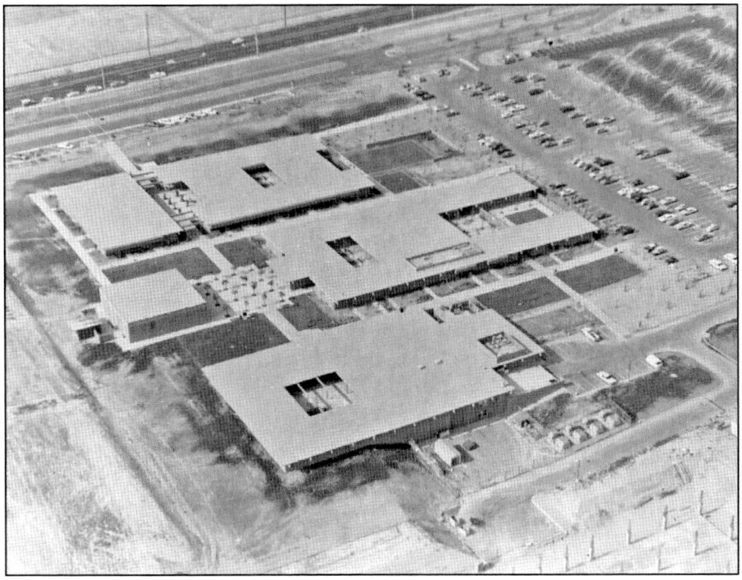

As other new campus buildings were completed, the Small College became home to an interdisciplinary and innovative accelerated academic degree program. Faculty members served as mentors, and students took courses such as the Chemistry of Nutrition or the Environmental Programs Workshops. The Small College operated until the 1980s.

Two

The College Becomes a University
The 1970s

What is the genius of Dominguez Hills? It may be in our past, brief as that is; it may be in our future as a comprehensive public urban university. But most likely it will be found in the people who were here, the people who are here now, the people who will be here, and in a commitment to quality, to responsive change, to the goals of a pluralistic, dynamic, and sometimes troubled society, and to the simple values of the life of the mind and of humaneness.

—Pres. Donald R. Gerth, March 11, 1977.

A month after 200 Dominguez Hills students had marched to a local bank to protest the killing of four students at Kent State University in May 1970, Pres. Richard Nixon sent a note to the university's graduating class that read, "You graduate at a time when established institutions and ideas are being questioned as they have never been questioned before in our history." And question they did. But as the 1970s progressed, those questions moved away from national issues. In the fall 1970 semester, 2,652 students were enrolled. Throughout the decade, the student government searched for common ground on how to spend student fees, who their leaders would be, and how best to address ethnic studies issues. The first phase of campus construction ended with the opening of three major buildings by 1973. The curriculum was expanded to include business classes as well as health courses. President Cain retired in 1976 and was replaced by Donald R. Gerth. Cain, with the help of Lyle Gibson, Harry Nethery, and the early faculty, had formulated a plan to create a unique college, and despite a few bumps, they had delivered. The college attained university status in 1977, and the next year, the second phase of campus construction was completed with the addition of a theater, health center, humanities building, and gymnasium. Campus funding plummeted in 1979 due to Proposition 13, a budget cut. President Gerth and the CSUDH Academic Senate worked together to avoid major layoffs by allowing faculty to teach classes outside their departments. Enrollment at the end of the decade was 7,173.

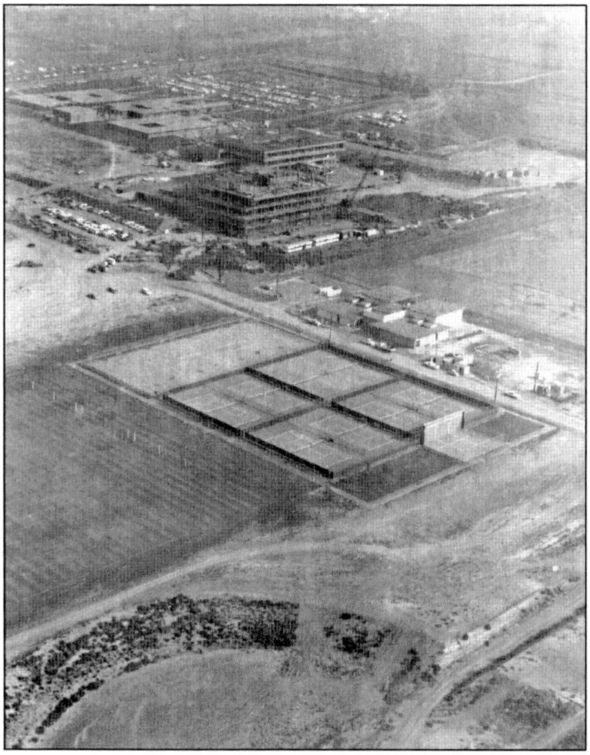

In this 1970 image from the air, CSC Dominguez Hills takes shape. At the bottom of the photograph is the outline of the future baseball field, then the tennis courts and the field house. In the upper part of the photograph are the Educational Resources Center/Library and Social and Behavioral Sciences building, both under construction.

Administrators, campus advisory board members, and local dignitaries don their hard hats to examine the progress of construction on the Educational Resources Center/Library. Included are, from left to right, Herman Graves, Lyle E. Gibson, Mary McFall, Samuel Stewart, Ted White, Robert Bersi, Curt Groninga, Gilbert Smith, Jim Bayer, Polly Watts, Pres. Leo Cain, Phillip Wesley, Assemblyman Leon Ralph, Donald P. Loker, and Donald MacPhee.

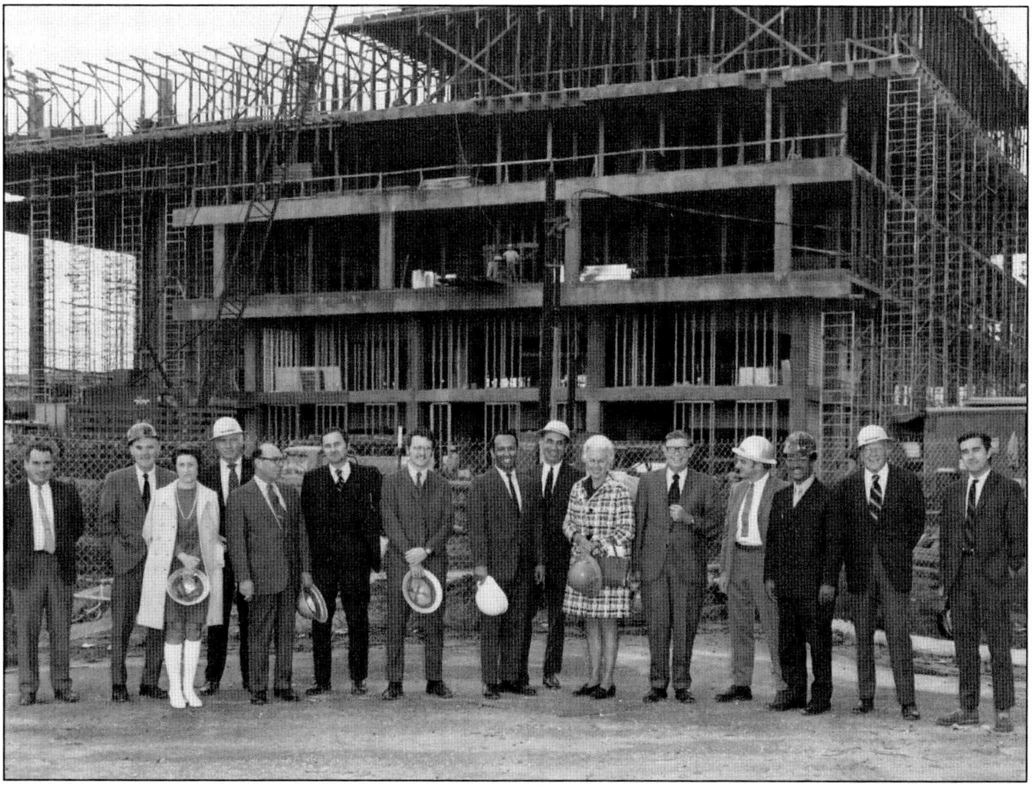

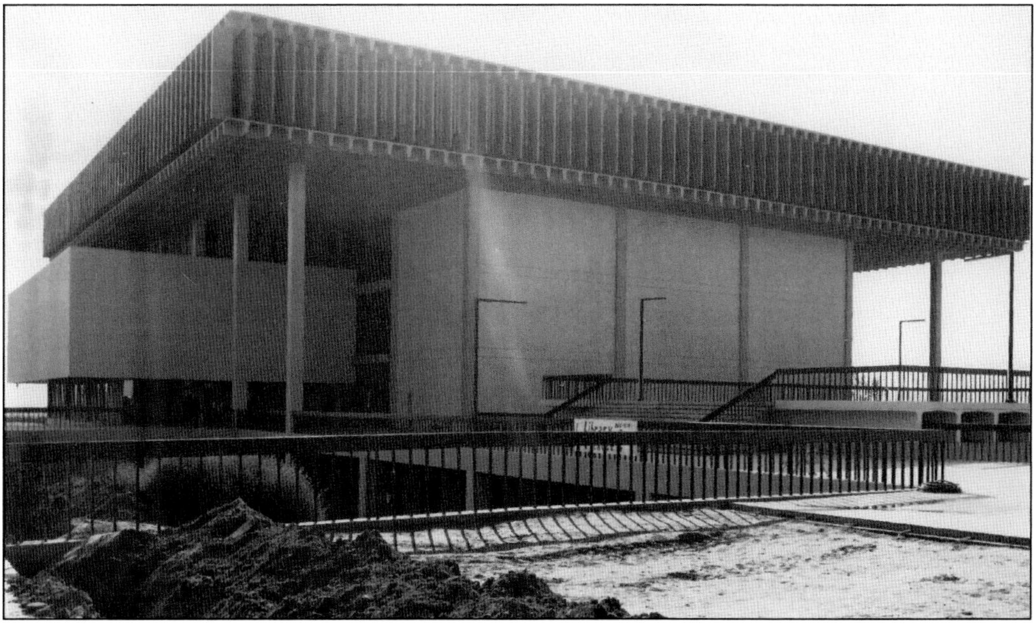

The Educational Resources Center (ERC) was completed in 1971 with a grand opening occurring on January 15, 1972. Library staff brought books from the other campus library locations with carts the size of library shelves for easy re-shelving. The ERC/Library addition was named for President Cain upon his retirement in 1976. A new library addition is scheduled to open adjacent to the current one in 2010.

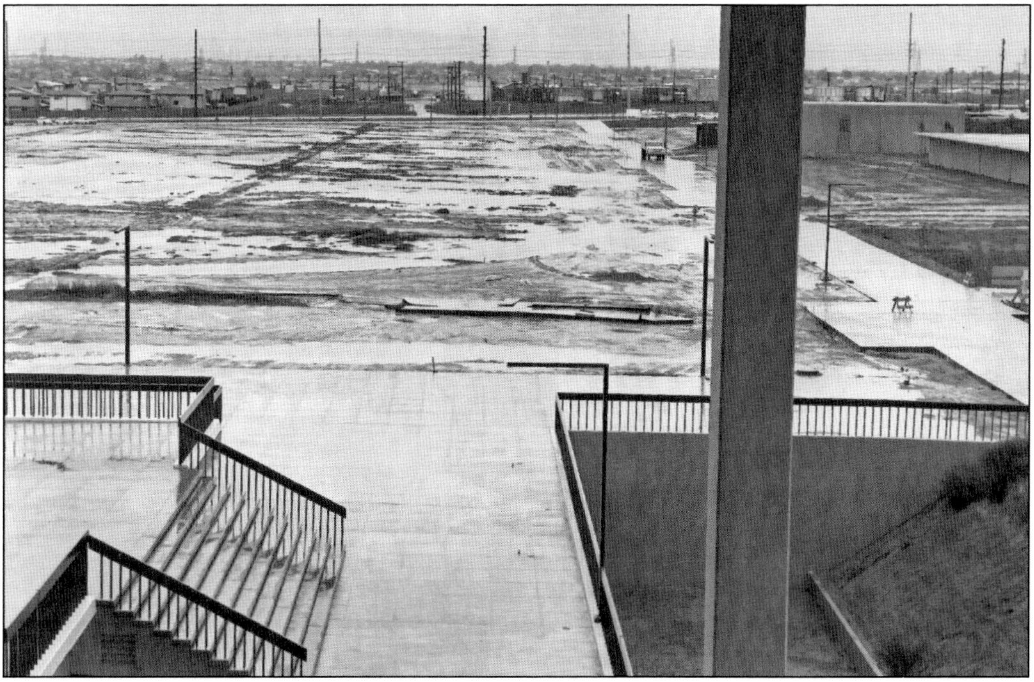

CSC Dominguez Hills' future campus mall, viewed toward Victoria Street, appears more like a lake in the midst of the first large segment of campus construction during the 1971–1972 academic year.

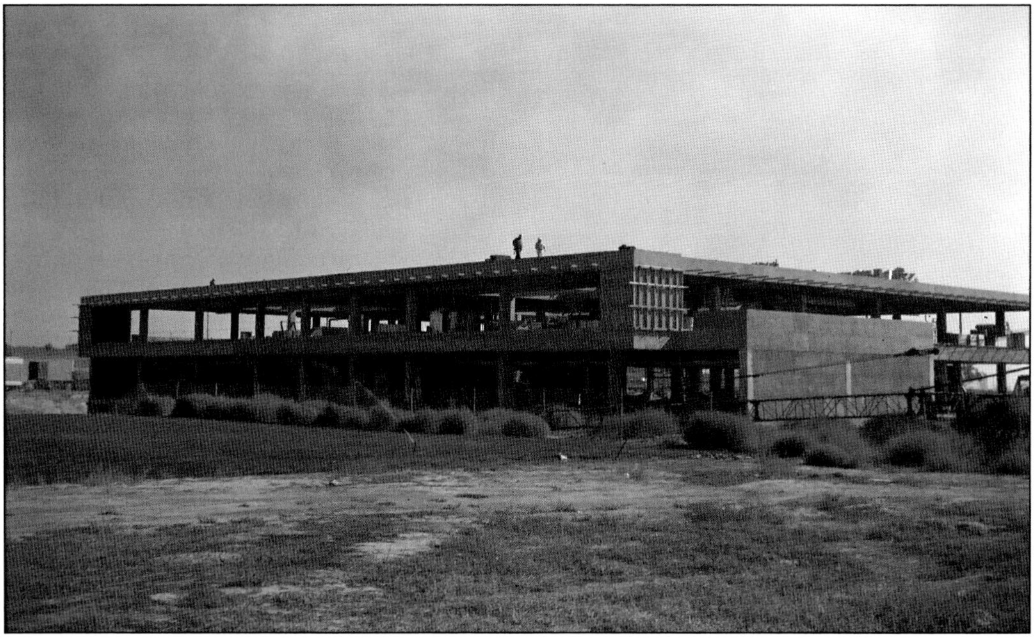

Pictured here is the Social and Behavioral Sciences building as seen during construction. The building opened in 1971 to house the School of Social and Behavioral Sciences, which included the departments of anthropology, economics, geography, history, political science, psychology, and sociology. The school also offered interdepartmental concentrations in African American studies, American studies, urban studies, and other areas.

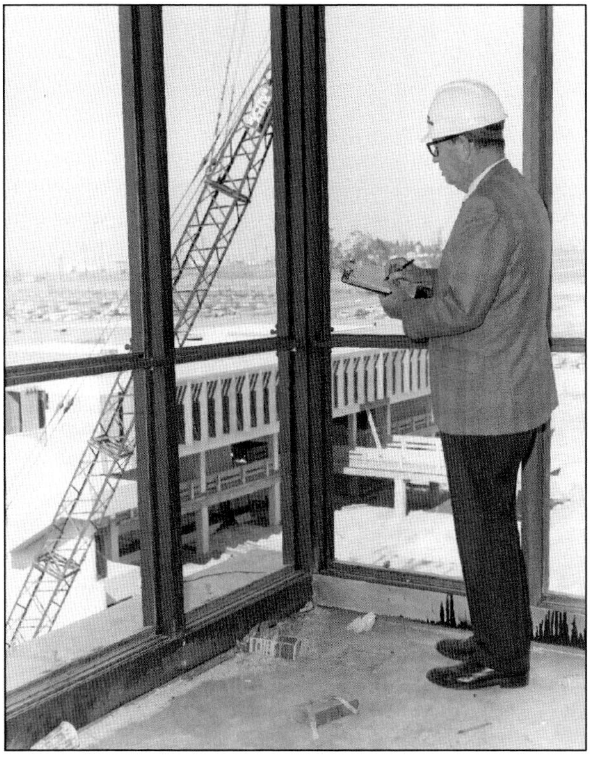

President Cain stands on the top floor of the Educational Resources Center in 1971 inspecting progress on the Social and Behavioral Sciences building across the way. Pres. James E. Lyons memorialized Cain in 2001 saying, "Because of all he did and all he stood for, people in our communities have access to a college education and a productive life."

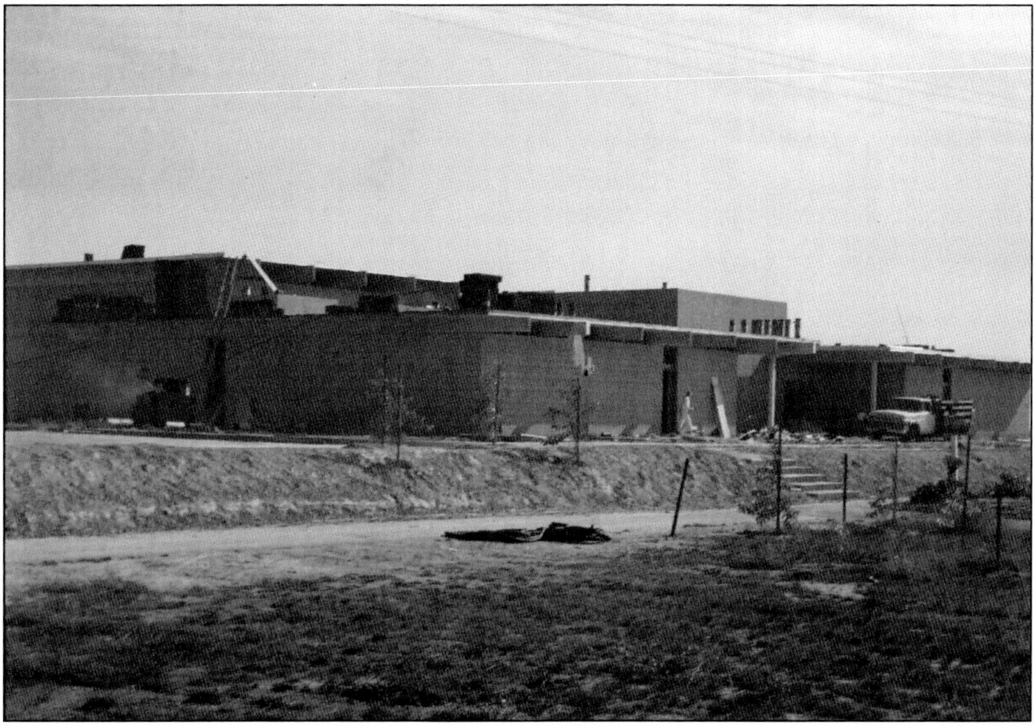

President Cain was determined to create a campus with a wide variety of athletic facilities. The field house, shown here during construction in 1970, contained two activity rooms as well as locker rooms and showers. Among the other facilities built in the early years of the new campus were tennis courts, a baseball field, a basketball court, and a track.

The Natural Sciences and Mathematics building, intended to coordinate laboratory programs, opened in 1973. The building included 34 laboratories for biology, chemistry, physics, and math classes, 57 faculty offices, a green house, and animal behavior rooms. At the time the building opened, the School of Natural Sciences and Mathematics included the departments of biological science, chemistry, health and physical education, mathematics, and physics.

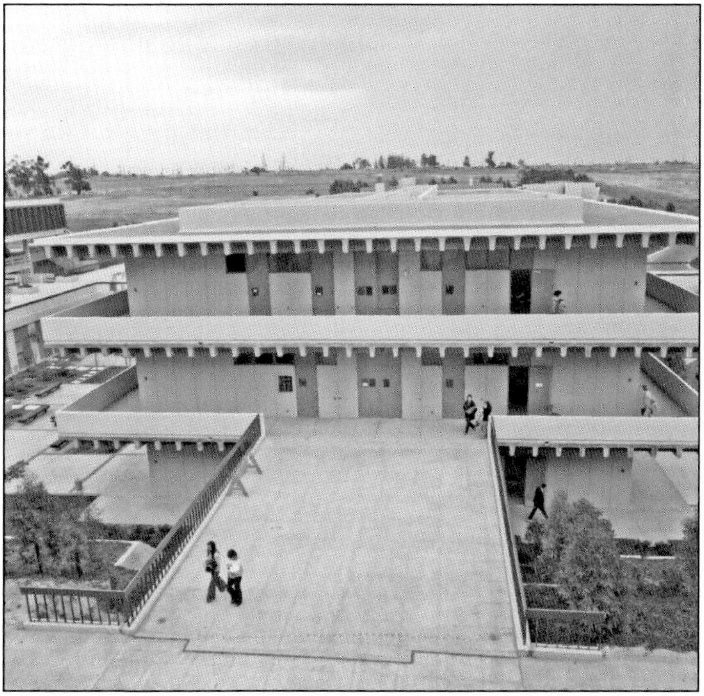

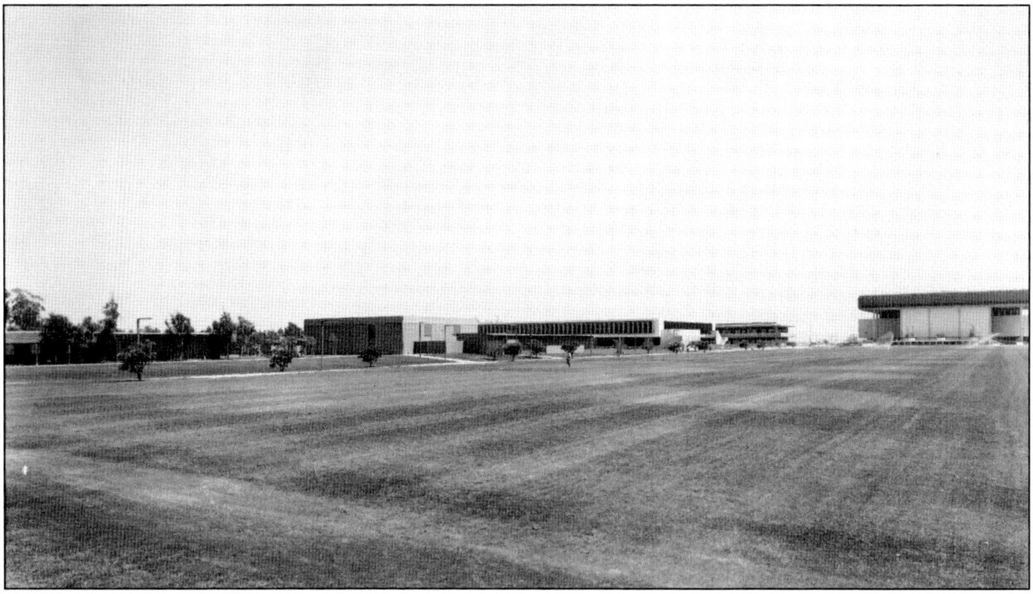

The well-manicured and growing campus is shown here in 1973. This photograph shows most of the buildings in the first phase of the construction of the campus nearly completed. Buildings to the left include the Small College Complex, Social and Behavioral Science, Natural Sciences and Mathematics, and the Educational Resources Center.

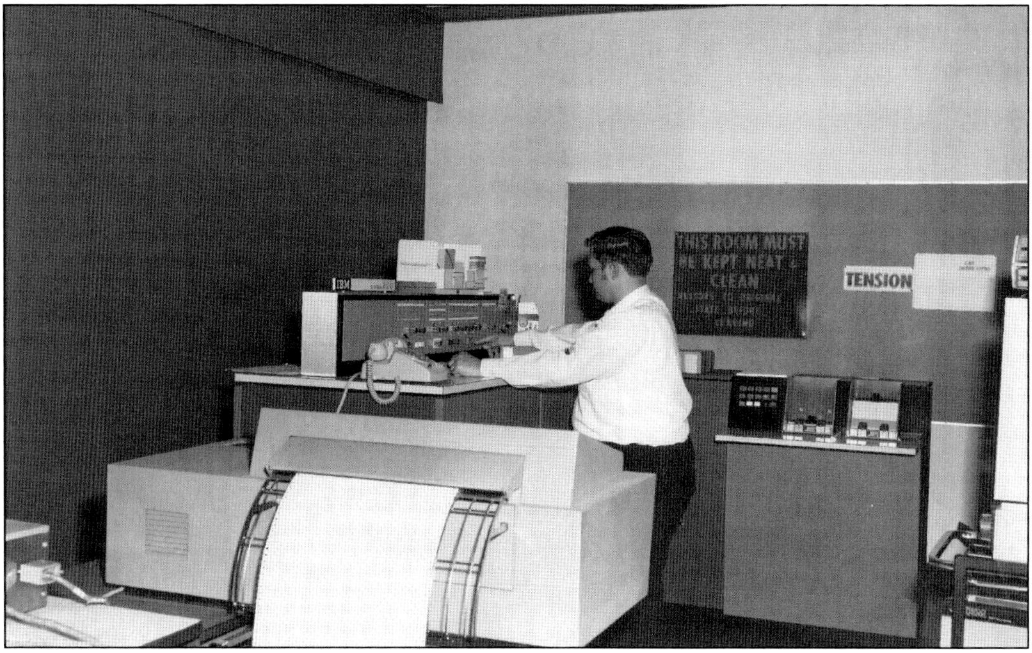

A college employee operates the IBM System 360 mainframe computer in the Campus Computer Center in August 1970. According to the 1970–1971 college catalog, "the Office of Institutional Studies and ADP [Automated Data Processing] provide technical assistance and data processing services for instructional support, research, and administration." Computer processing was also available for students enrolled in information systems, an interdepartmental field of study.

An innovative set of five lectures titled "In Search of Identity: The Japanese in America," took place at the college in 1970 to stimulate campus and community interest in courses on East Asian culture and history. Additional events that spring included photographic exhibitions and a Kabuki play. Pictured here, from left to right, are Nadine Hata, program organizer and history professor, Harry Kitano, a speaker from UCLA, and Don Hata, history professor.

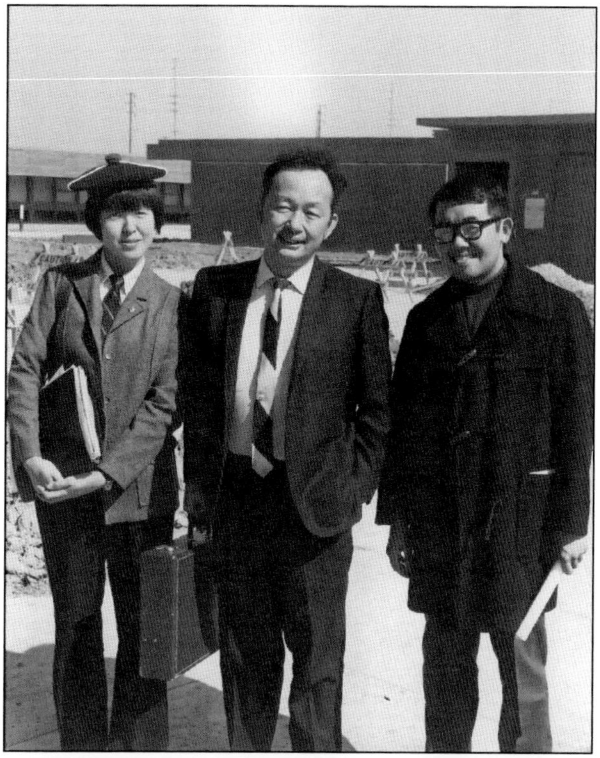

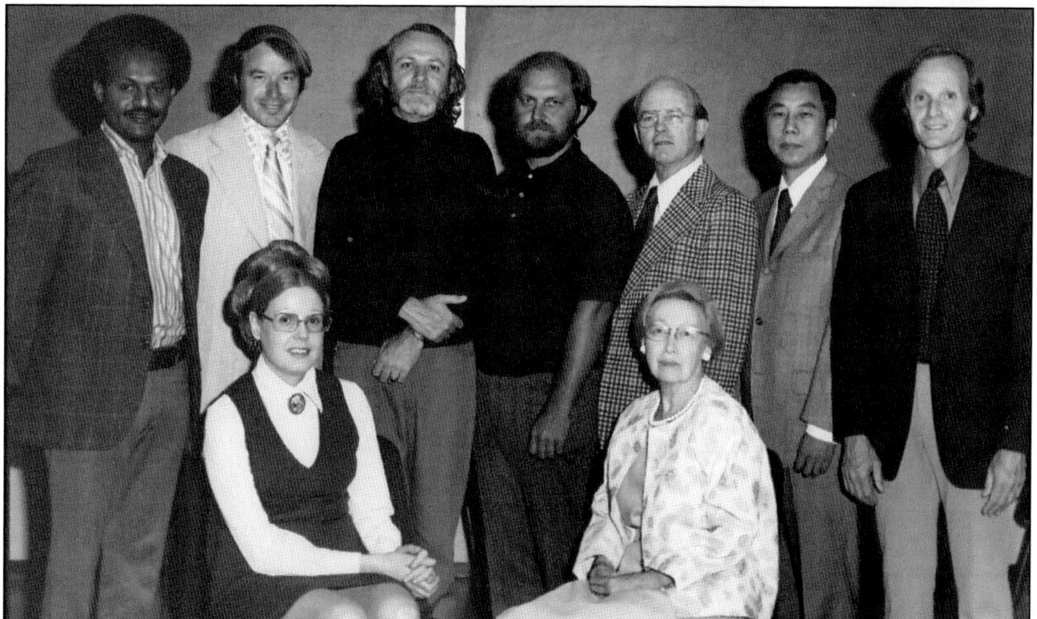

Professors and others in economics and business administration departments are shown here in the 1970s. Included, from left to right, are (first row) unidentified and Marion Buck; (second row) C. W. Lee, Abe Kidane, Frank Billes, Jim Harris, George Clawson, George Wong, and Herb Milgrim.

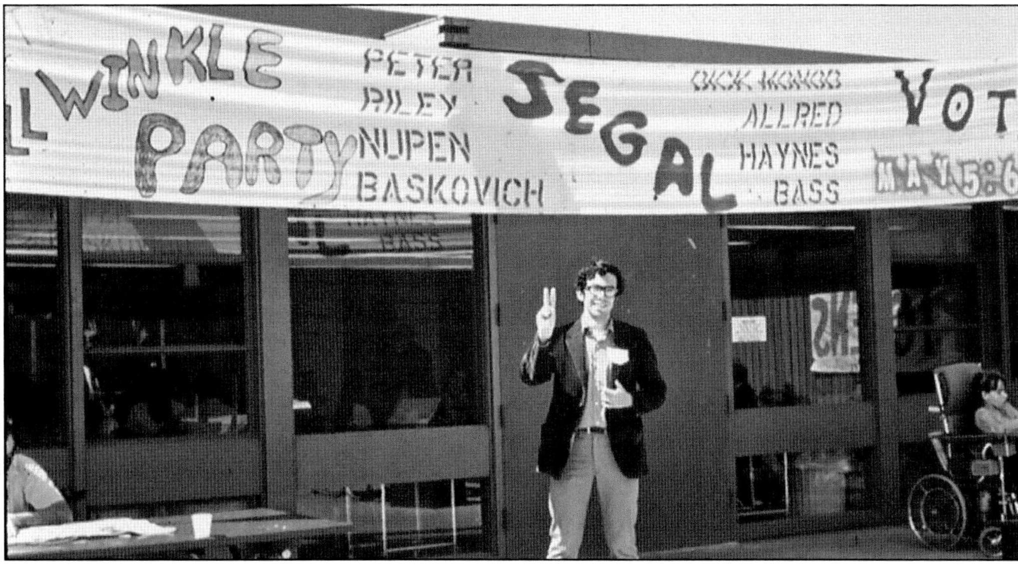

Ed Segal campaigns for student body president in 1970. Segal's Bullwinkle Party won the election. Segal founded a satirical underground newspaper entitled the ***Bullsheet*** that was aimed at lampooning various aspects of the college community. After he was elected, Segal was quoted as saying "we had much more fun running for office than being in office."

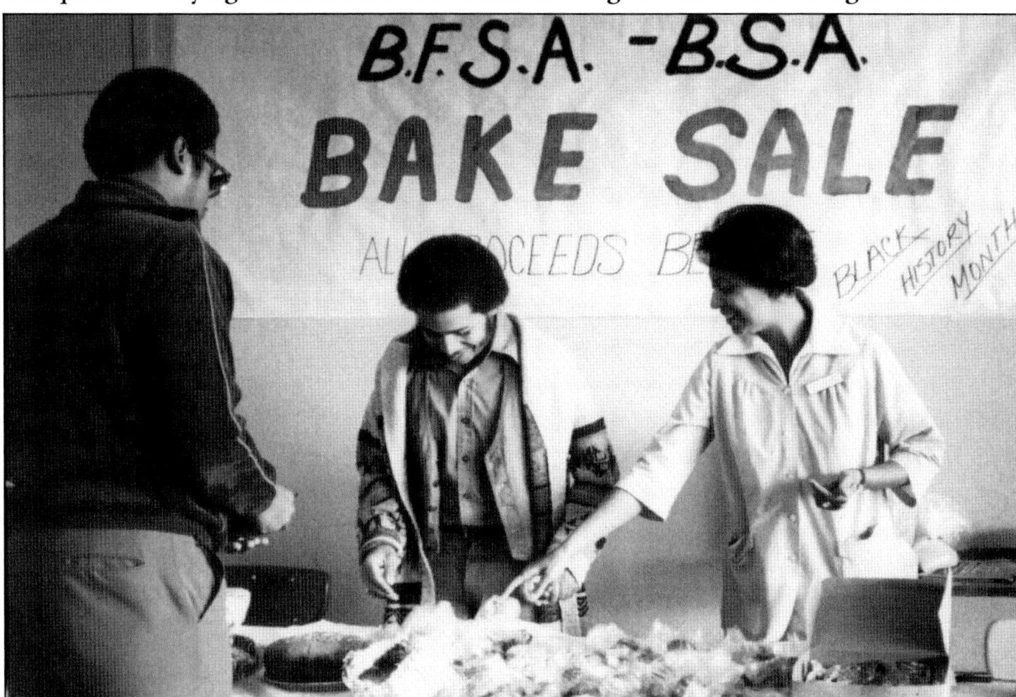

The Black Student Association was among the sponsors of a bake sale to raise funds for a Black History Month during the early 1970s. According to the 1971–1972 catalog, Afro-American Studies was an interdepartmental field "designed to provide an understanding of the cultural and social roots of African-Americans as well as the political, social, and economic factors that have influenced their development in American culture."

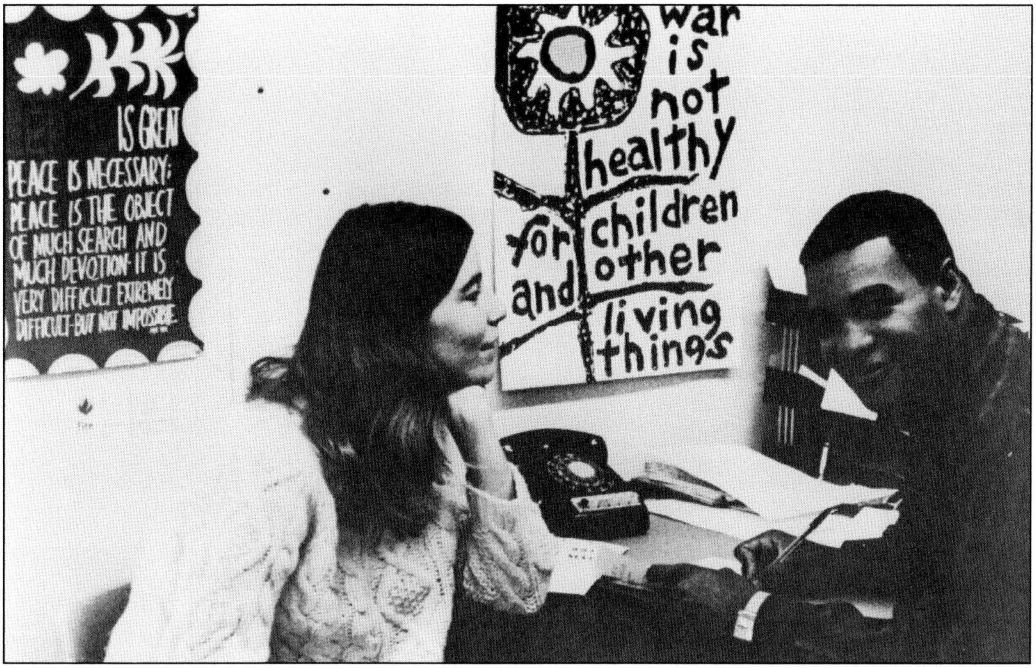

A source of antipathy between the administration and student activists developed with the refusal of President Cain to allow student resource fees to be used for draft counseling in 1969. After a change in CSC policy, counseling was funded by the student government and offered by the Draft Counseling and Peace Education office during 1970.

In June 1970, the Asian Studies Society sponsored a luncheon that attracted 250 people at the Watt Campus. The Japanese-American band the Invaders entertained during the event. An interdepartmental East Asian field of study was designed to provide students an understanding of social, political, and cultural patterns of East Asia, with an emphasis on China and Japan. The 1970–1971 college catalog offered six Japanese and seven Chinese language courses.

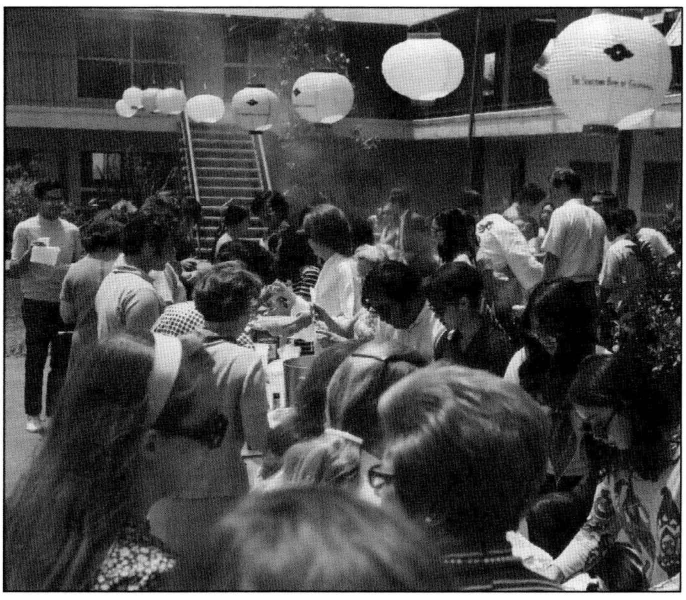

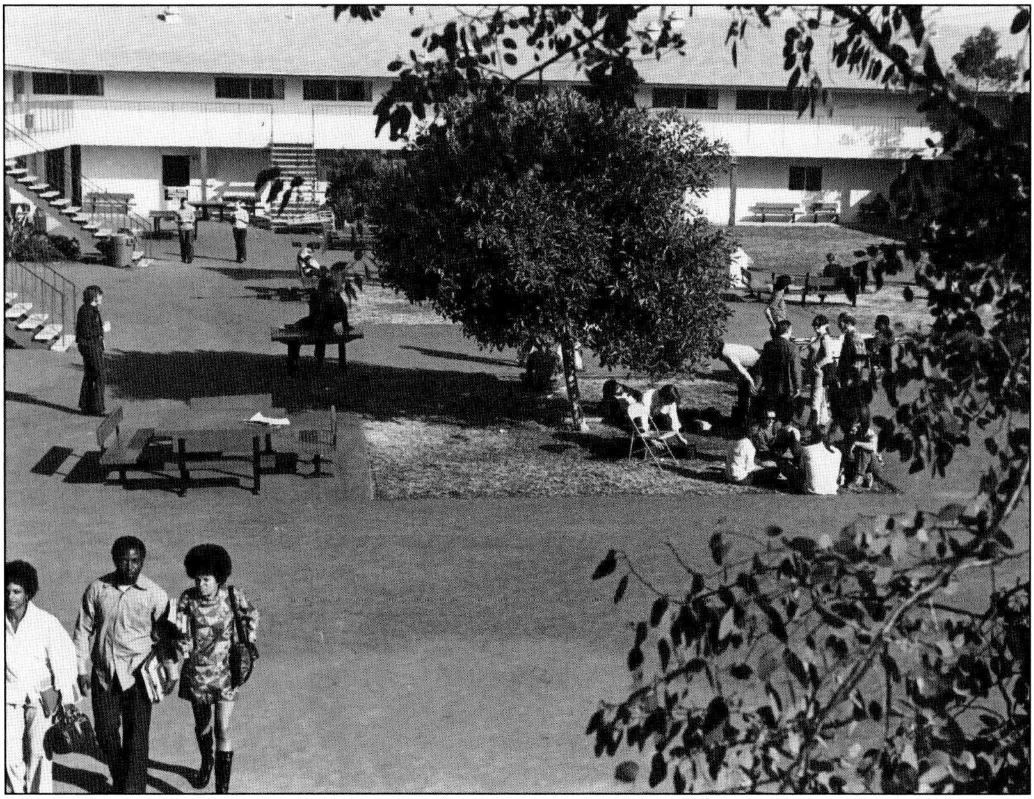

By 1971, the Watt Campus was now called the "old campus" and the foliage appears to have matured. The new campus was still under construction, and building openings occurred on a semi-annual basis. The Watt Campus was used by CSC Dominguez Hills until mid-1972. It was later occupied by the South Bay University College of Law and was then dismantled to make way for a condominium complex in the 1980s.

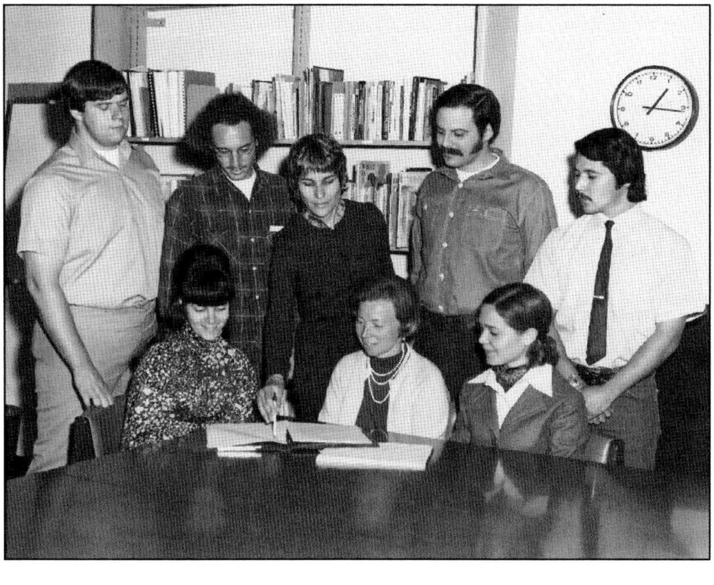

Among other reasons for joining the History Club in April 1970, a student newspaper article explained that students could get firsthand knowledge of faculty members' idiosyncrasies. Special lecture topics that year included "Norman Thomas and his Influence on America," "The Mexican-American and Modern Society," and "Russia in 1917—Revolution or Evolution."

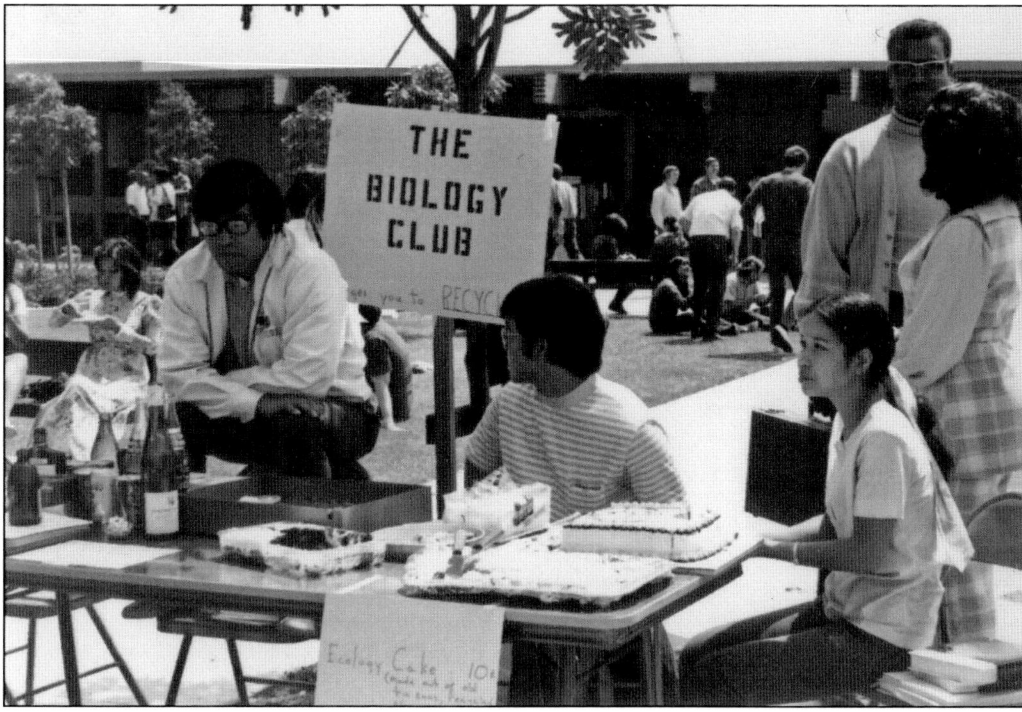

In 1971, the new campus provided a larger venue for campus organizations to showcase their clubs and raise funds. The Biology Club offered an "Ecology Cake" for 10¢. The first Earth Day, April 22, 1970, was celebrated with an environmental teach-in. The student newspaper devoted several pages to Earth Day and stated that, "Ecology Action is . . . creating new lifestyles to reduce the waste and destruction of our environment."

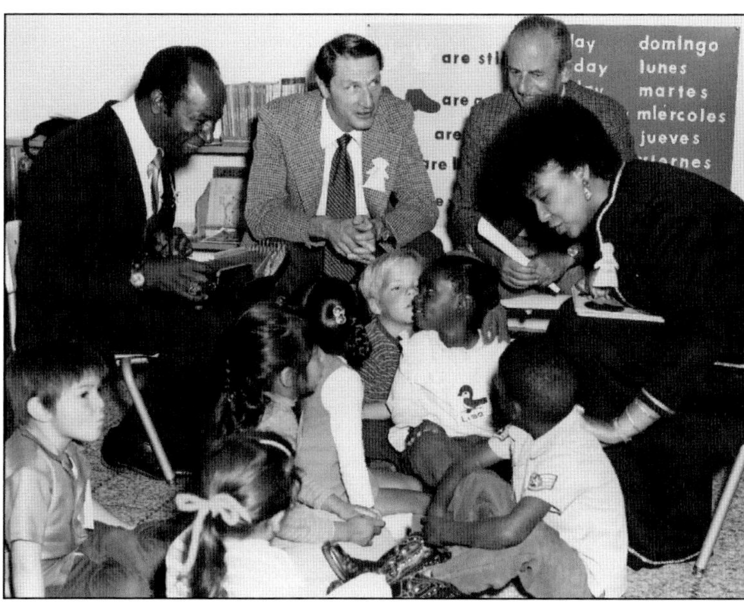

Teachers and administrators gather around children at the opening of the Head Start Day Care Center in 1973. Harry Nethery, dean of College Services and Facility Planning, is at the back right, alongside Milo Milfs, dean of students.

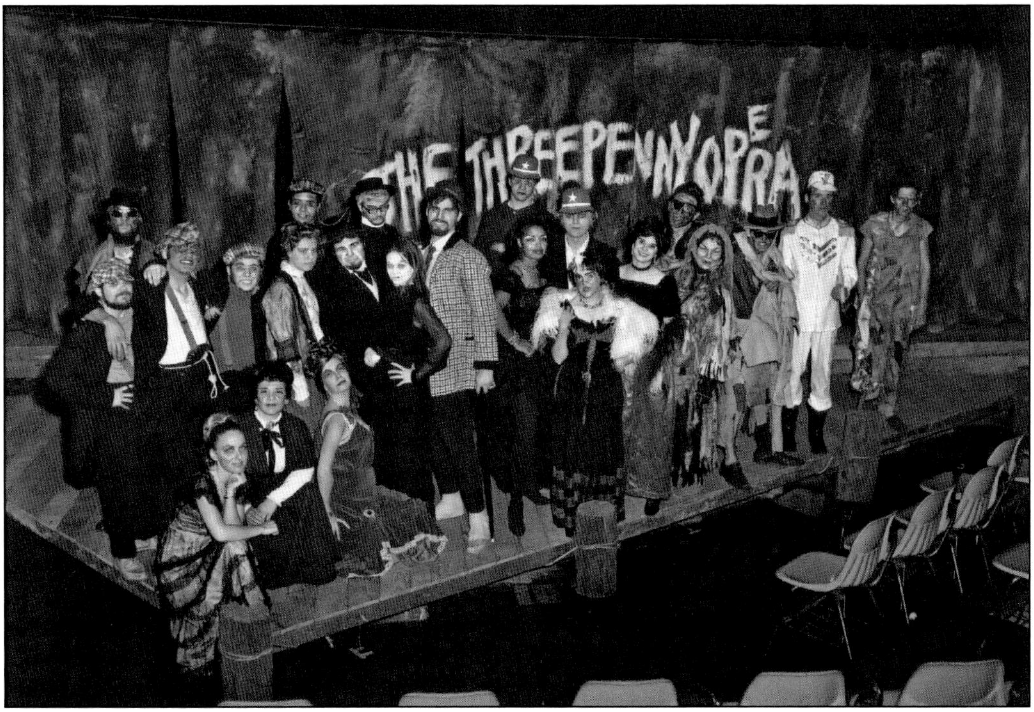

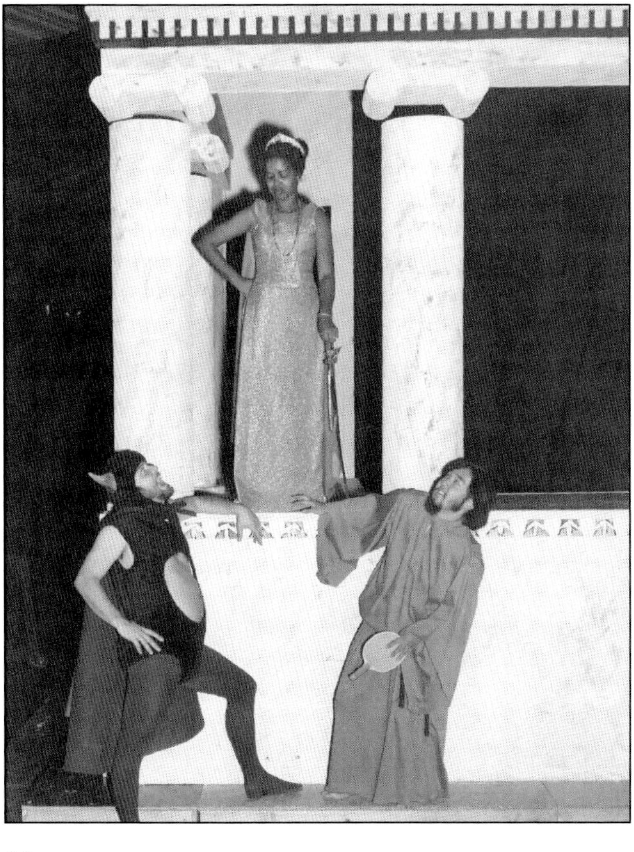

The Dominguez Players presented a production of Kurt Weill and Bertolt Brecht's *The Threepenny Opera* at the college's Playbox Theater in 1970. Hal Marienthal directed the production with Frances Steiner as musical director. The *Los Angeles Times* reviewed the play and wrote that the cast sang both "beautifully" and "terribly."

A Surprising Uprising opened in the Little Theater on campus in February 1972. Incorporating several elements of a burlesque rock musical revue, the play was based on *Lysistrata* by Aristophanes and featured a ping-pong game between Nixon and Mao. In an attempt to bring in an audience and stir up controversy, the playwright warned that the show might be shut down because of its subject matter. It wasn't.

This advertisement for GiGi's Mod Mod World, which was located around the corner from campus in the Alpha Beta Shopping Center, is indicative of businesses opening in the campus area that catered to students. The advertisement appeared in the student newspaper in October 1971.

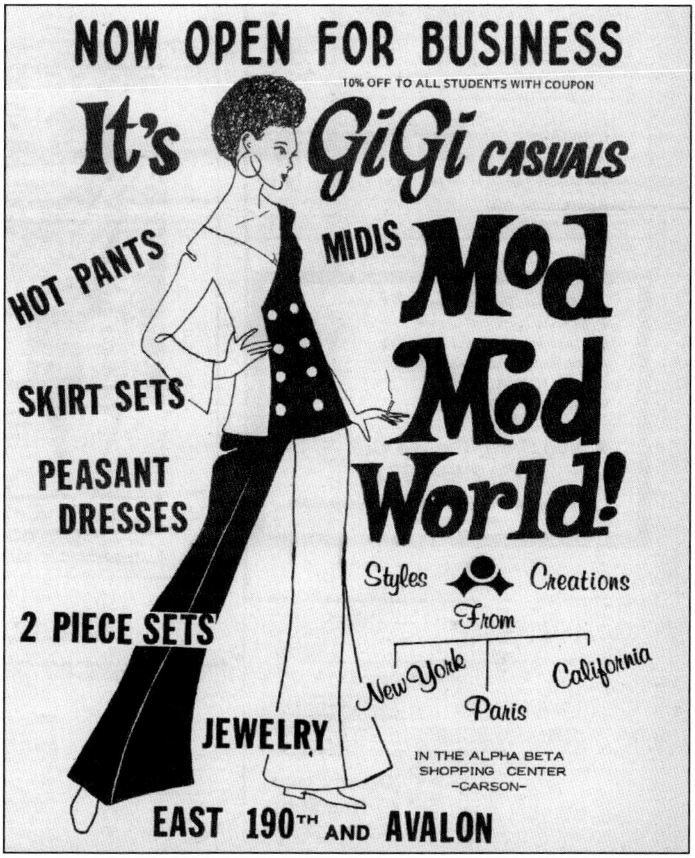

A 1975 exhibition titled "Locale as Laboratory" took an interdisciplinary approach to the history of the Dominguez Hills area. Ten separate collections were featured, including materials on Native American village sites, African American history, the 1910 air meet at Dominguez Field, the history of Compton, and Japanese Americans in Los Angeles.

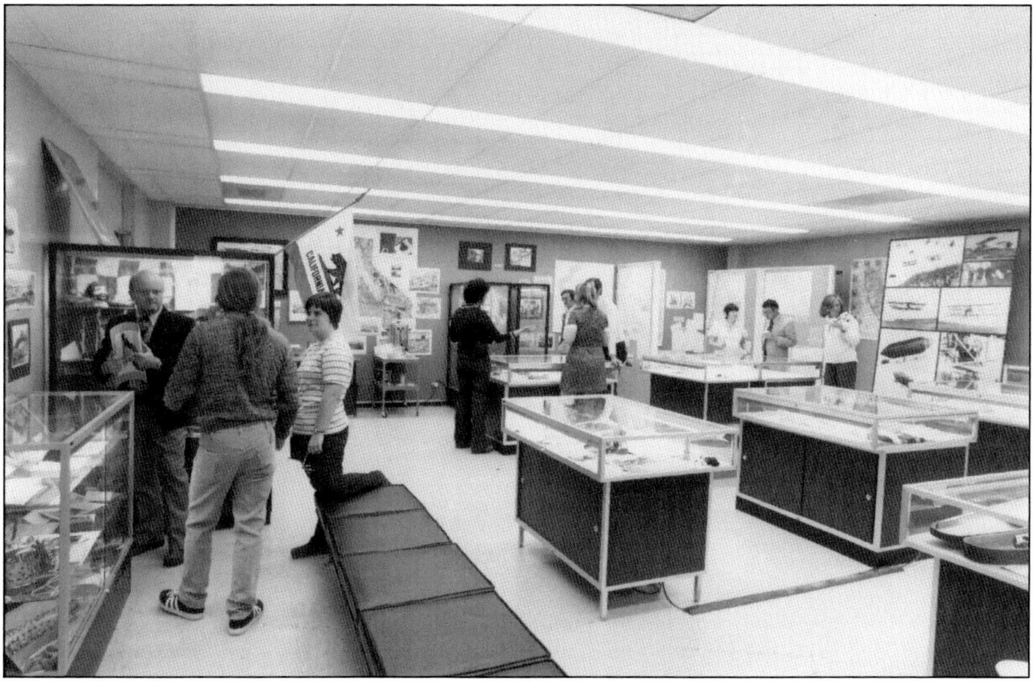

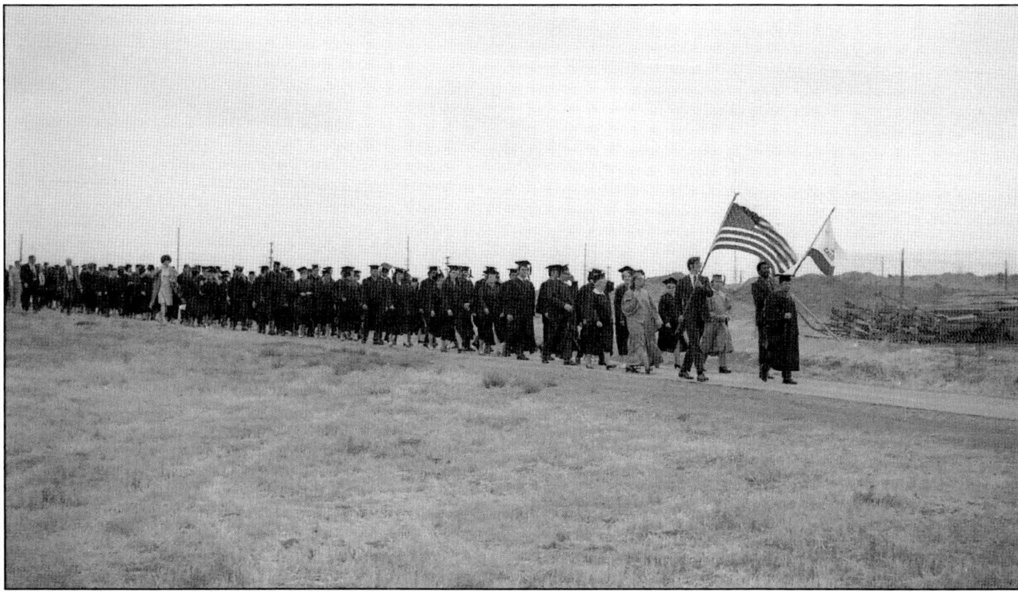

Faculty marshal Dr. Jack Vaughn (in cap and gown at front of the processional) leads students through a field from the old campus to the new one prior to morning commencement exercises in 1970. Dr. Philip Buck, retiring chair of the Political Science Department, delivered the main commencement address.

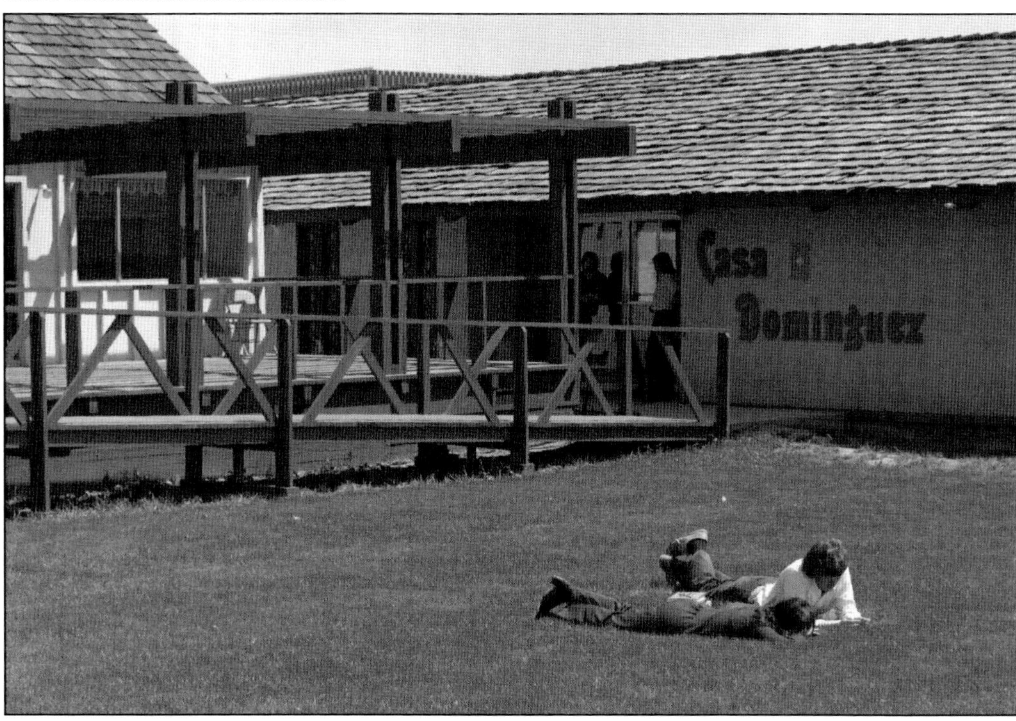

A former housing development sales office, the Casa Dominguez was donated to the Student Association in 1972. It was the site of many heated discussions throughout the 1970s as the student government debated curriculum developments, how to divide student fees, and various controversies surrounding campus personnel.

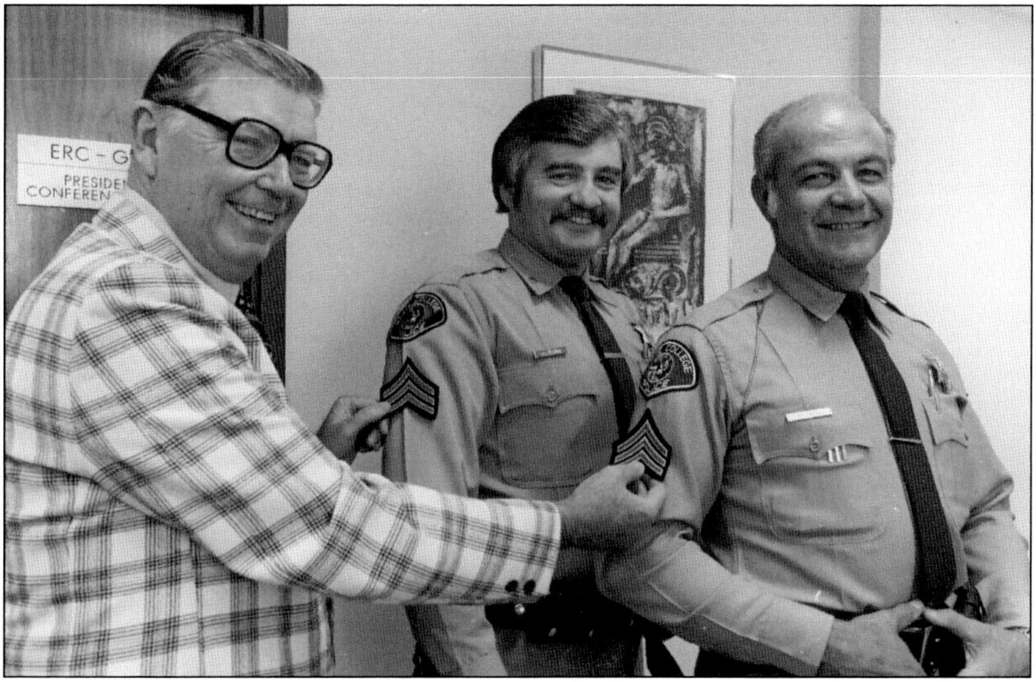

President Cain presents sergeant stripes to campus police officers Jack Peconic (center) and Mike Pappas (right) in 1976. The officers were the first to be named sergeants. In 1976, the college police department consisted of 12 officers, a chief, and five parking officers. By 2009, the police department had more than 20 officers and five parking officers.

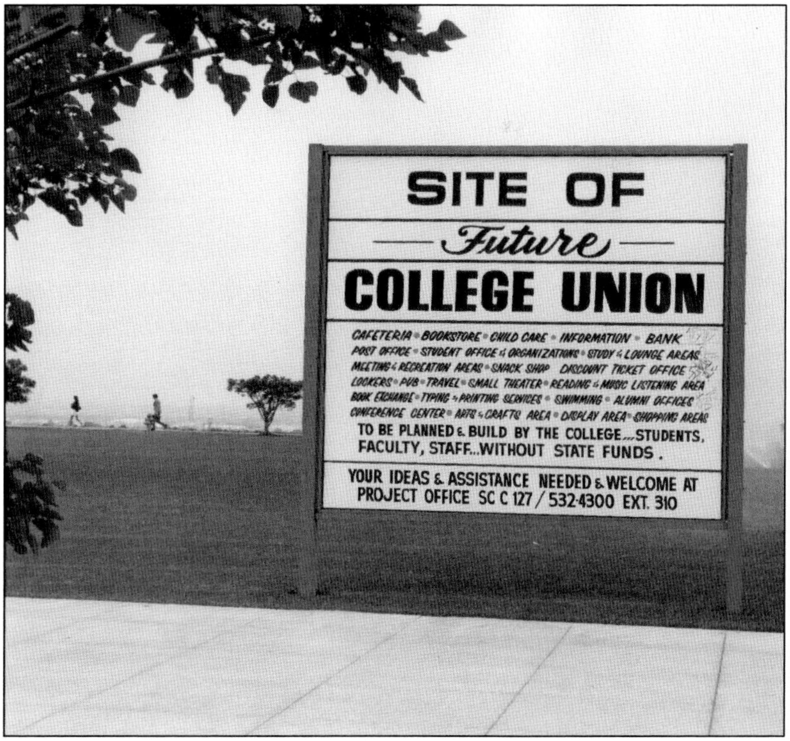

This image was used throughout the 1970s in the student newspaper to lobby for funding for a student union. By 1978, a temporary union had been established in the Small College, but it would be the mid-1980s before a student referendum to increase incidental fees was approved. At that time, a capital campaign to raise enough money to build a student union also commenced.

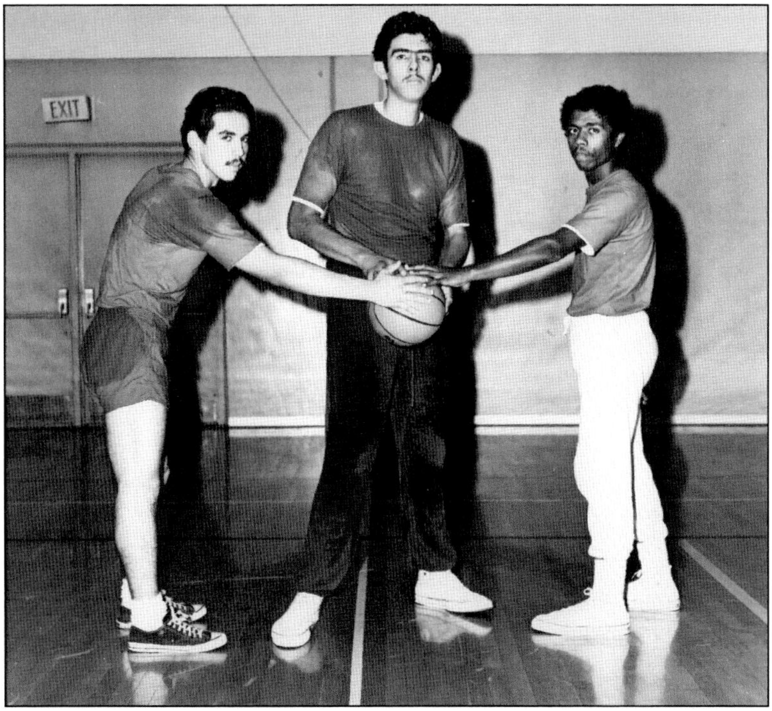

The college's first basketball team was coached by history professor Henry Orozco. The freshman squad in the early 1970s consisted of nine members and lacked a gym for practice. Pictured here, from left to right, are Manuel Guerrero, Enrique Herrera, and Leonard Thompson.

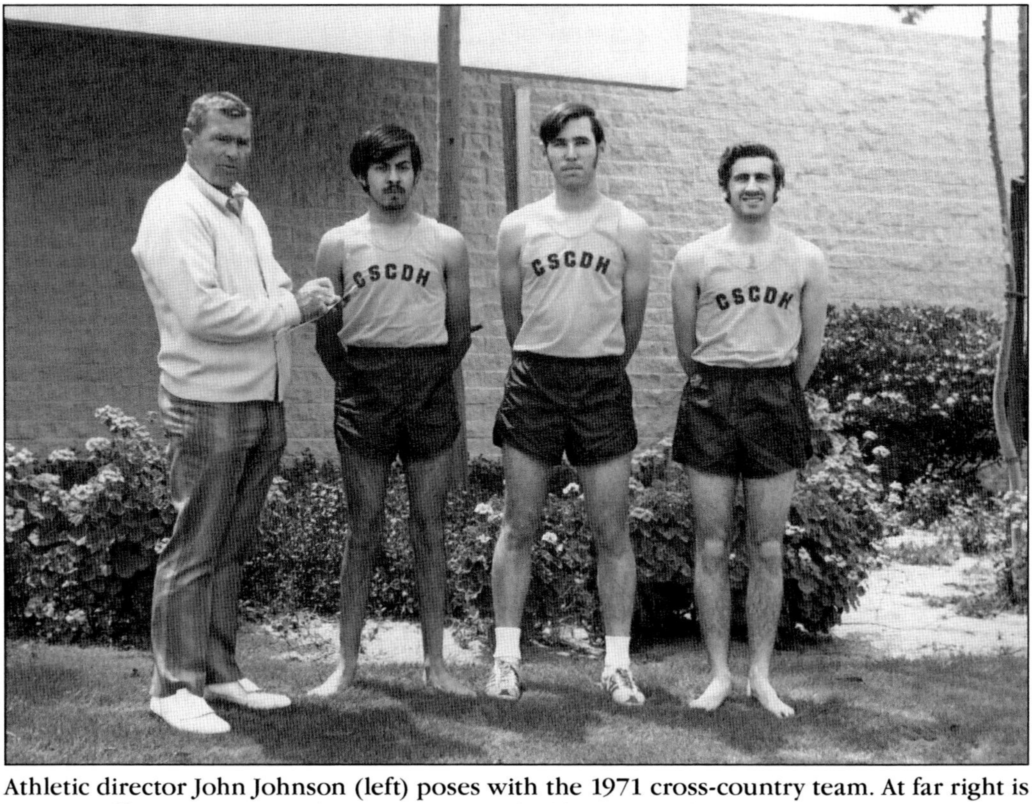

Athletic director John Johnson (left) poses with the 1971 cross-country team. At far right is Terry Graff, team captain. The team was coached by Ron Easley (not pictured).

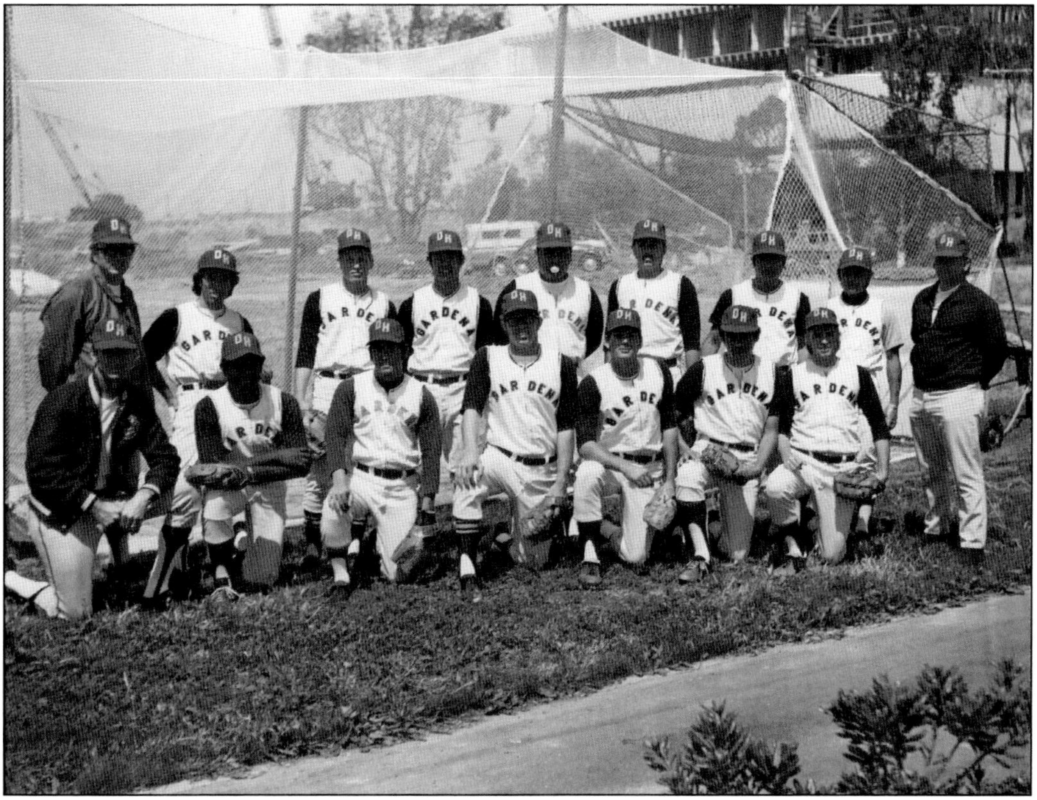

The 1971 varsity baseball team poses for a photograph in front of the batting cages and the yet-to-be-completed Educational Resources Center. While their caps read "DH," their jerseys are borrowed from Gardena High School.

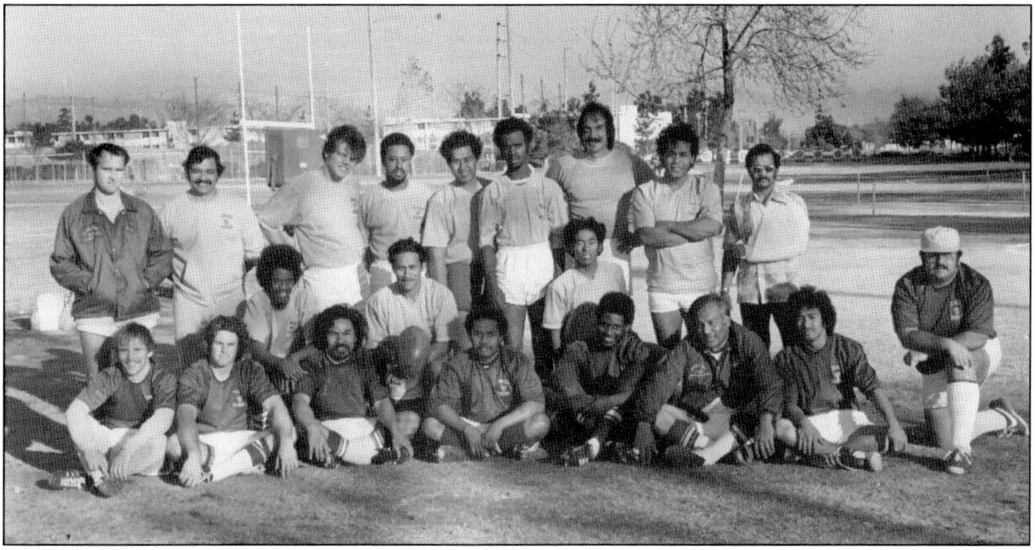

The 1973–1974 campus rugby team is pictured here with their coaches. In 1976, a writer for the student newspaper stated that rugby, given the game's international standing, was the third most popular sport on campus.

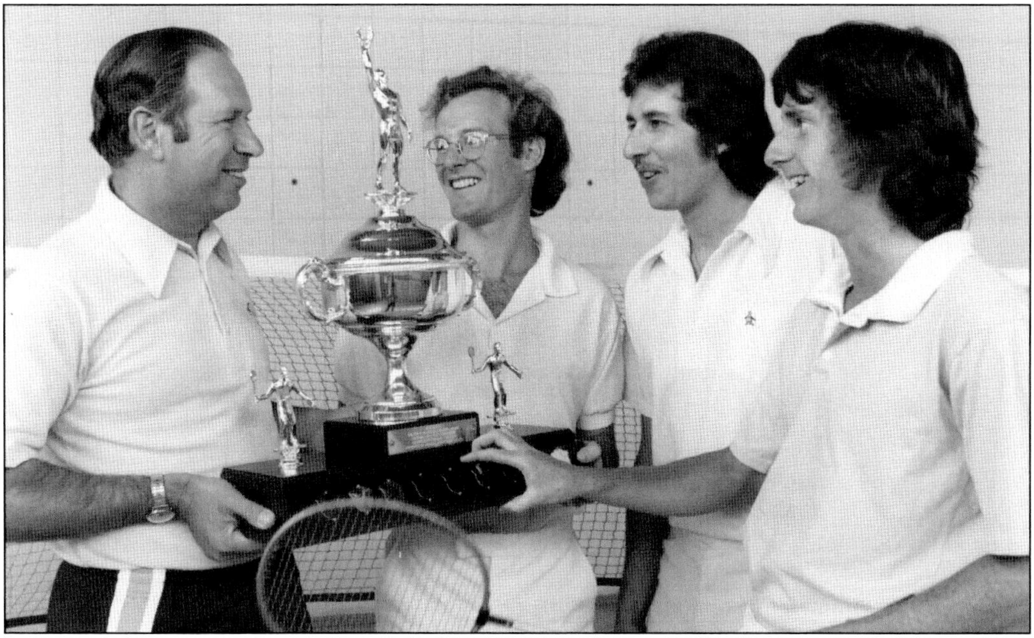

Head coach Jim Poole, left, holds the Badminton National Title trophy in May 1975 with (from left to right) Pete Steinbroner, Mike Kelly, and Tom Luevano. It was the first national title won by a Dominguez Hills team.

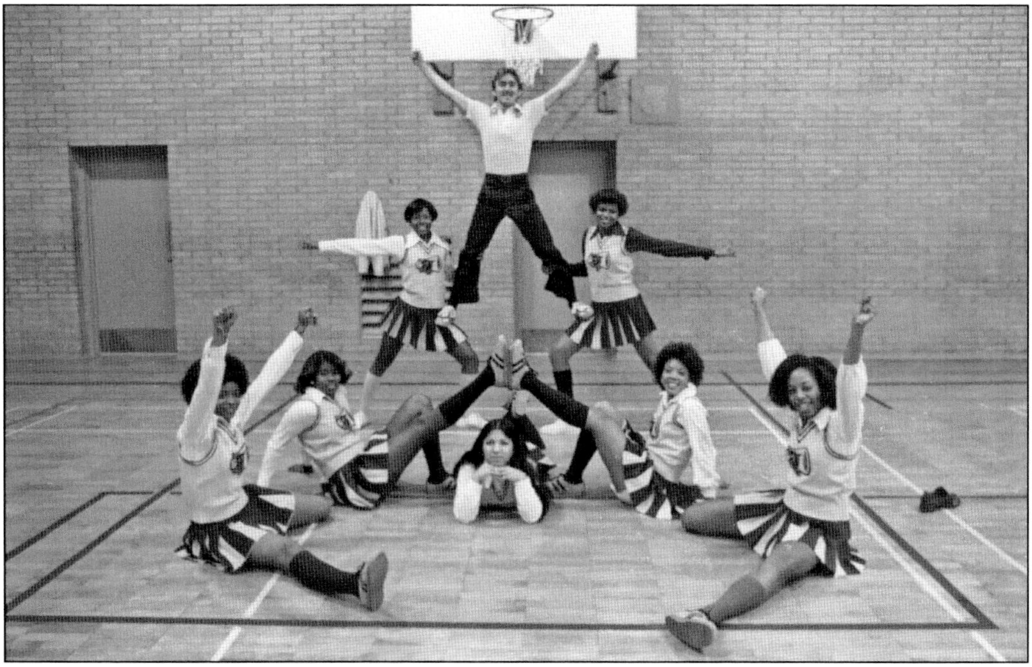

The Toro Cheerleaders form a pyramid in the gymnasium in the late 1970s. A campus committee recommended that the college symbol be a bull and have a connection to the Dominguez Family cattle brand. The nickname "Toros" was introduced in 1969. A memo noted that the college mascot would be a bull but discouraged students from keeping a "live example of one on campus as a pet."

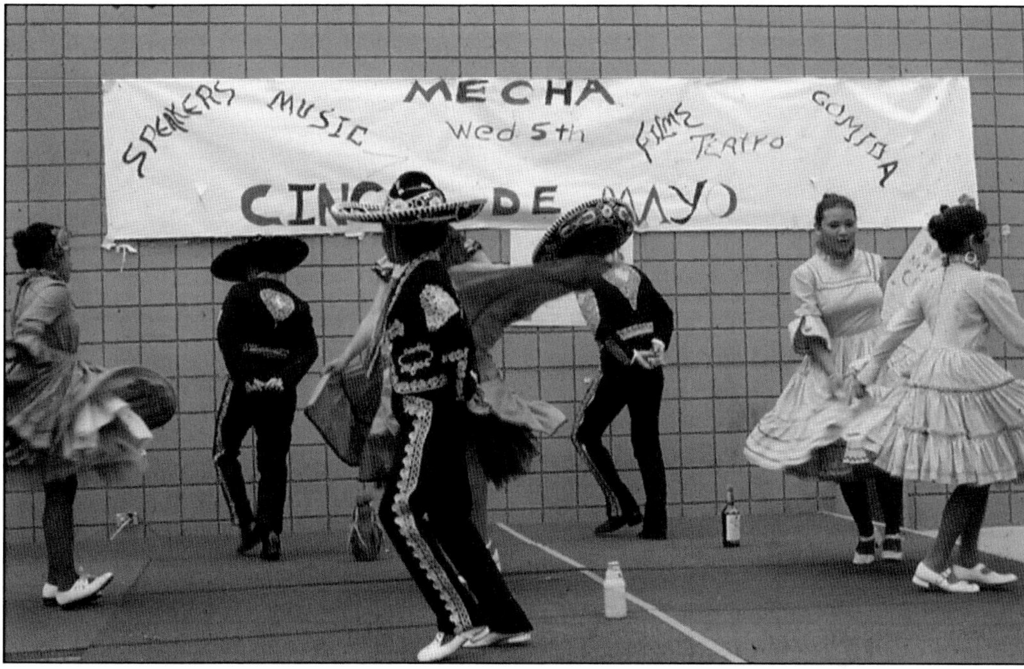

Founded in the late 1960s, the campus chapter of the Mexican American student organization Movimiento Estudiantil Chicano de Aztlán (M.E.Ch.A) consisted of over 40 students in its first year. Providing volunteer tutors and advisors, members also sponsored an annual Cinco de Mayo celebration for many years. Shown here is the celebration in 1976, which, according to the student newspaper, drew one of the largest crowds to the college up to that point.

The 1970 Cinco de Mayo celebration consisted of three days of events with speakers, music, and dance. Students from high schools throughout Los Angeles attended the event. The speakers included activist and educator Sal Castro, historian and former CSU Dominguez Hills professor Roldolfo Acuña, educator and politician Richard Alatorre, and sociologist Jaime Raigoza.

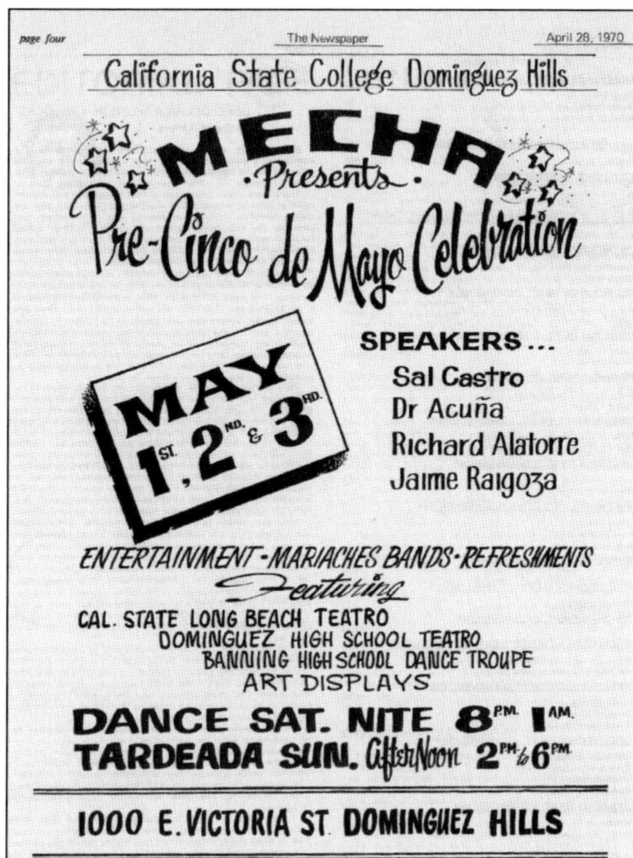
page four The Newspaper April 28, 1970

California State College Dominguez Hills

MECHA
Presents
Pre-Cinco de Mayo Celebration

MAY 1st, 2nd & 3rd

SPEAKERS...
Sal Castro
Dr Acuña
Richard Alatorre
Jaime Raigoza

ENTERTAINMENT-MARIACHES BANDS-REFRESHMENTS
Featuring
CAL. STATE LONG BEACH TEATRO
DOMINGUEZ HIGH SCHOOL TEATRO
BANNING HIGH SCHOOL DANCE TROUPE
ART DISPLAYS

DANCE SAT. NITE 8 P.M. 1 A.M.
TARDEADA SUN. AfterNoon 2 PM to 6 PM

1000 E. VICTORIA ST DOMINGUEZ HILLS

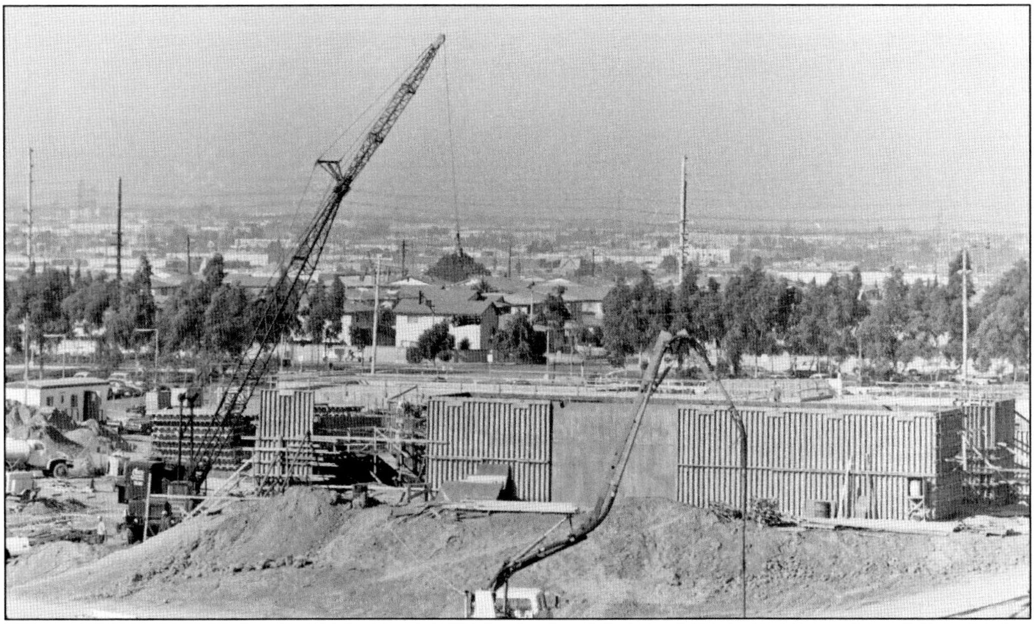

The second round of campus construction began in the mid-1970s. Ground was broken on the Student Health Center on August 1, 1975. The building was to contain over 20,000 square feet of space for examination and treatment rooms, X-ray facilities, an emergency room, medical laboratories, and a pharmaceutical dispensary.

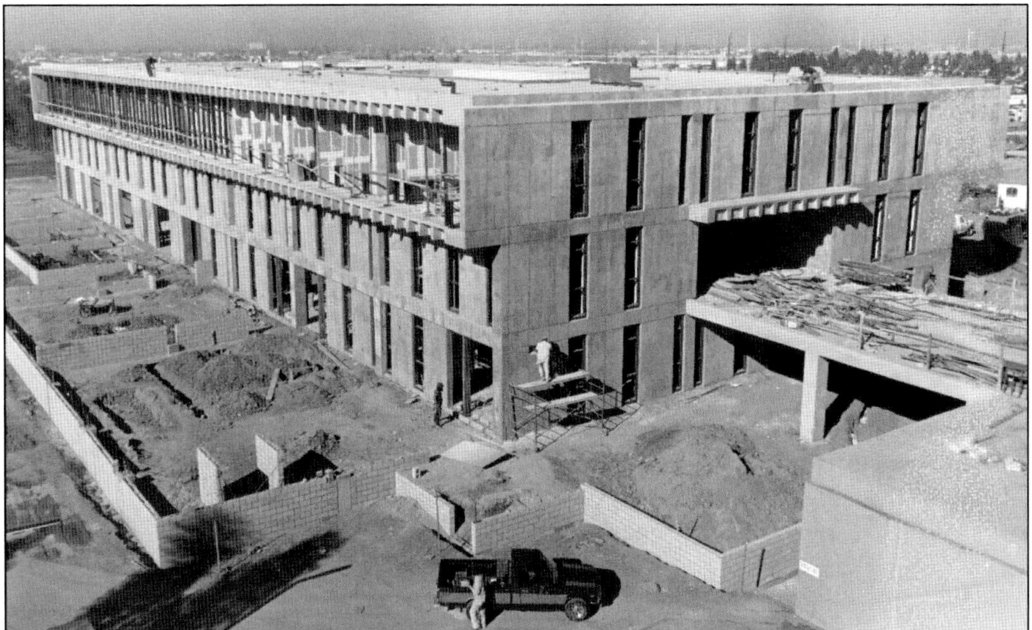

The three-story Humanities and Fine Arts building is shown here during construction. The building included a musical recital hall, an art gallery, art studios, music instruction facilities, language laboratories, various classrooms, and about 100 faculty offices. In 1994, the building was renamed John N. and Marion L. LaCorte Hall in honor of the parents of philosophy professor John LaCorte.

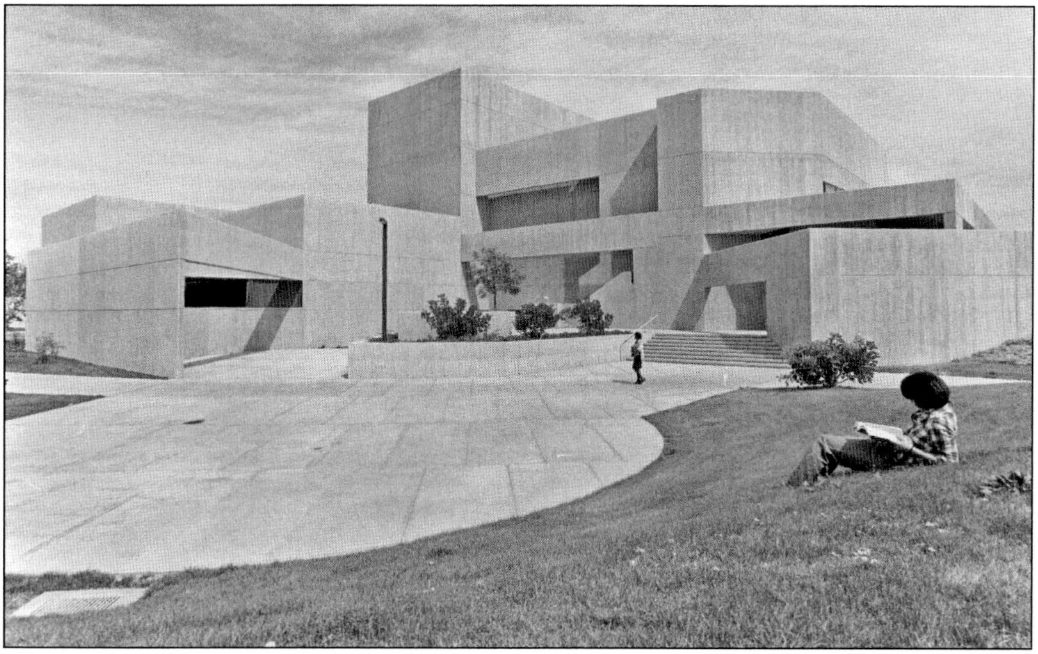

After several years of being written out of the state budget, the funds to build the University Theatre made it into the 1975 budget. The 500-seat theater included a full stage, rehearsal and dressing areas, and a large scene shop. It was completed in 1977.

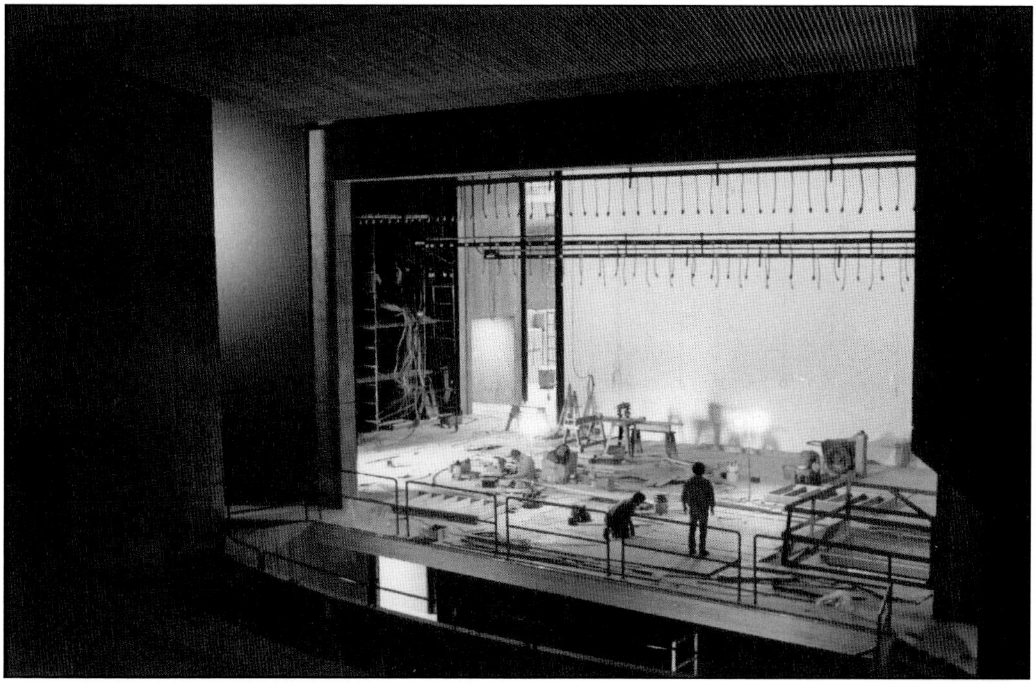

The construction of the stage of the University Theatre is shown here prior to the Dominguez Players' opening production of *My Fair Lady* in November 1977. The Playbox Theater in the Small College Complex had been a smaller venue but had served as the home for theater productions at CSC Dominguez Hills for eight years.

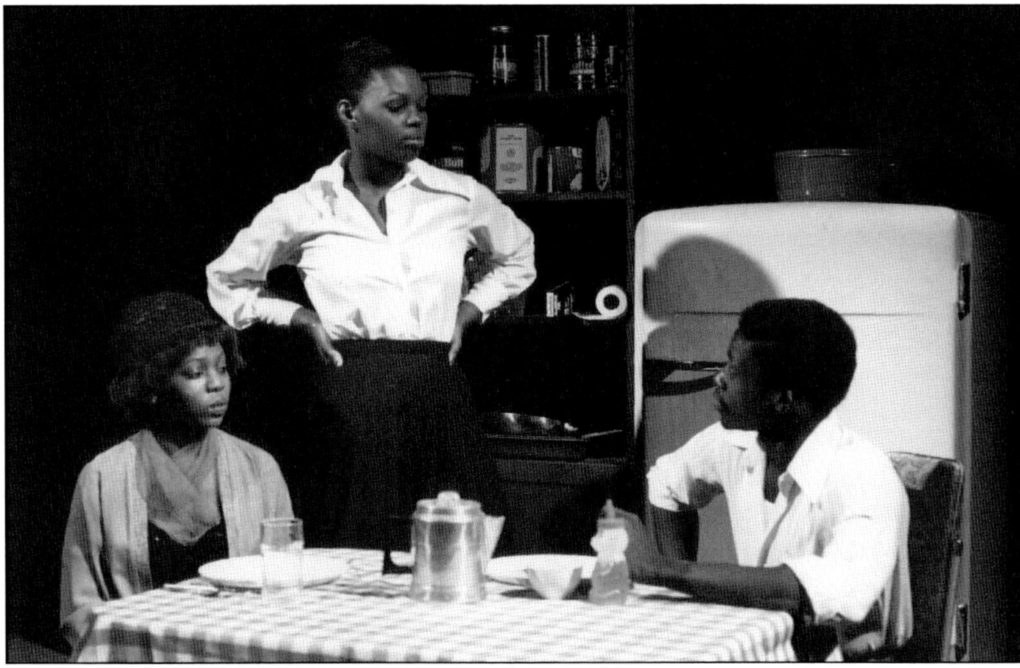

Directed by Luther Whitsill, a local teacher, the Dominguez Players' 1978 production of Lorraine Hansberry's *A Raisin in the Sun* featured Toni White (left), Willa Osby (center), and Clint Crosby.

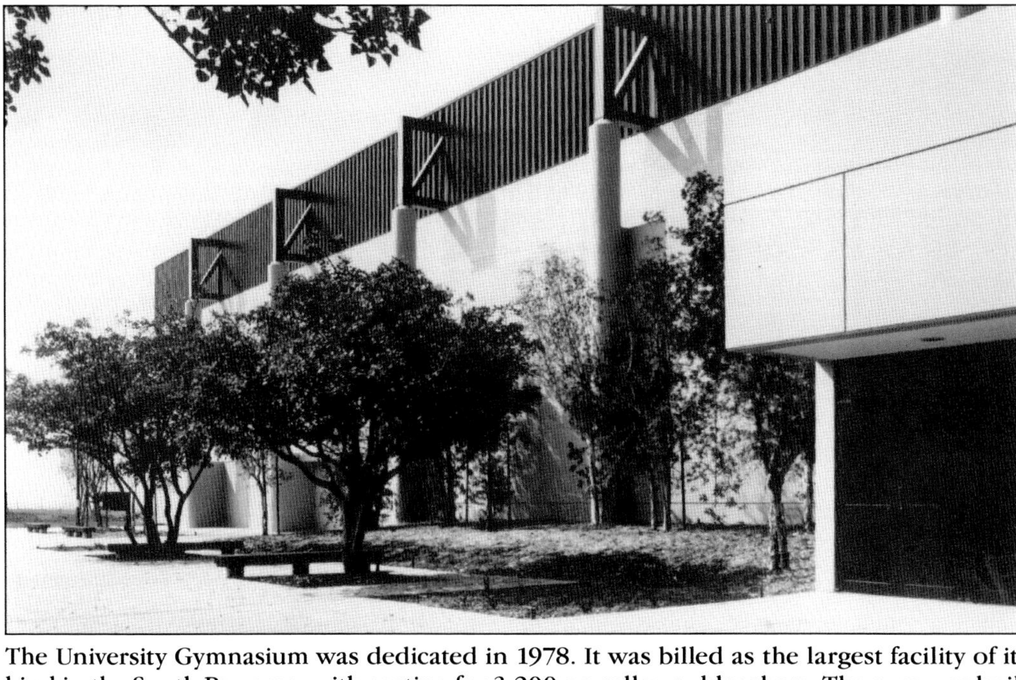

The University Gymnasium was dedicated in 1978. It was billed as the largest facility of its kind in the South Bay area, with seating for 3,200 on rollaway bleachers. The gym was built to accommodate several basketball, volleyball, or badminton games simultaneously as well as to have rooms for dance and combative activities. An outdoor pool was built next to the gym. Completion of the sports complex ended the university's initial building program.

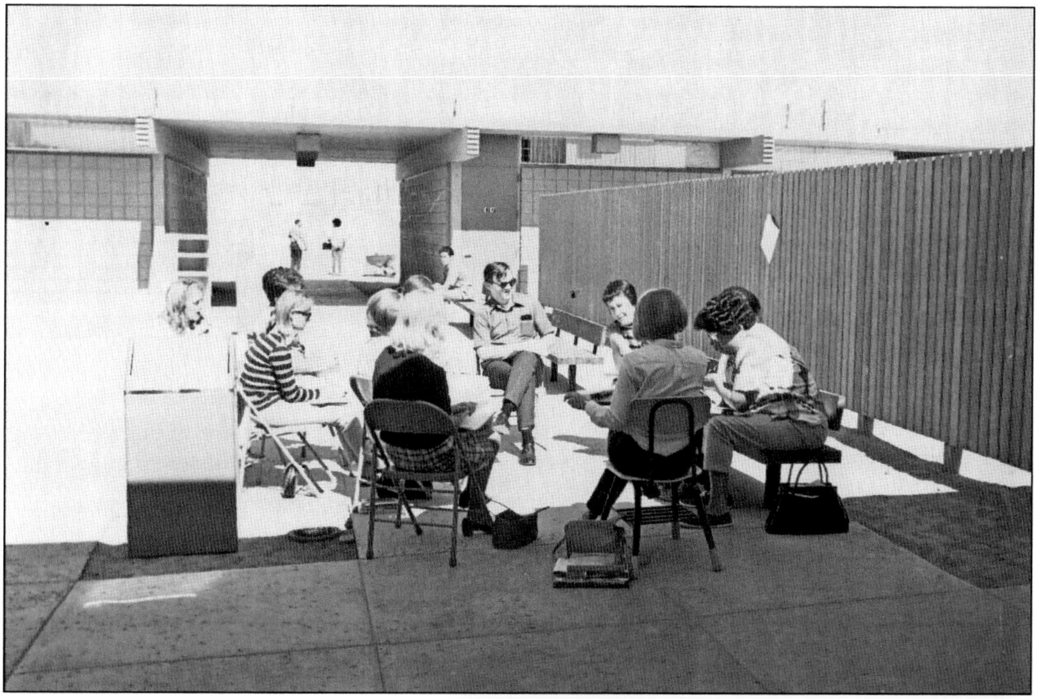

A class takes place outdoors adjacent to the Small College Complex in the 1970s. In its initial years, Small College courses were taught in modules of three or six weeks. General education requirements for the Small College included elementary computer programming, study skills, and writing. Areas students could concentrate on included civilizations, human studies, and environmental studies.

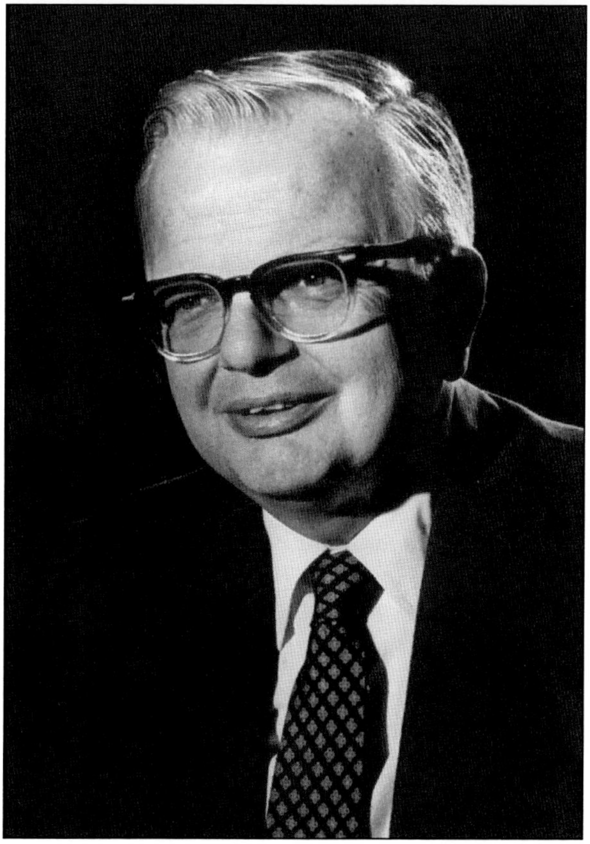

Donald R. Gerth became president in 1976 and served until 1984. Gerth served in teaching and administrative roles within in the CSU system for over 50 years, including as president of Sacramento State University for 20 years. During his tenure at CSU Dominguez Hills, Gerth guided the college toward university status, instituted new management policies to help the campus become a full-fledged urban university, and brought the 1984 Olympics to campus.

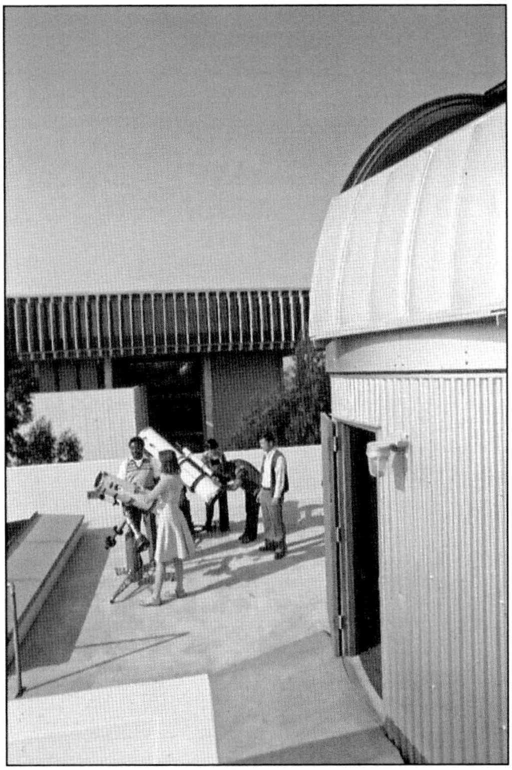

Students under the tutelage of Dr. Keith Lee look through telescopes next to the campus observatory atop the Natural Sciences and Mathematics building. The observatory opened for stargazing in 1977.

Upon reaching an enrollment of 6,500 students—25 percent of whom were graduate students—and with 45 degree programs, the college met the criteria to become a university. President Gerth displays a bumper sticker announcing the news in 1977. "University status for Dominguez Hills is a signal . . . that the campus has the level of maturity and capability to offer programs which enrich . . . this community," he said.

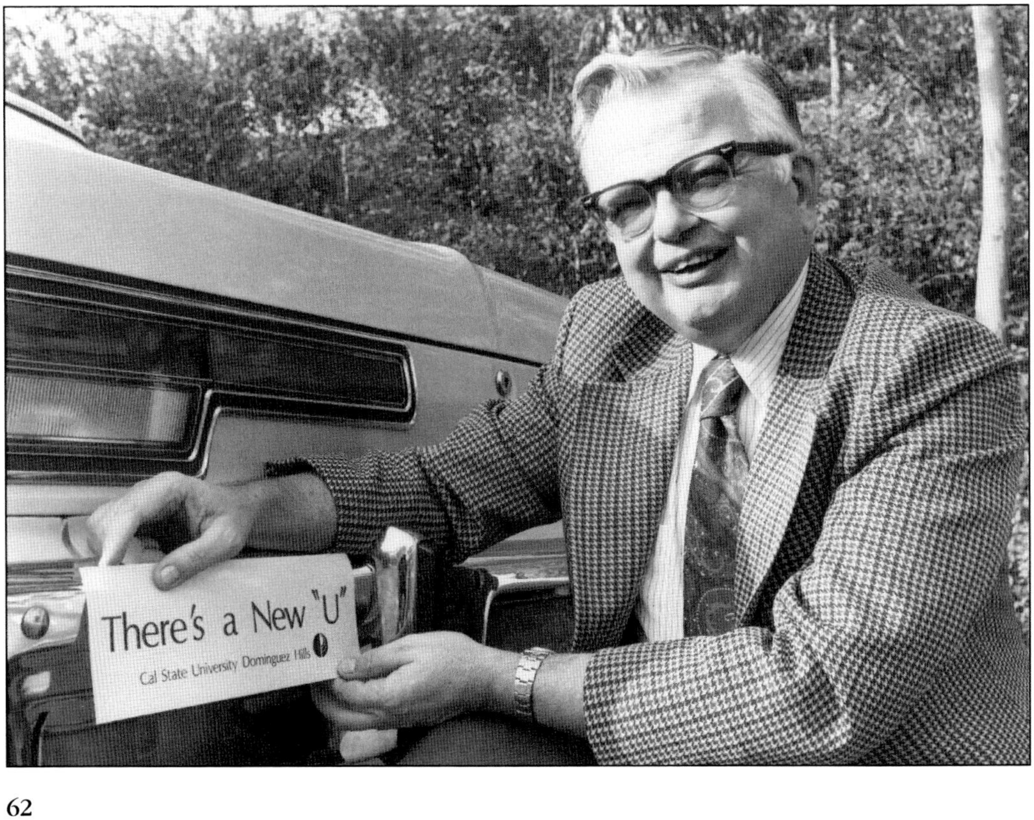

Sen. Joseph Biden speaks in the University Theatre on October 24, 1977, 31 years before being elected vice president of the United States. Biden described his experiences on the Senate Foreign Relations Committee as its youngest member. He explained that the United States was going through a period of the "aftermath of the aftermath of Vietnam." Donald MacPhee, dean and university vice president, sits in the front row.

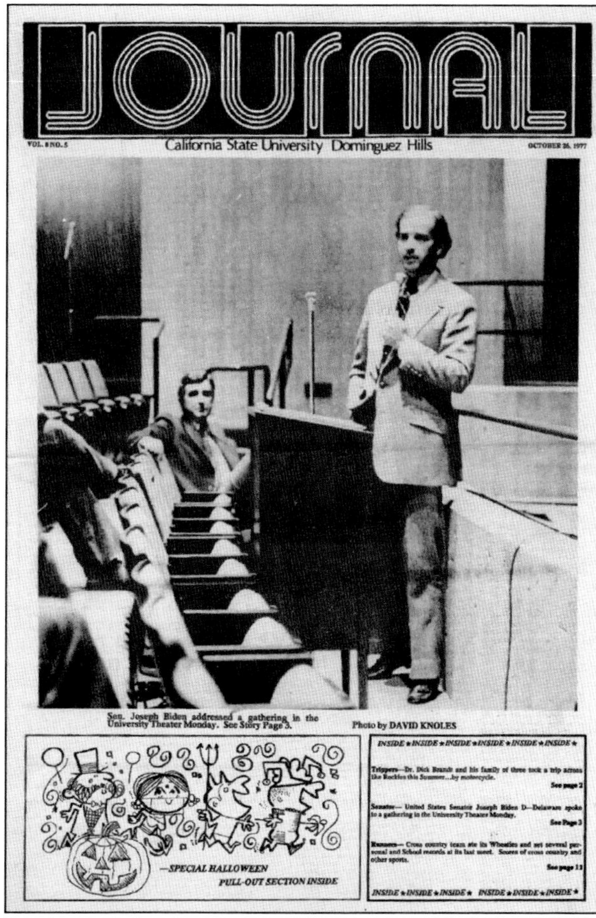

JOURNAL

VOL. 8 NO. 5 California State University Dominguez Hills OCTOBER 26, 1977

Sen. Joseph Biden addressed a gathering in the University Theater Monday. See Story Page 3.

Photo by DAVID KNOLES

—SPECIAL HALLOWEEN PULL-OUT SECTION INSIDE

INSIDE ★ INSIDE ★ INSIDE ★ INSIDE ★ INSIDE ★ INSIDE ★

Trippers—Dr. Dick Brandt and his family of three took a trip across the Rockies this Summer…by motorcycle.

See page 2

Senator— United States Senator Joseph Biden D—Delaware spoke to a gathering in the University Theater Monday.

See Page 3

Runners— Cross country team ate its Wheaties and set several personal and School records at its last meet. Scores of cross country and other sports.

See page 11

INSIDE ★ INSIDE ★ INSIDE ★ INSIDE ★ INSIDE ★ INSIDE ★

President Gerth hosts the dedication of the Japanese Garden in November 1978. Working from a design by landscape architect Haruo Yamashiro, the garden was created through the work of members of the Gardena Valley Gardeners Association and others. "The garden will serve as a symbol of the importance of Japanese culture to the rich and diverse heritage of all Americans," Gerth said.

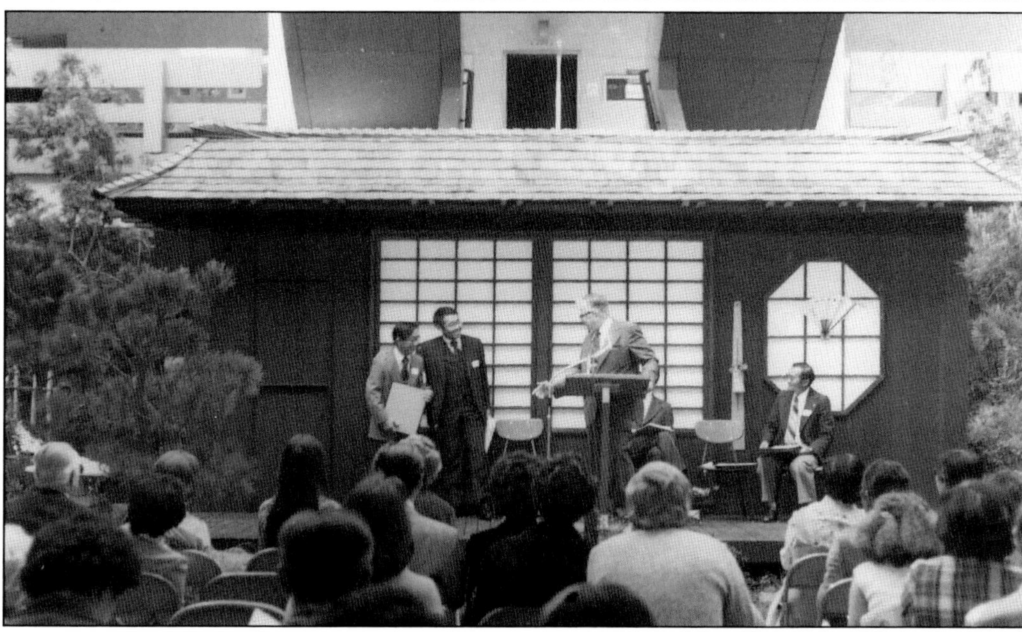

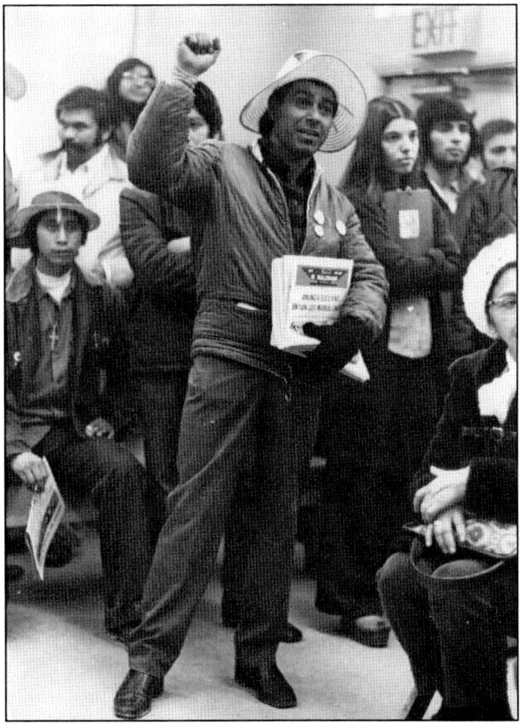

A Chicano activist holding copies of *El Malcriado*, the newspaper of the United Farm Workers, makes a point during a presentation as a crowd of students listens. During this period, Mexican American studies at CSU Dominguez Hills incorporated classes from 10 departments. The curriculum was focused on "training leaders, both inside and outside the minority communities, who are capable of working in minority affairs."

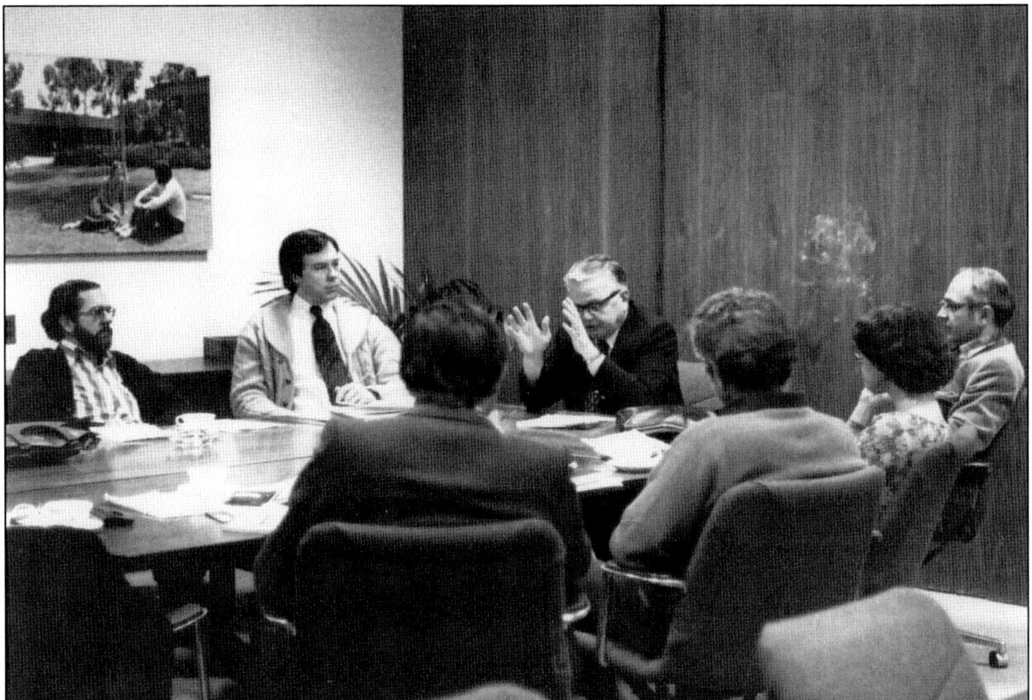

A room in the ERC/Library adjacent to the president's office was christened the "Peace Room" during the administration of President Gerth. In this 1979 photograph, Gerth meets with the CSU Dominguez Hills Academic Senate.

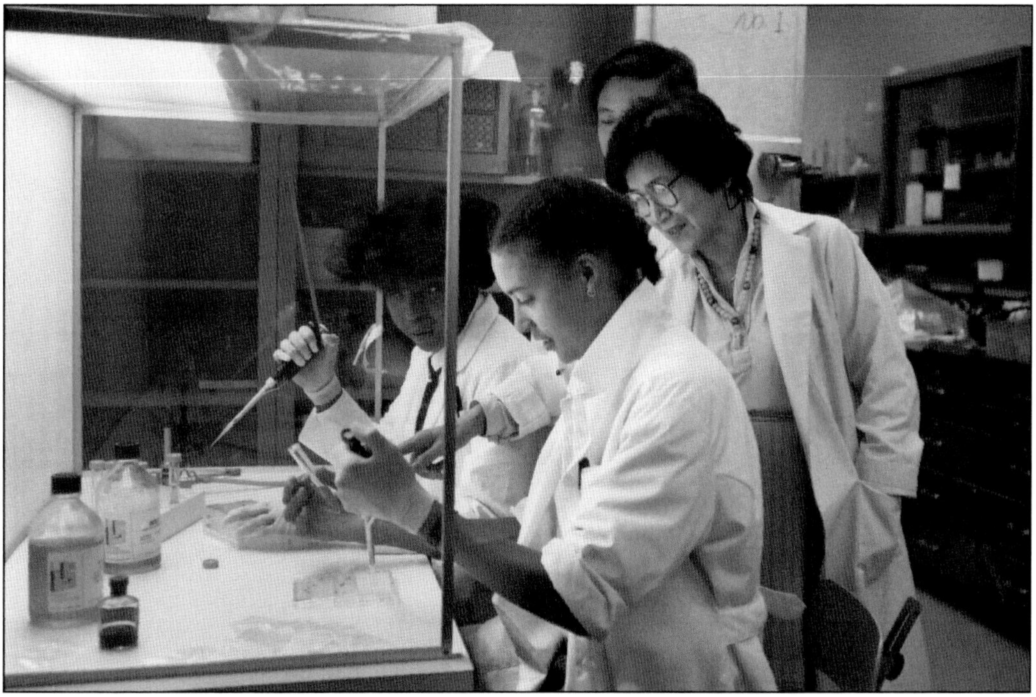

Biology professor Dr. Lois Chi (at right) directs students as they prepare samples for class in this *c.* 1979 photograph. Biology student Rebecca Yates is in the foreground. A founding member of the Biology Department, Dr. Chi's research into parasitology and the disease schistosomiasis has been recognized internationally.

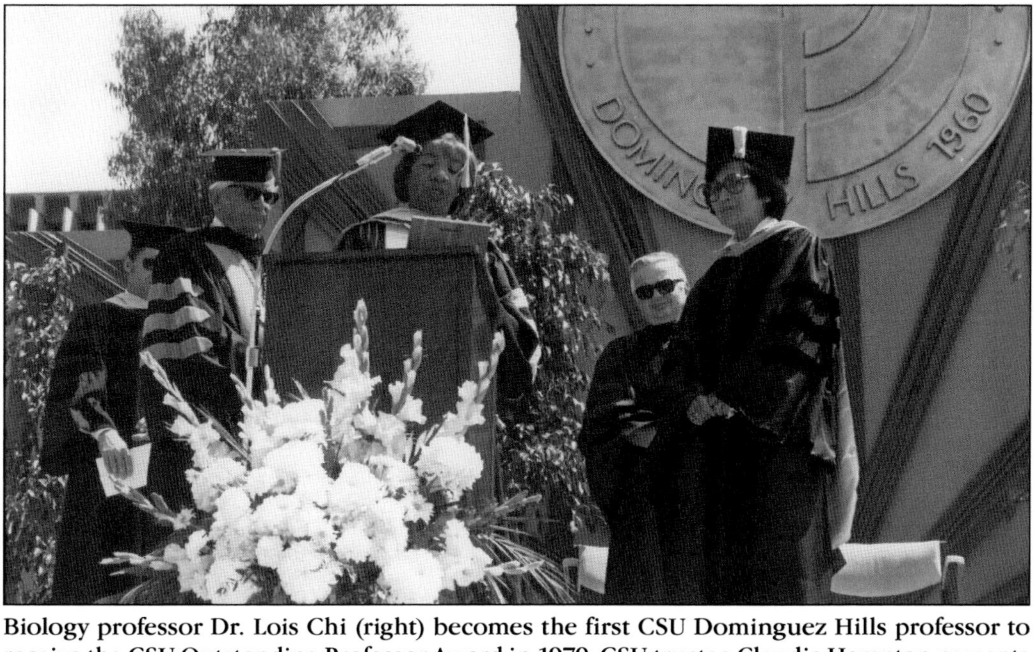

Biology professor Dr. Lois Chi (right) becomes the first CSU Dominguez Hills professor to receive the CSU Outstanding Professor Award in 1979. CSU trustee Claudia Hampton presents the award from the podium. CSU chancellor Glenn Dumke (left of podium) and President Gerth (behind Chi) are also on stage.

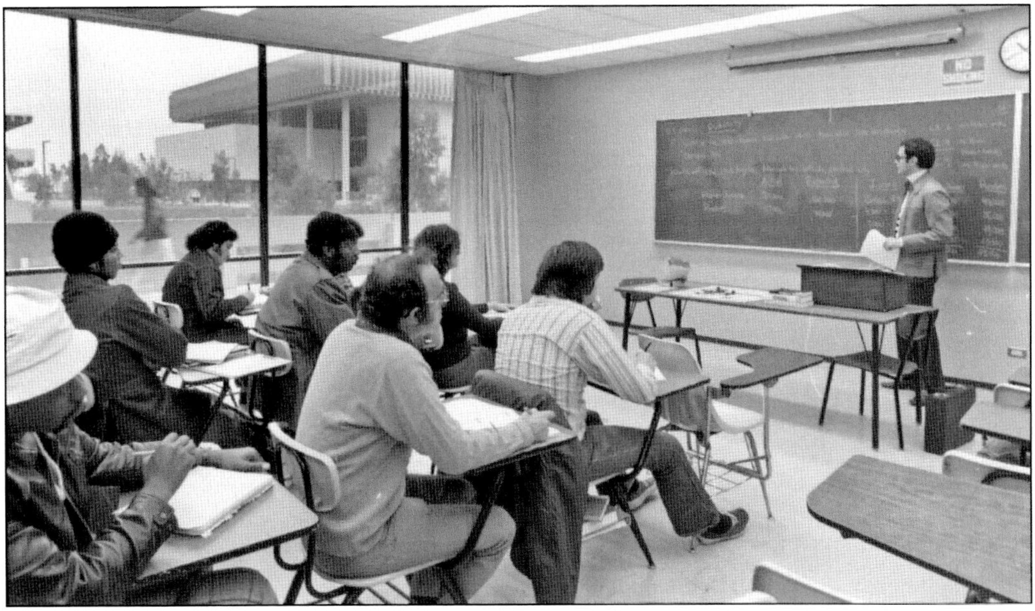

A faculty member lectures on housing in Los Angeles in the Social and Behavioral Sciences building. The Educational Resources Center building is in the background. In a 1977 student newspaper, an article reported on a survey of campus women that found the main reason women attended the college was its location. Other reasons for attending included the size of college enrollment and because certain majors were available.

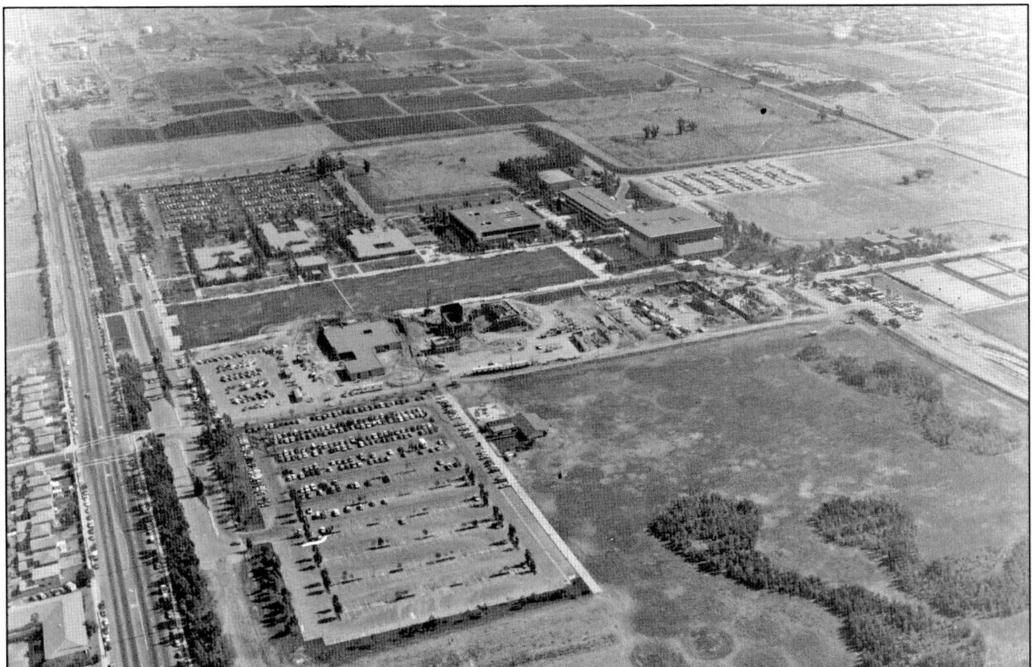

This image shows the later phase of construction on campus in 1976. The Humanities and Fine Arts building (now known as LaCorte Hall), the University Theatre, and the Student Health Center are shown in various stages of construction.

Three

Serving New Communities
The 1980s

This university is committed to its people, to the urban community in which it is located, and to the concept that higher learning is not something in which only a few, for economic or social reasons, can productively be participants. . . . One of the fundamental conditions of this university's existence is the multi-ethnic and multi-cultural nature of our setting. We seek to enhance and indeed, celebrate that pluralism: in academic programs, in the makeup of our student body, faculty and staff, and in programs offered jointly with the community.

—Mission and Goals of CSU Dominguez Hills, University Catalog, 1980–1981.

Enrollment stayed around the 7,000–8,000 mark throughout the decade, and four university presidents served CSU Dominguez Hills during the 1980s: Donald Gerth left for the presidency of Sacramento State University in 1984, Richard Butwell became president in 1984 and stayed until his death in 1987, John Brownell was acting president for two years, and Robert Detweiler was named president in 1989. Although no major academic buildings were constructed during the 1980s, a good deal of construction and new campus programs came to fruition. The Older Adult Center opened in 1981 for students over the age of 55. Student housing opened for occupancy in 1982. To acknowledge the 20th anniversary of the California State University, a system-wide archive was established at the University Library. The 7-Eleven Olympic Velodrome was constructed on the land west of the main campus for cycling competition during the 1984 Los Angeles Olympics. U.S. bicyclists won nine gold medals at the velodrome. As the 25th anniversary of the founding of the campus approached, students voted to increase fees for the construction of a student union. Student Affirmative Action programs were accelerated in 1985 to focus on enrolling additional Hispanics, Filipinos, and Samoans. In 1986, the campus was the recipient of a $276,000 NIH (National Institutes of Health) Minority Biomedical Research Program grant; this program continues to operate today. In 1987, the Statewide Nursing Program, dedicated to furthering the education of practicing nurses, was established at the university. It became quite important in showcasing health-related programs at the university.

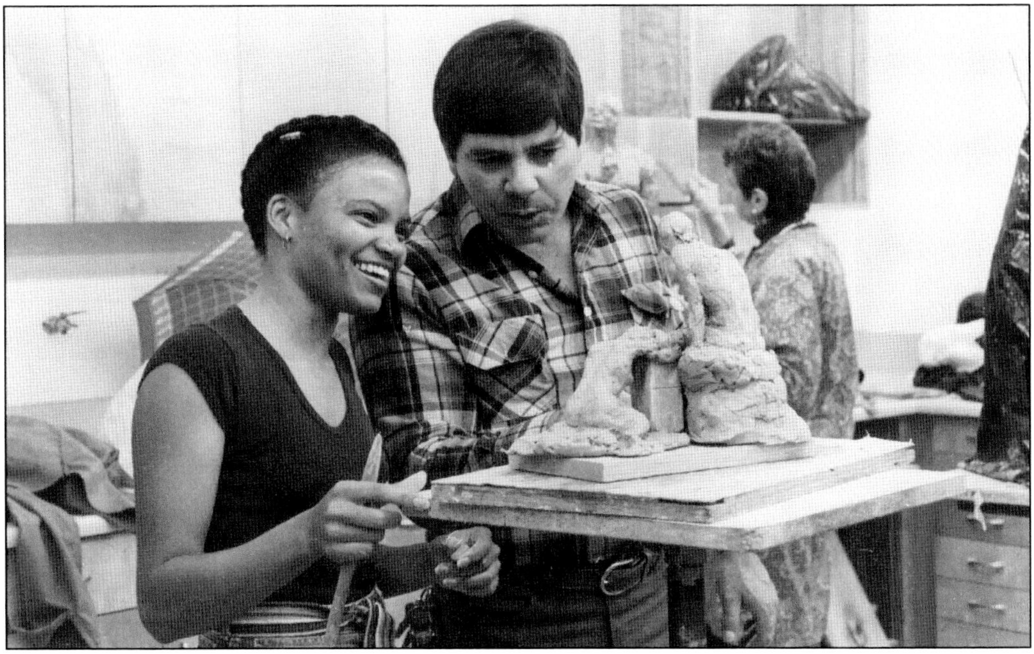

Prof. John Goders offers advice to a student about her clay sculpture during a sculpting class with a model in 1983. According to the 1983–1985 catalog, the art program at CSU Dominguez Hills was "marked by the close correlation of the art history, art studio, and design programs, and by the strong connection between different studio areas."

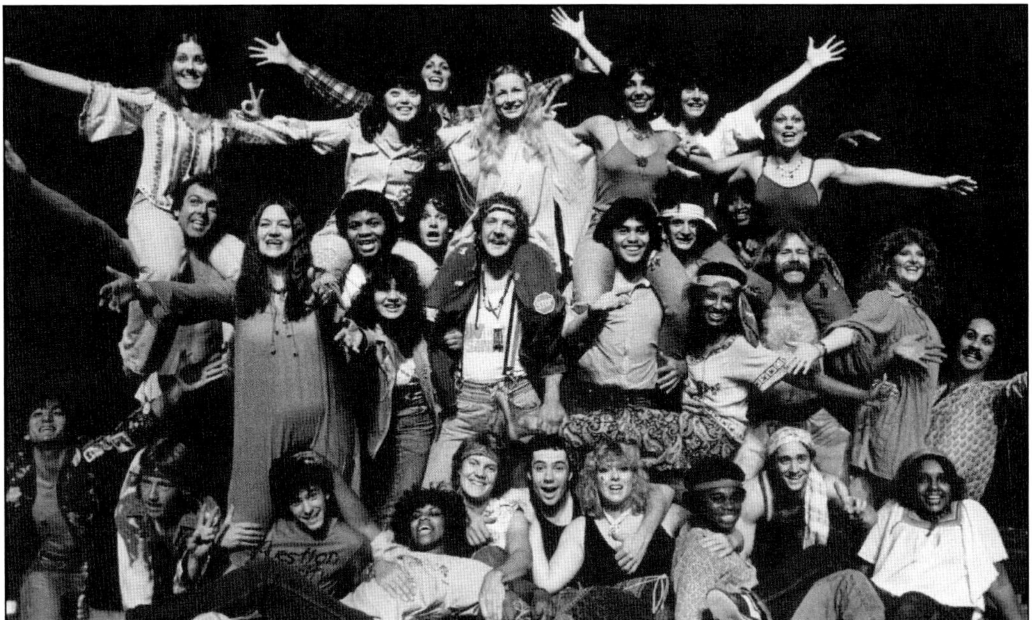

The Dominguez Players started the 1980s with a production of the 1960s musical *Hair*. The play was the last production in the college's Celebration of the American Musical series. Theatre Arts chair Peter Lach directed the cast of 32. Musical direction was by Marjorie Poe, and Collie Valadez choreographed the play.

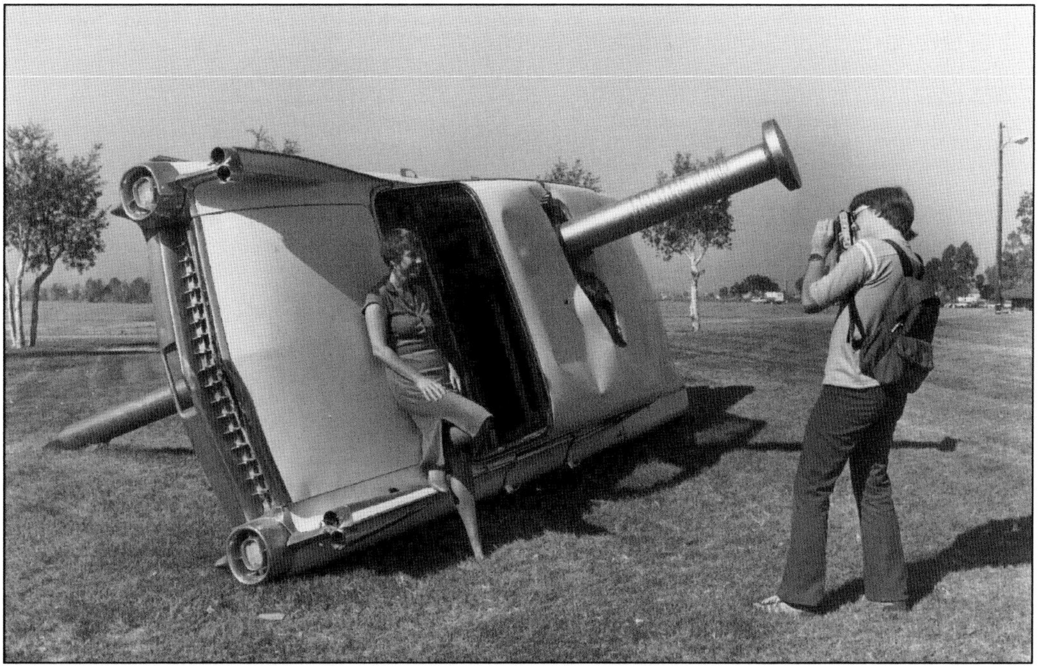

A photographer snaps a picture of a woman leaning against the *Death of an Era* art installation. Displayed throughout 1980 on campus, the Dustin Shuler work consisted of a 1959 Cadillac impaled with a large nail through its body. It was meant to symbolize the end of an era of endless energy consumption.

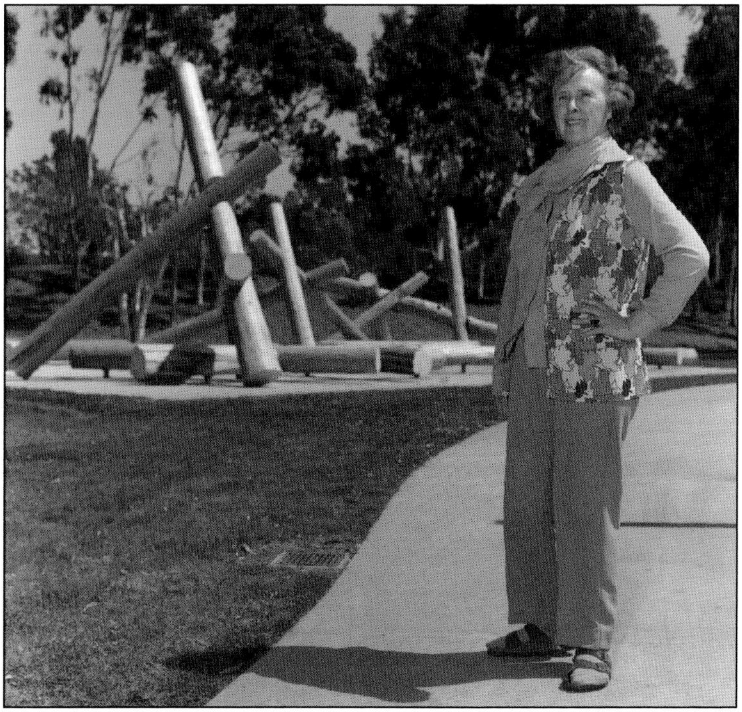

Prominent artist Claire Falkenstein poses in front of *The Forum*, a "socio-sculpture environment" consisting of cedar logs from Oregon on a concrete platform in the CSU Dominguez Hills Sculpture Garden. The sculpture was created as a memorial to A. Quincy Jones, the campus architect who died in 1979. The dedication took place in May 1987. *The Forum* was removed in the early 2000s.

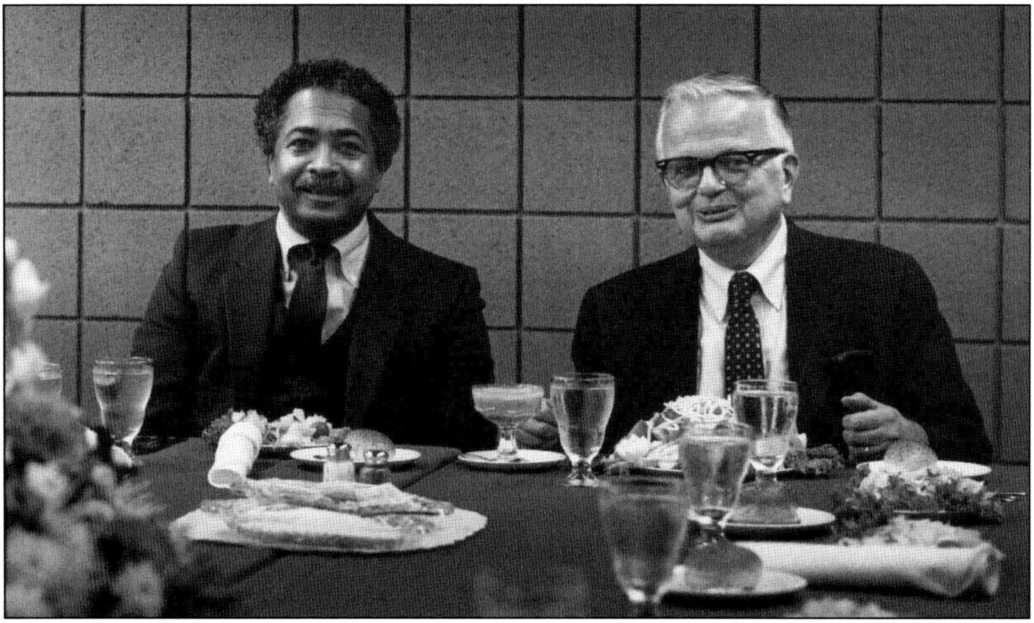

Former lieutenant governor and congressional candidate Mervyn Dymally is seated with President Gerth (right) prior to a candidate forum in 1980. Dymally was later instrumental in bringing the California African American Political and Economic Institute to the university in 2003.

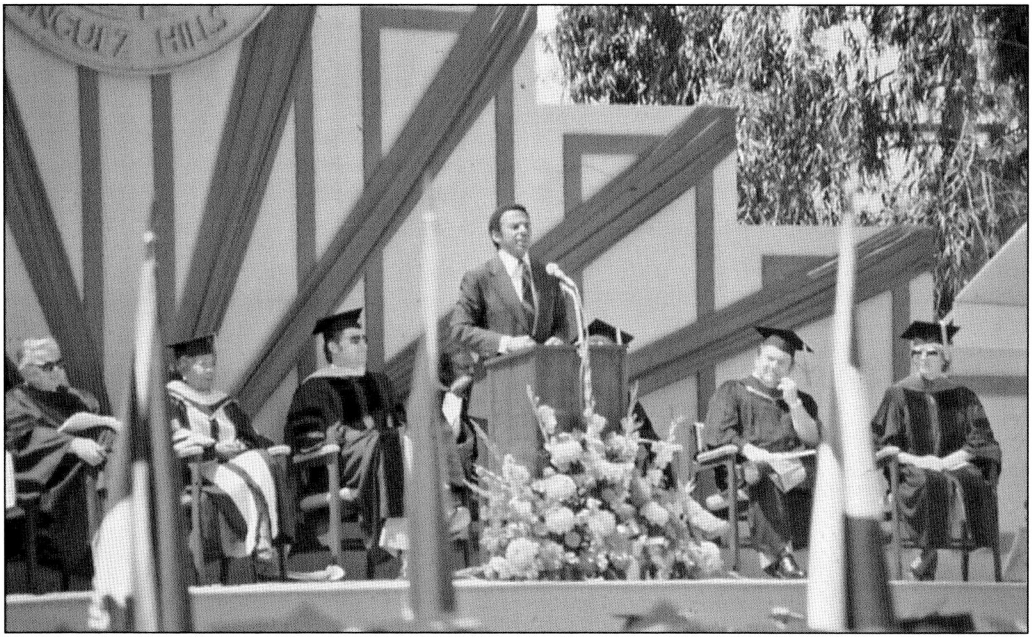

Former ambassador to the United Nations and civil rights leader Andrew Young speaks at the 1980 commencement. Also on the dais, from left to right, are President Gerth, CSU trustee Claudia Hampton, Vice Pres. David Karber, Dean George Walker, and Dean Suzanne Gemmell.

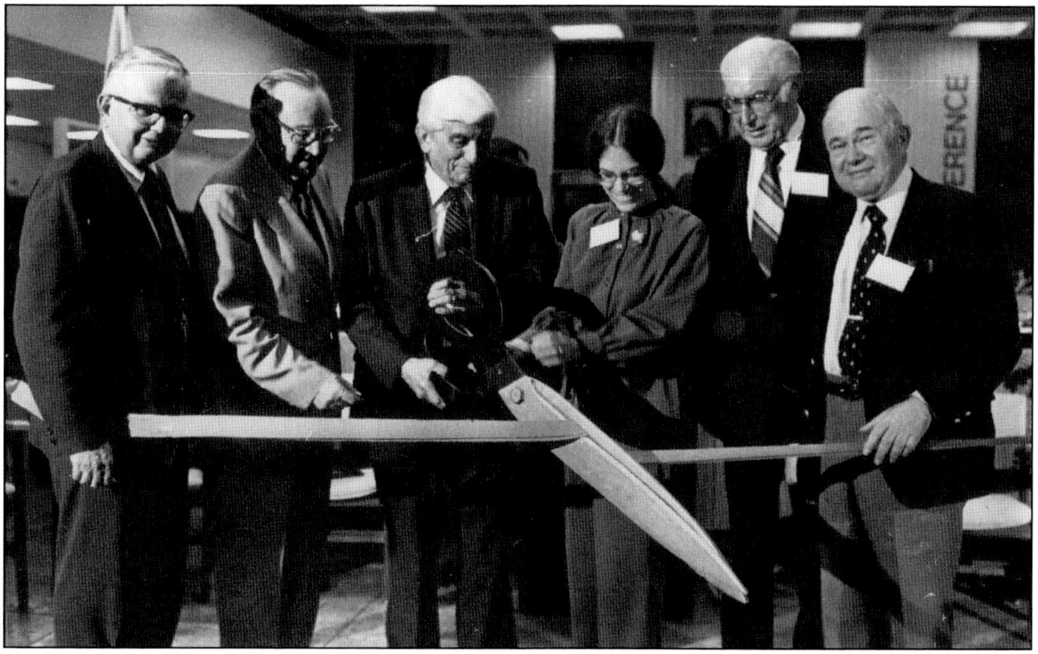

The CSU Historical Archives was created by the CSU Board of Trustees in 1979 and dedicated in 1981 at the University Library. Attending the ceremony was former governor Edmund "Pat" Brown (second from left) as well as Glenn Dumke (with the scissors), Louis Heilbron (right), and others. The archives is now one of the largest archival repositories devoted to the history of higher education planning in the western United States.

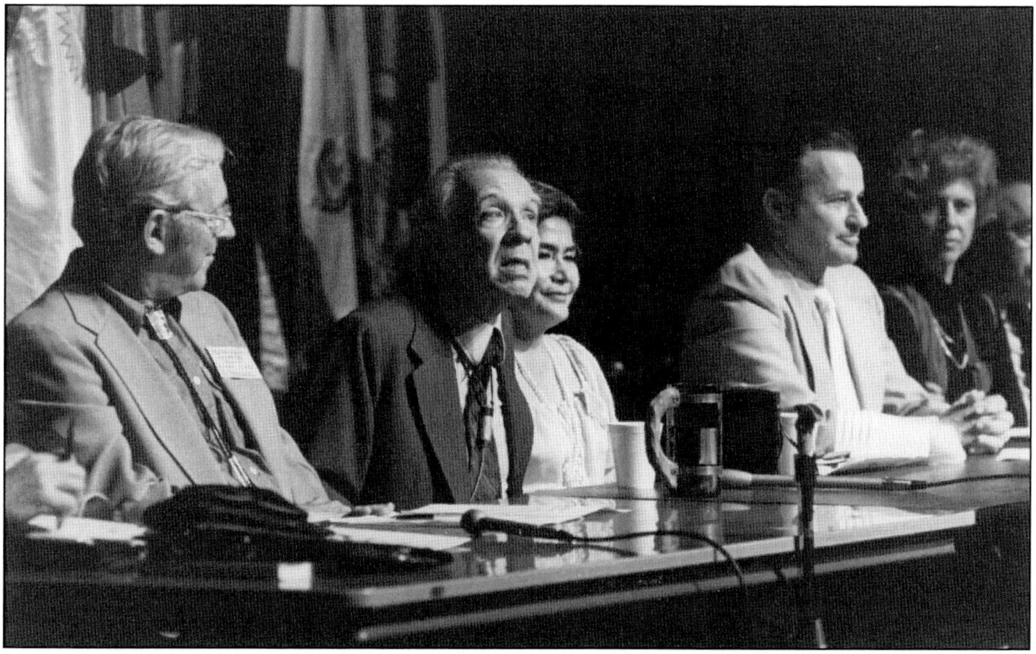

Jorge Luis Borges, considered one of the literary world's foremost writers, came to CSU Dominguez Hills in April 1980 as keynote speaker at the Hispanic Conference on Pacific and Caribbean Literature.

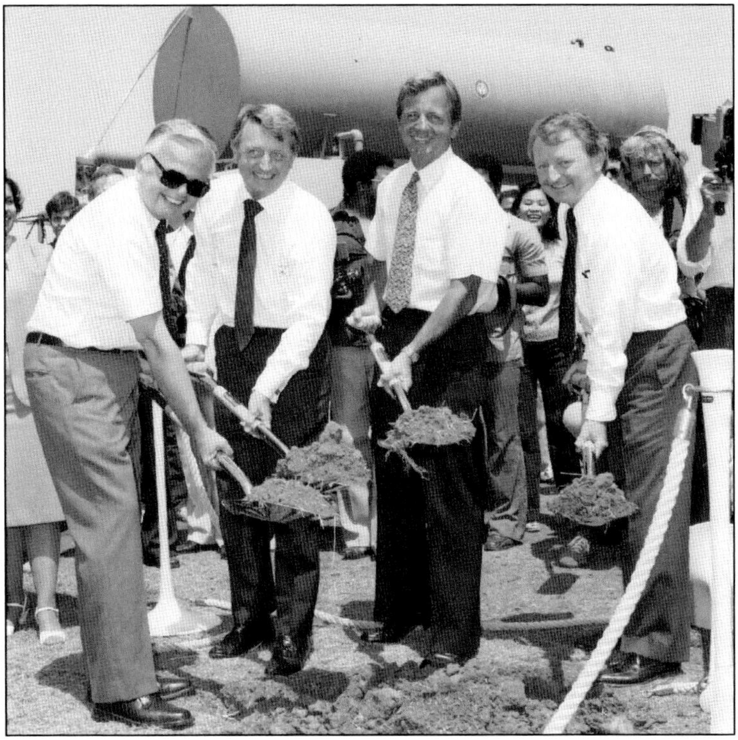

As Peter Ueberroth, organizer of the Los Angeles Summer Olympics, was planning the 1984 event, President Gerth offered campus land as a venue. During a conversation, Ueberroth asked Gerth, "How would you like to have the Olympic Velodrome?" Gerth said, "We'll take it. What is it?" Gerth then agreed that the cycling competitions would be welcomed at CSU Dominguez Hills. Pictured at the groundbreaking are President Gerth (left), Peter Ueberroth (second from right), and others.

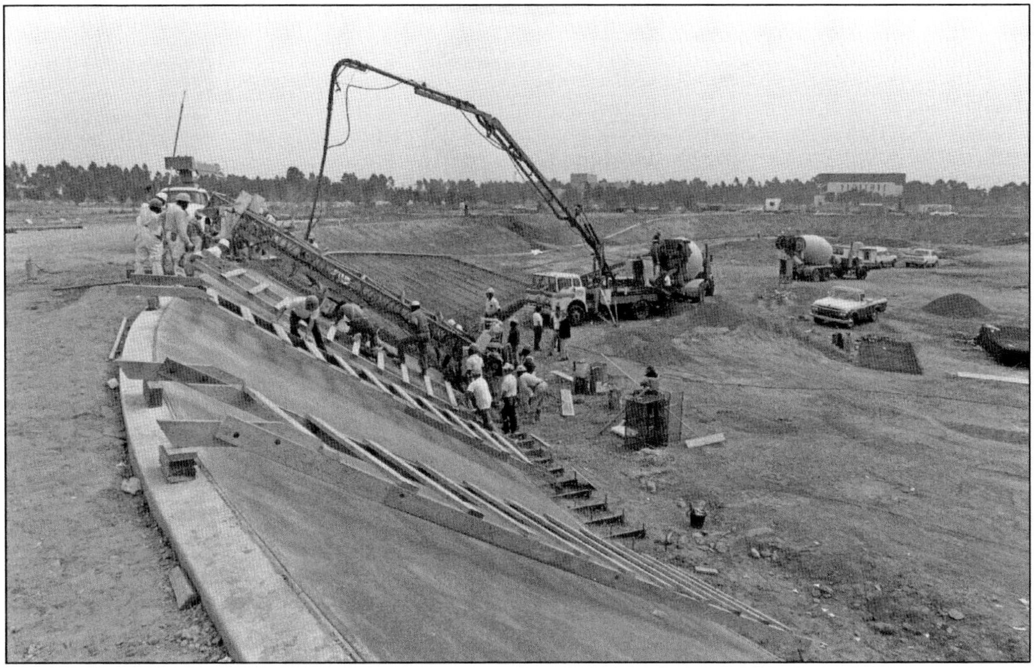

Ground was broken for the velodrome in 1981. At a cost of $3 million, the cycling facility was financed by a gift from the Southland Corporation. The track had permanent seating for 2,000 and temporary seating for 6,000 during the Olympics.

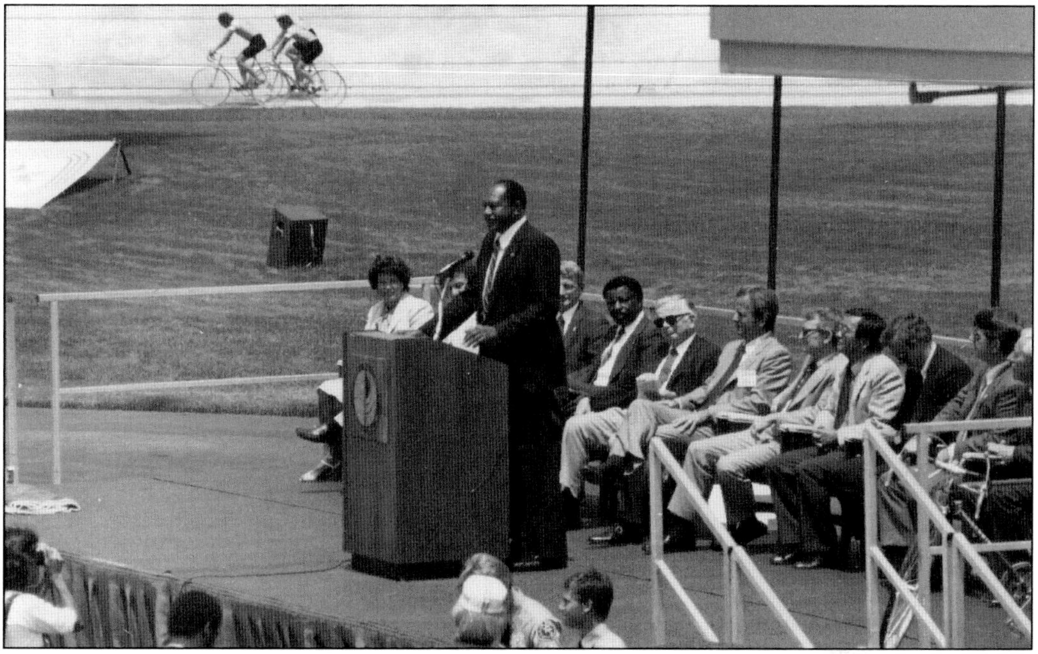

Los Angeles mayor Tom Bradley welcomes dignitaries and cyclists to the opening of the velodrome track on July 8, 1982. The university booked a number of cycling events prior to the 1984 games to ensure that the track and facility was in line with Olympic standards. Olympians Eric Heiden and Sheila Young Ochowicz pedaled the first lap. The next day the 7-Eleven/*Bicycling* Magazine Grand Prix became the venue's first competition.

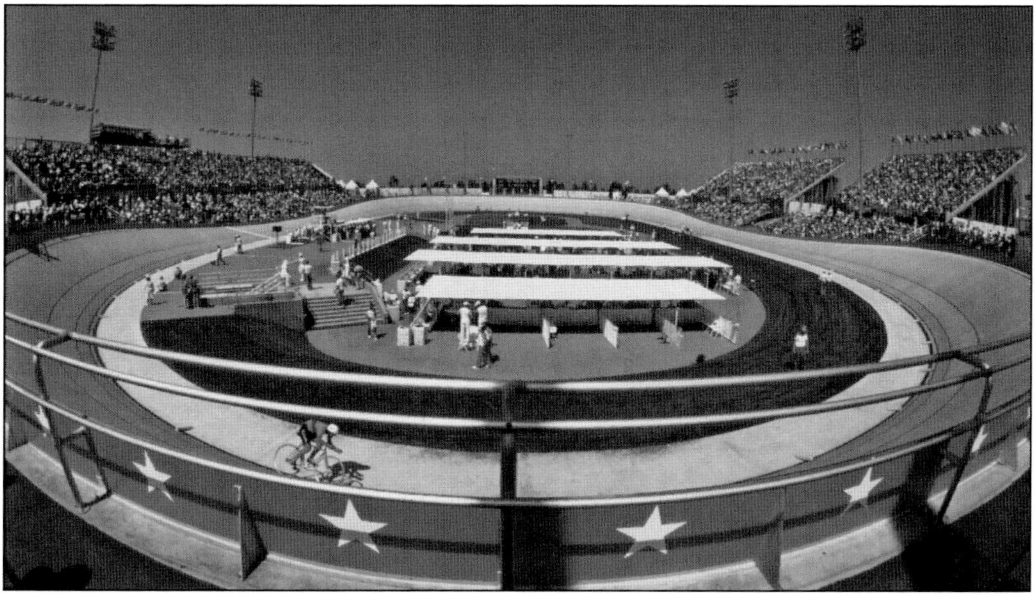

Sellout crowds enjoyed the excitement of the Olympics at CSU Dominguez Hills. On August 3, 1984, Americans Mark Gorski and Nelson Vails fought for the gold in the finals of the sprint competition. Gorski won, but both cyclists held the same American flag as they circled the track after the race. Cyclists for the United States took a total of nine gold medals during the 1984 competition.

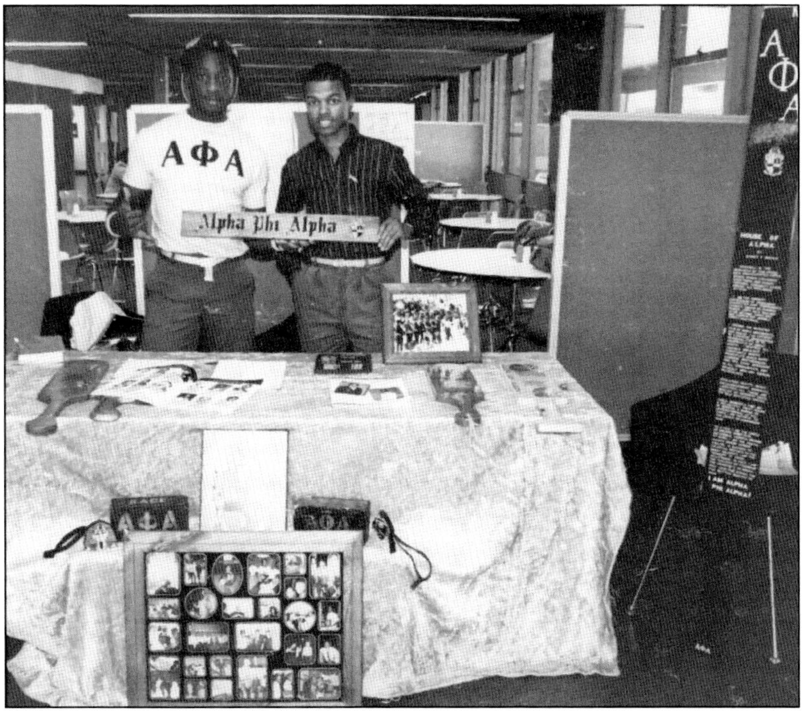

Two students represent Alpha Phi Alpha fraternity at a display table in the student cafeteria during the 1980s. Founded in 1906, Alpha Phi Alpha is the oldest African American fraternity in the United States.

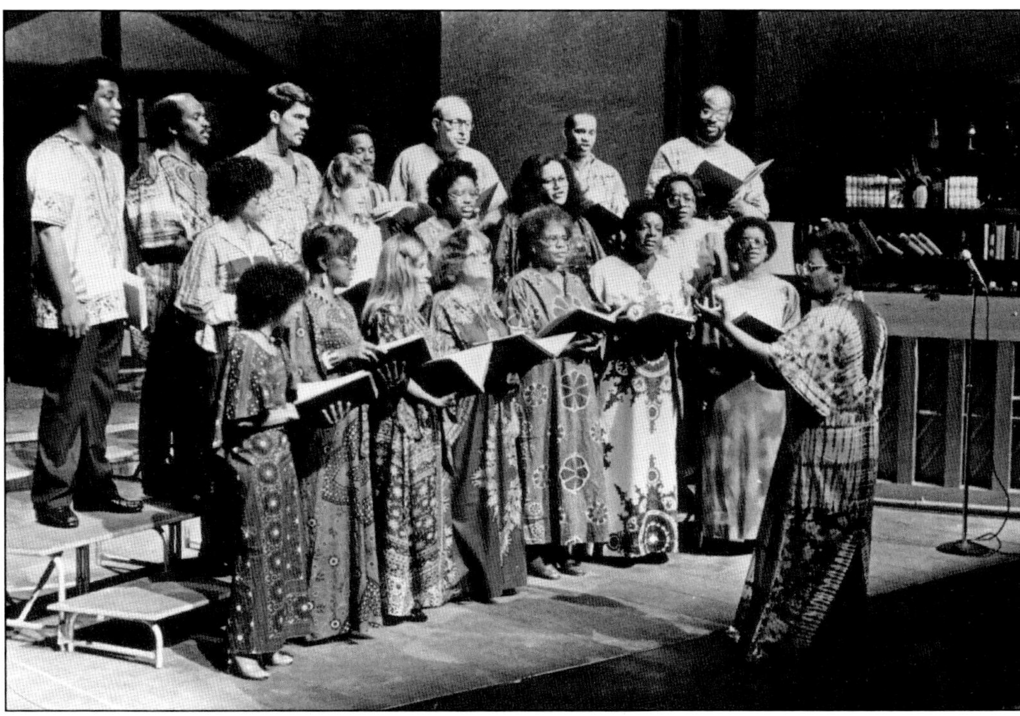

Hansonia Caldwell, a faculty member and former dean, has conducted the university's Jubilee Choir since 1978. The choir (pictured here in 1982) consists of students, faculty, and community members and performs music from the African Diaspora, including spirituals, gospel, and ragtime. In 1999, the choir performed at Carnegie Hall in New York City.

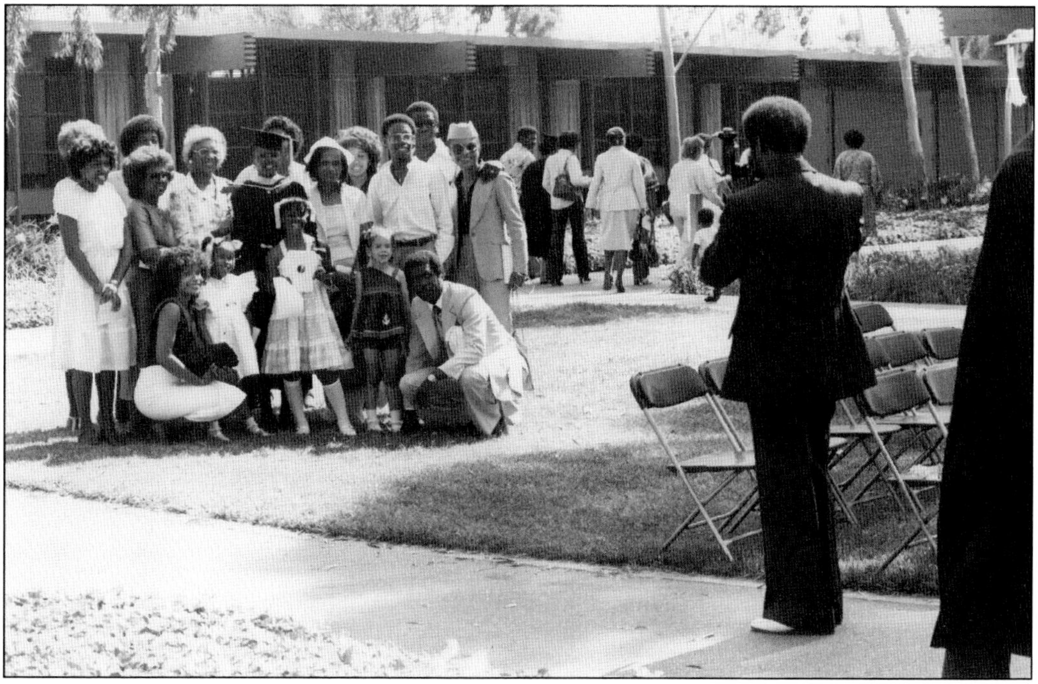

Family members gather around a graduate after commencement near the Small College Complex on June 12, 1982. Congressman Glenn M. Anderson spoke at the commencement and said, "We are in the mini-skirt age of education budgets . . . the cloth is being cut close to the edge of indecency." More than 2,000 graduates received diplomas among the approximate 10,000 students who had graduated from CSU Dominguez Hills since 1966.

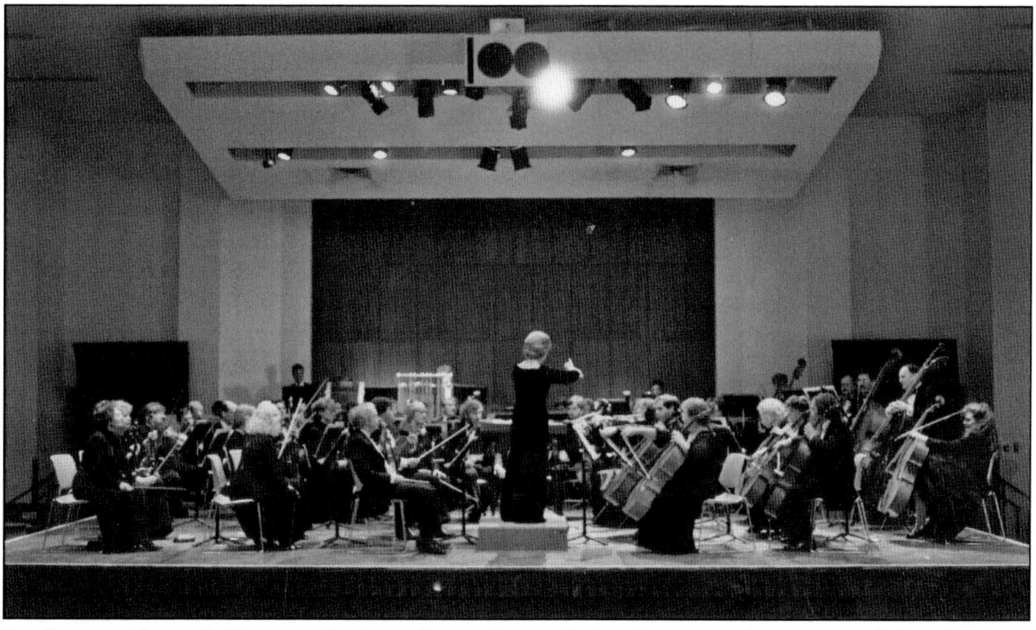

Professor of music Frances Steiner (center) conducts the annual concert of the Carson–Dominguez Hills Symphony Orchestra in the University Theatre, a tradition she established in 1977.

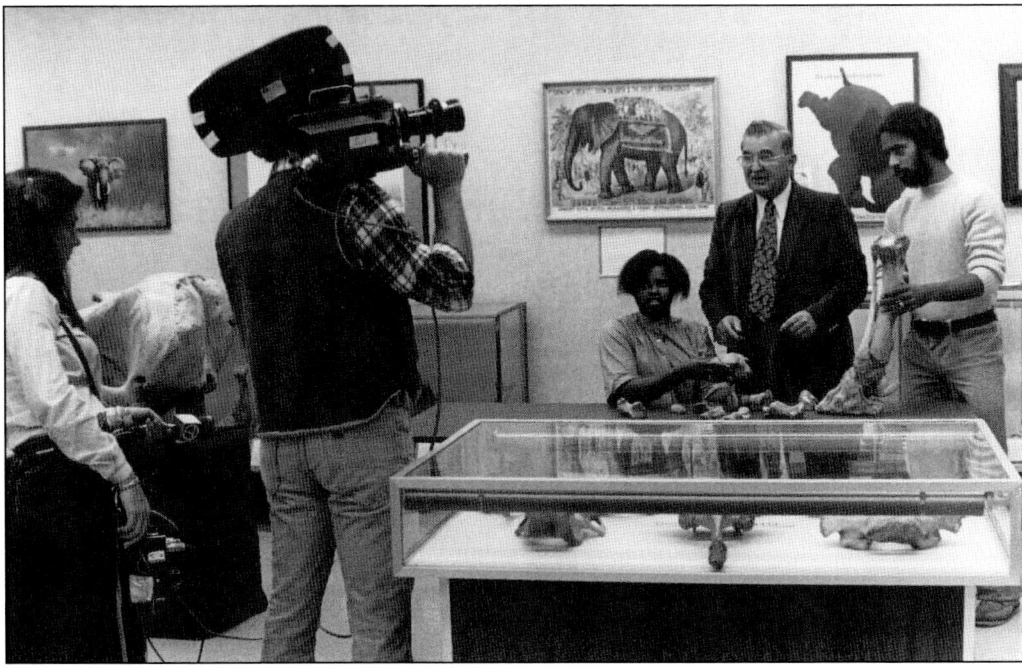

In 1980, psychology professor Jack Adams was interviewed about his exhibition on elephants. Dr. Adams's research into elephants led him to bury an elephant and a rhinoceros on campus for later skeletal research after the animals had decomposed.

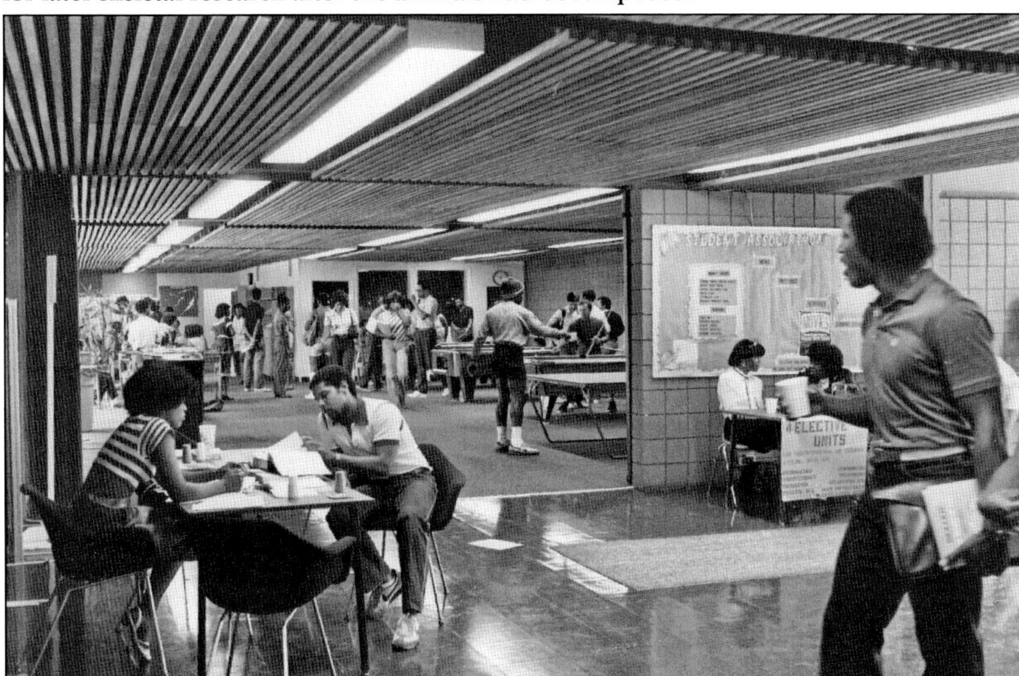

A temporary student union was set up in the late 1970s in the space formerly occupied by the university bookstore in the Small College Complex. This 1983 image shows continued student interest in ping-pong.

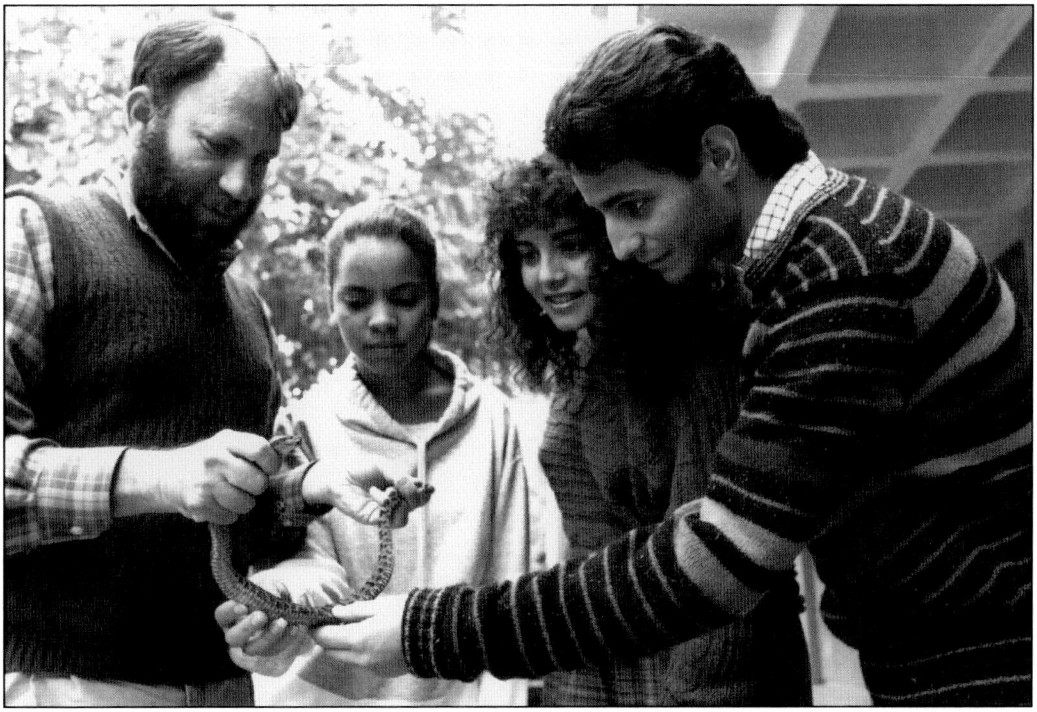

David Morafka, professor of biology at the university from 1972 to 2001, shows a snake to his students. Morafka was a prominent biologist whose research involved rattlesnakes, lizards, and desert tortoises.

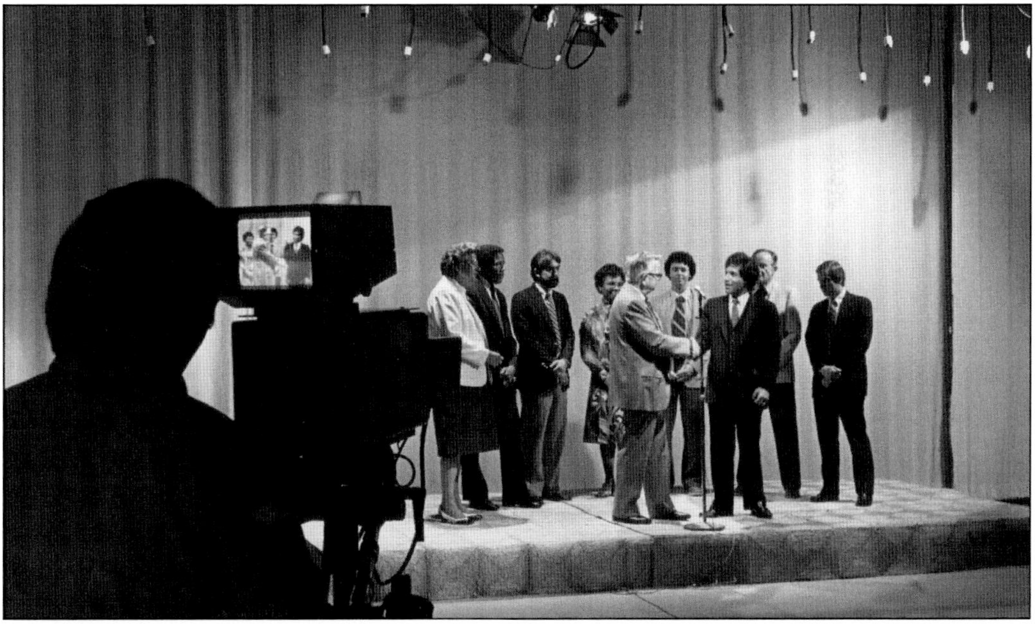

An initial step in the university's use of cable television for classes was a grant from a Torrance cable company. President Gerth and Larry Windsor (right, shaking Gerth's hand) of Group W Cable are photographed with others. An early venture in CSU Dominguez Hills television (DHTV) was the show *Comline*, hosted by Frank Paine.

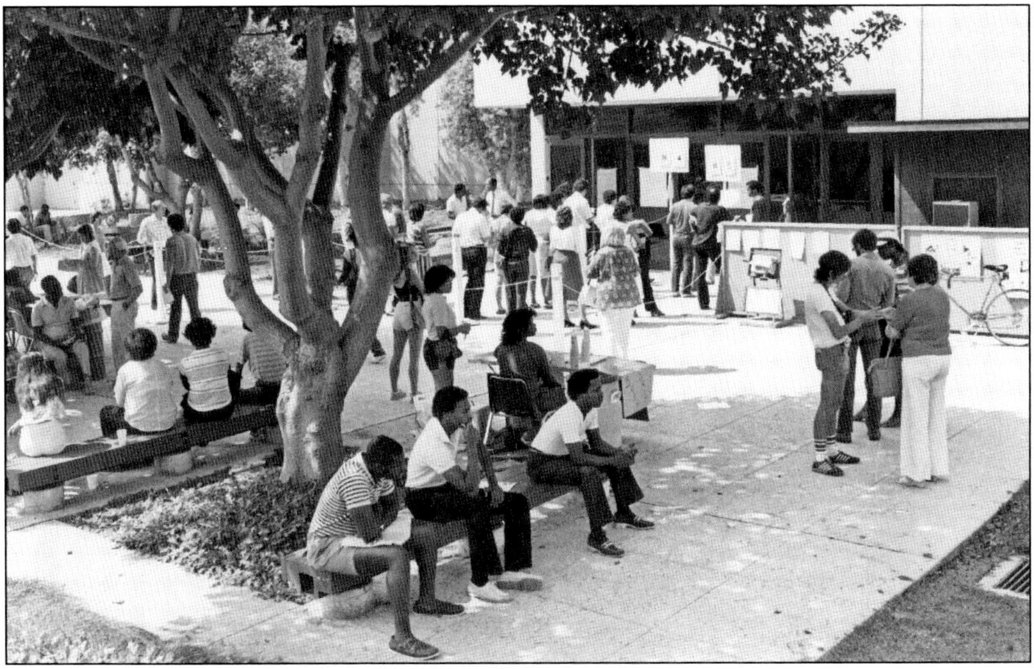

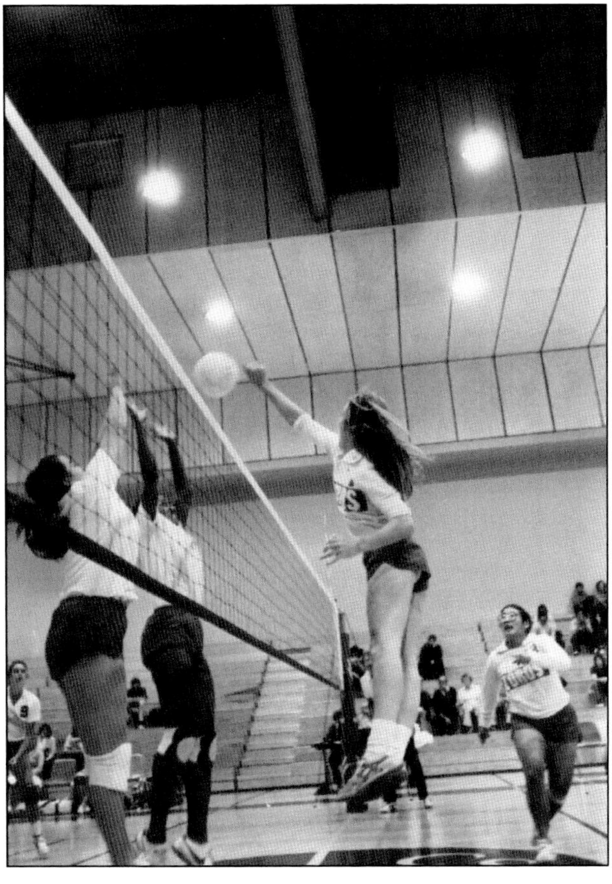

The annual ritual of students lining up to register for classes was in full swing in 1983 as students waited their turn. By 1987, CSU Dominguez Hills was one of the most ethnically diverse universities in the country. White students consisted of 40 percent of enrolled students, while African Americans made up 34 percent, Chicanos 7.4 percent, Asians 9 percent, other Hispanics 4 percent, Filipinos and Pacific Islanders 3.5 percent, and Native Americans 2.1 percent.

A member of the Toro women's volleyball team spikes the ball during a 1982 game in the university gymnasium.

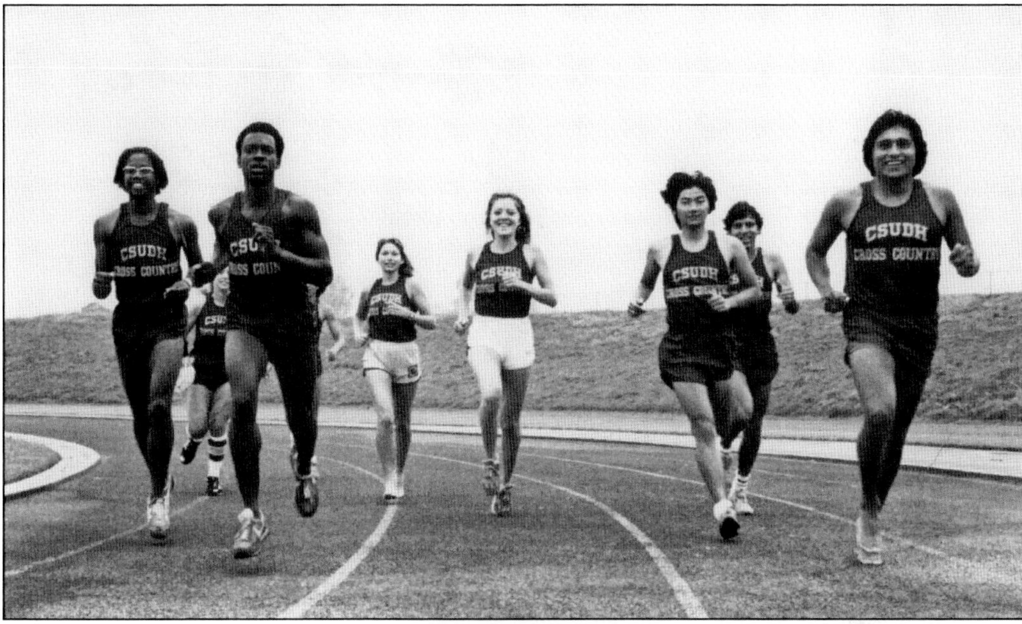

Members of the men's and women's cross country teams train together on the university track in the fall of 1983.

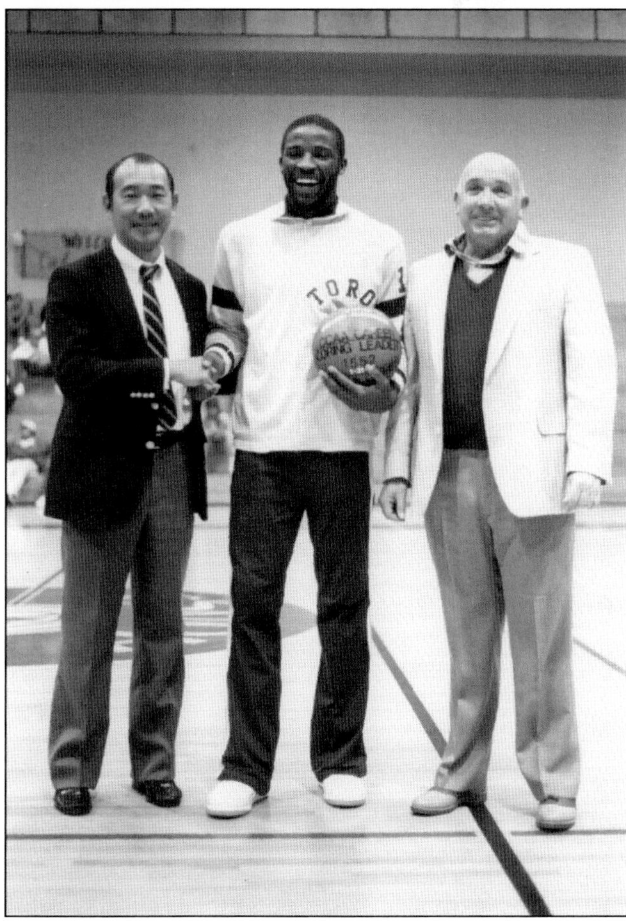

Coach Dave Yanai (left) congratulates William Alexander (center) upon becoming the all-time leading scorer in California Collegiate Athletic Association history in 1987. Dave Yanai spent 19 seasons (1977–1996) as basketball coach at the university. His teams advanced to the 1981, 1987, and 1989 National Collegiate Athletic Association (NCAA) Tournaments and won the 1979 National Association of Intercollegiate Athletics (NAIA) district title. Also in the photograph is Tom Morgan, California Collegiate Athletic Association (CCAA) commissioner.

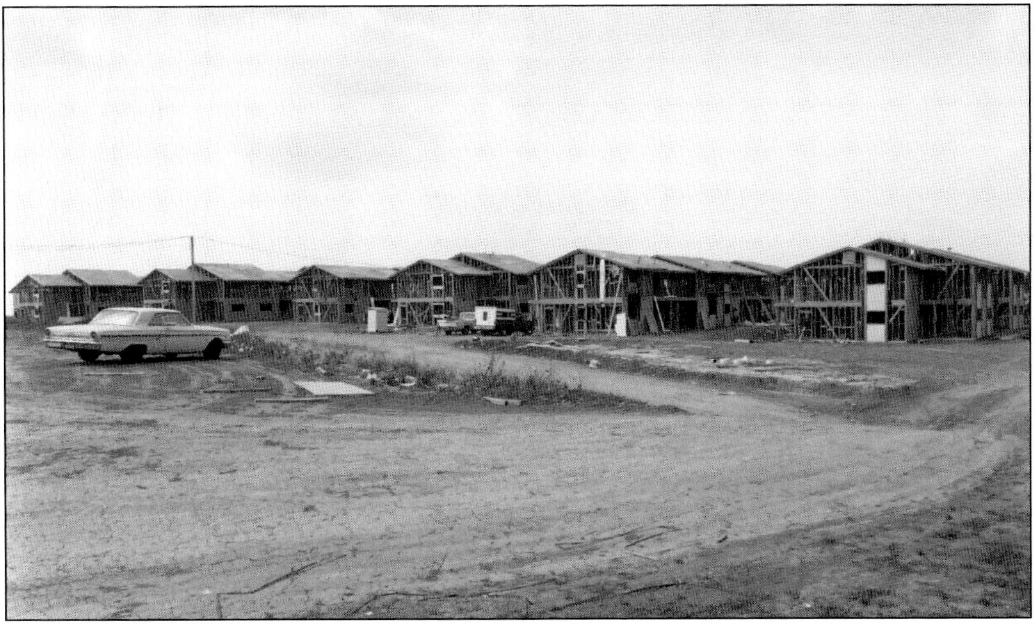

Ground was broken in 1981 for student housing on the east side of campus. Upon completion, the facility consisted of 15 two-story structures that accommodated 352 students in 104 apartments.

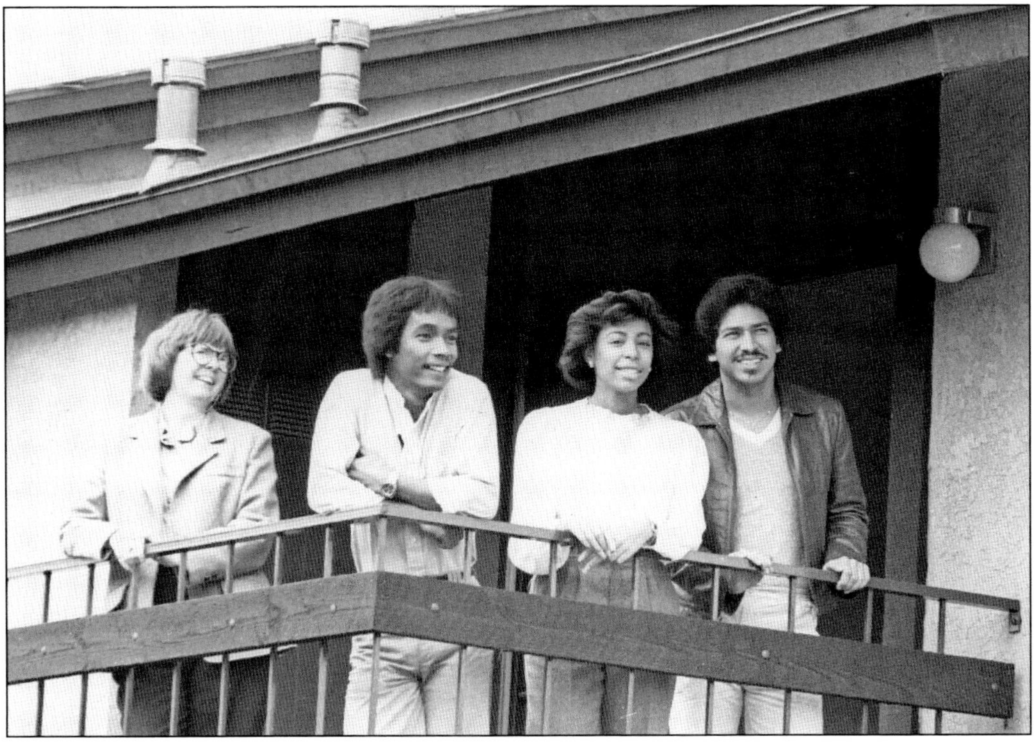

Students survey the surroundings from a balcony of one of the new student housing apartments during the open house and ribbon-cutting ceremony in 1982. Though CSU Dominguez Hills is popular with commuters and older students, many students live on campus.

Richard Butwell was named the third president of the university on July 10, 1984. A scholar of Southeast Asia, Butwell came from the University of South Dakota. Donald Gerth left CSU Dominguez Hills for the presidency of Sacramento State University, where he served for 20 years.

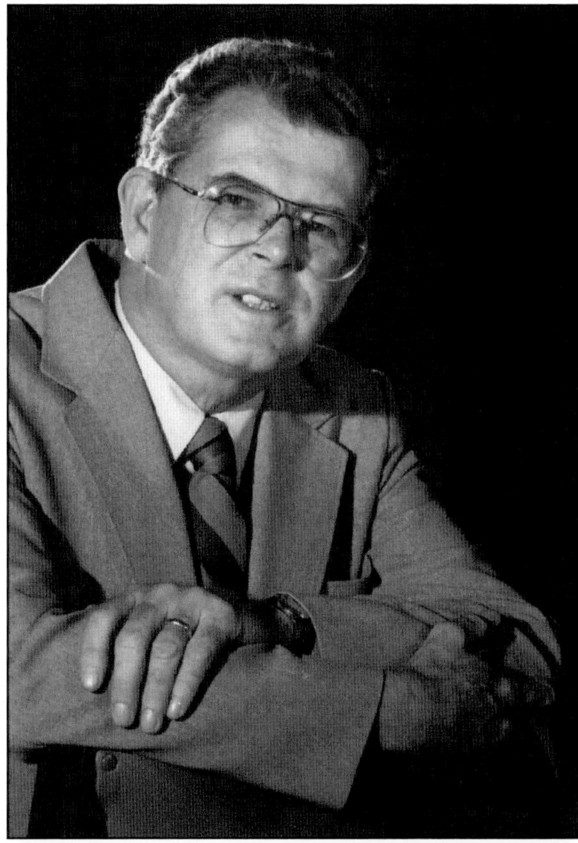

Formed as a result of the 1984 report "Hispanics and Higher Education, A CSU Imperative," the CSU Dominguez Hills Hispanic Advisory Council was created in 1985 and chaired by Dr. Raul Aceves, dean of Urban and Community Affairs.

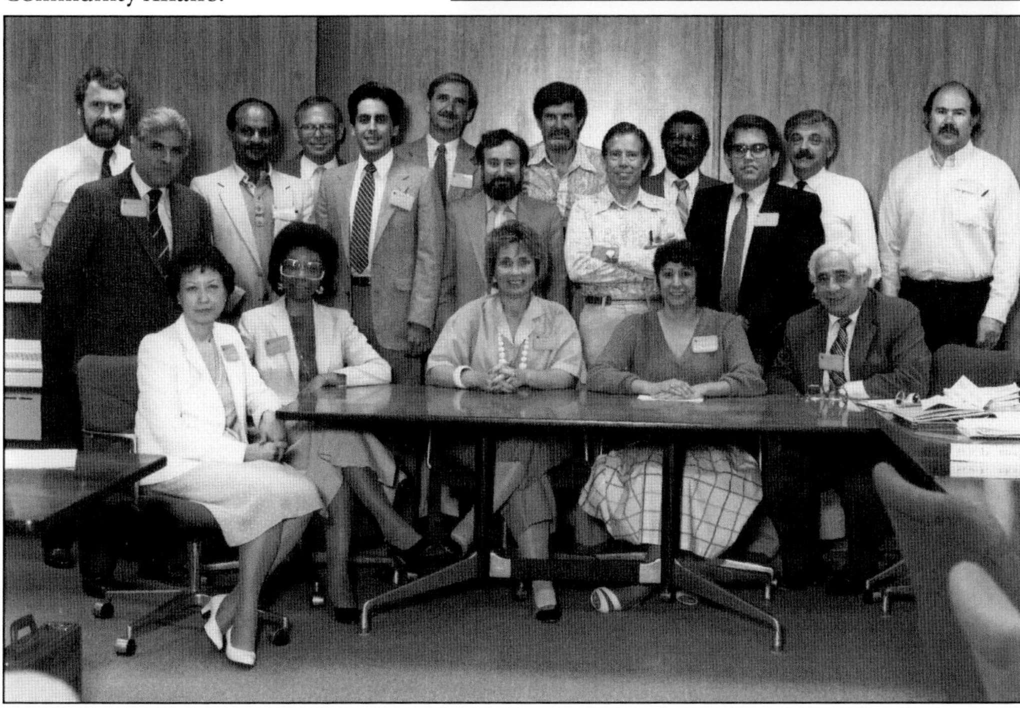

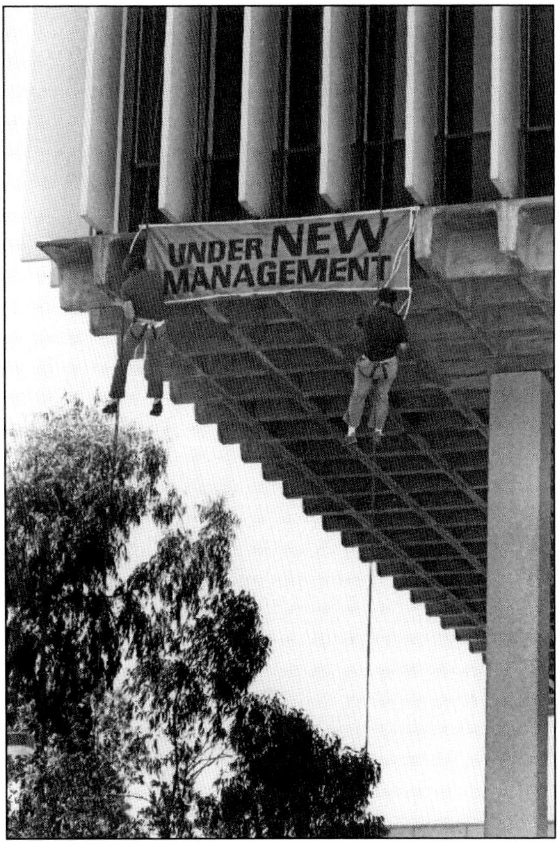

Sign hangers dangle from the Educational Resources Center/ Library as they place an "Under New Management" sign to welcome new president Richard Butwell to campus in August 1984.

Students dressed in formal wear participate in the 1983–1984 CSU Dominguez Hills homecoming event in the university gymnasium.

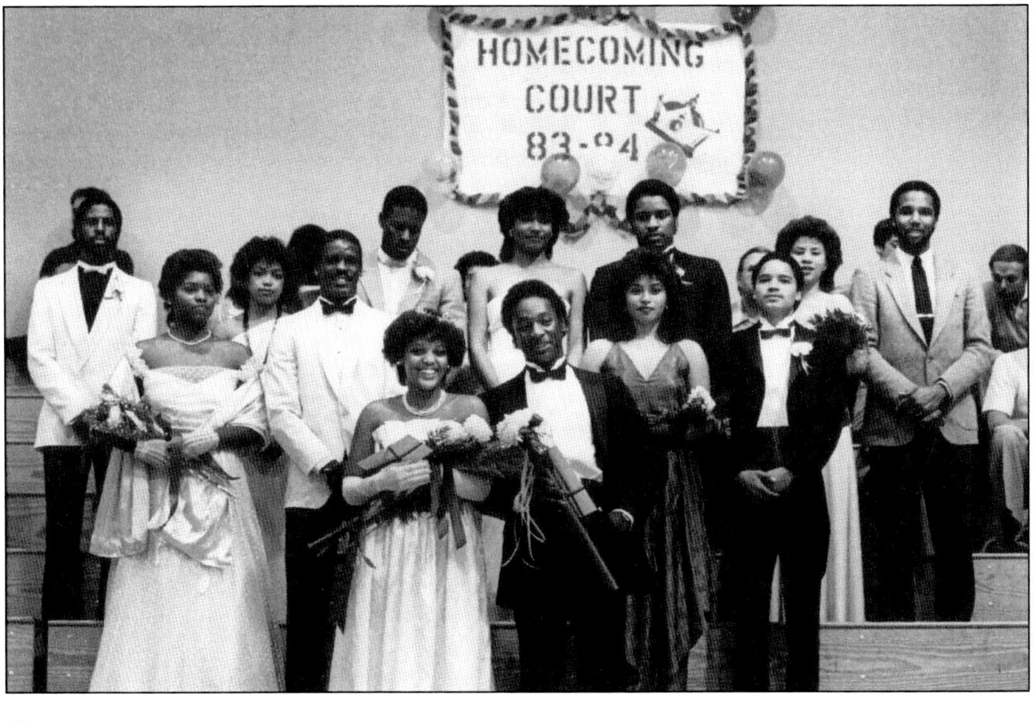

In 1985, the campus celebrated its 25th year. A history of the campus was written by history professor Judson Grenier titled *The Rainbow Years 1960–1985: The First Quarter Century of California State University, Dominguez Hills Carson, California*.

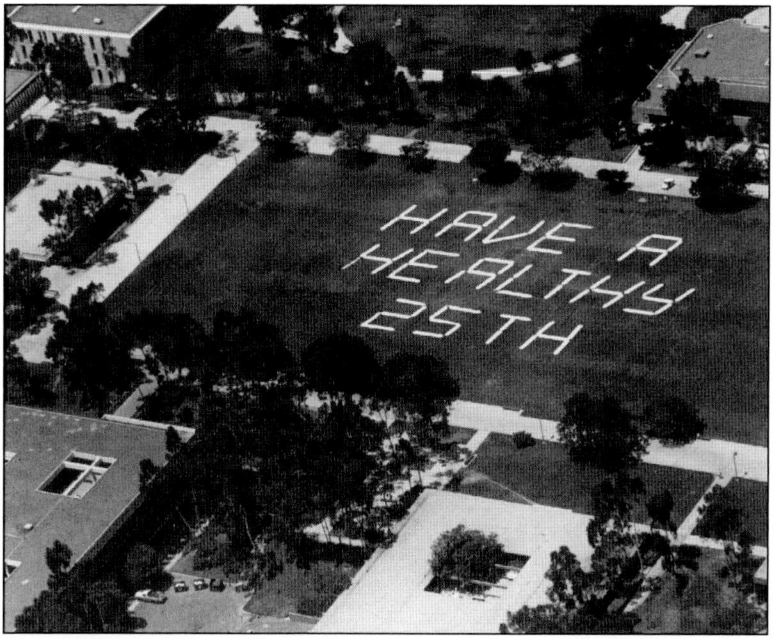

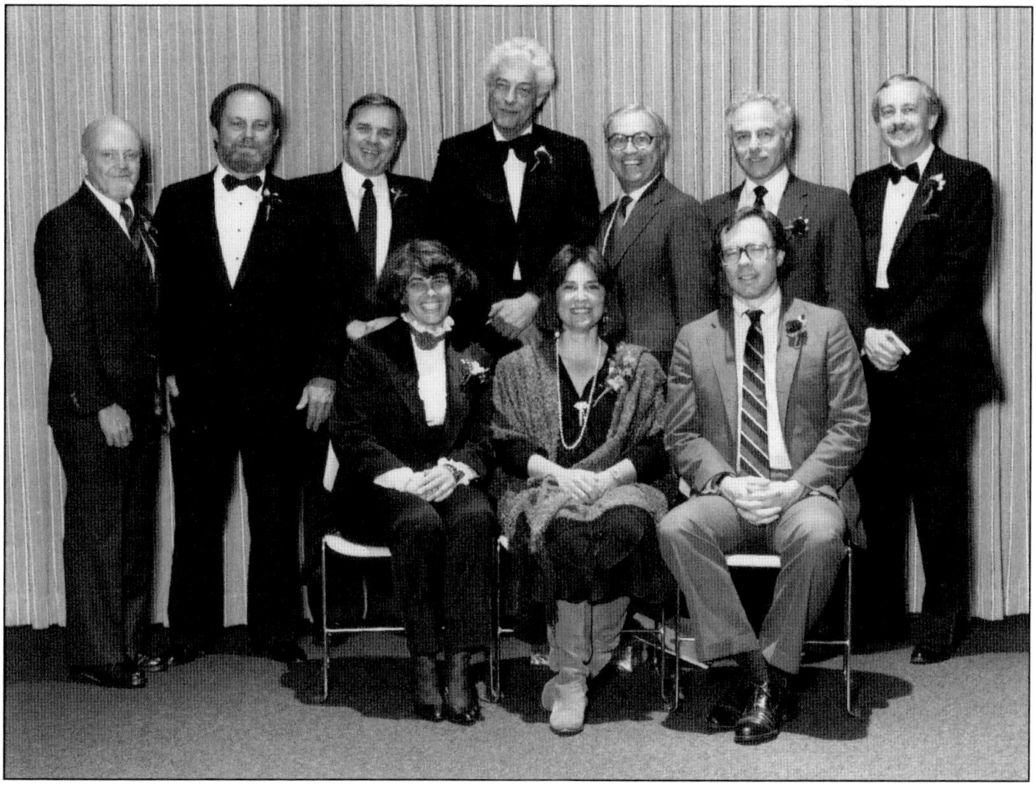

During a 25th-anniversary celebration, the campus honored the past chairs of the CSU Dominguez Hills Academic Senate. From left to right are (seated) Ellen Gerry, Sandy Wilcox, and Tom Pyne; (standing) Judson Grenier, James Harris, Ken Gash, Jack Foote, David Rankin, Hal Charnofsky, and Sam Wiley.

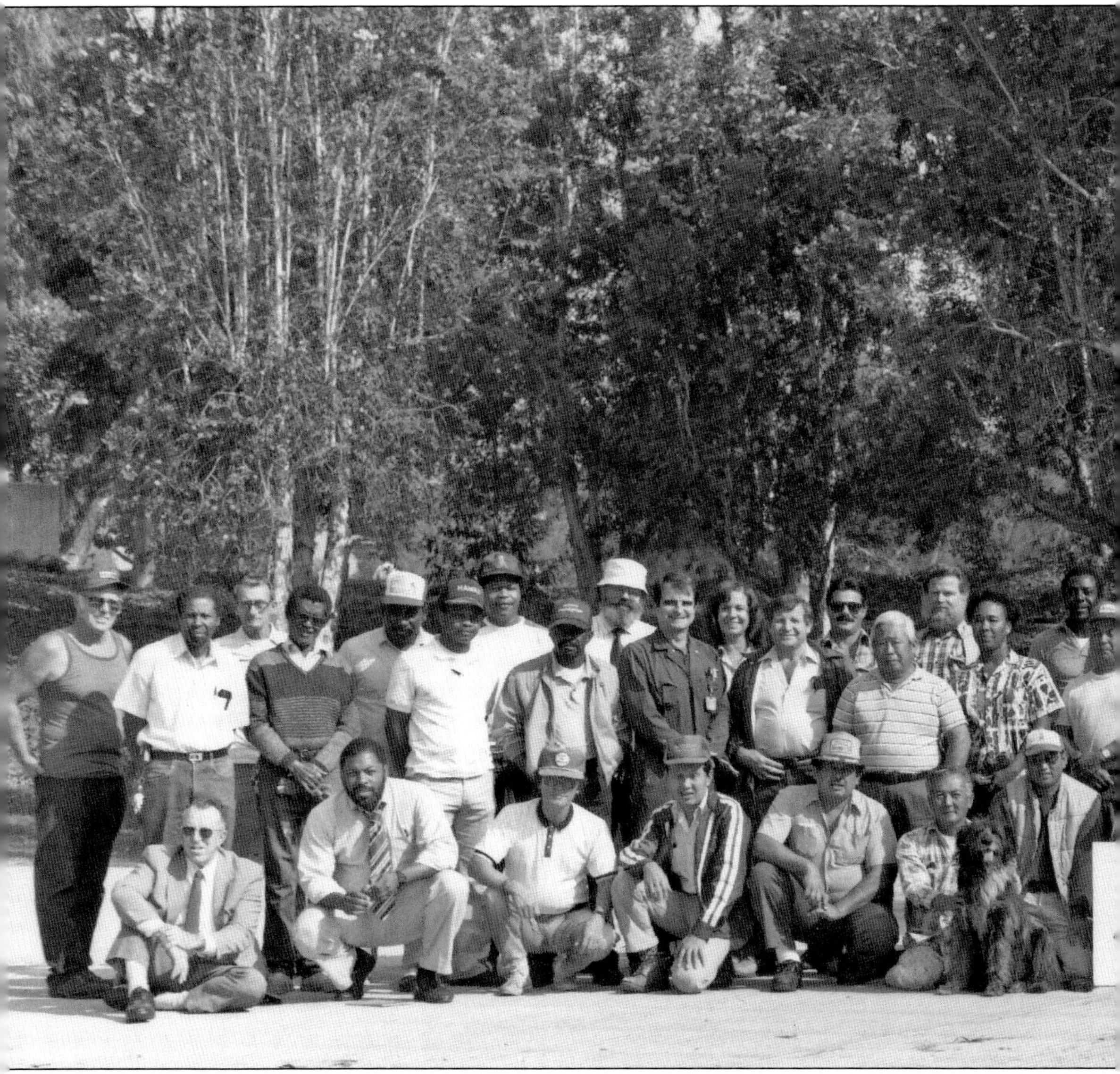

The CSU Dominguez Hills Plant Operations staff gathers for a group photograph in November 1986. Plant Operations (now known as Physical Plant) has the job of maintaining the campus

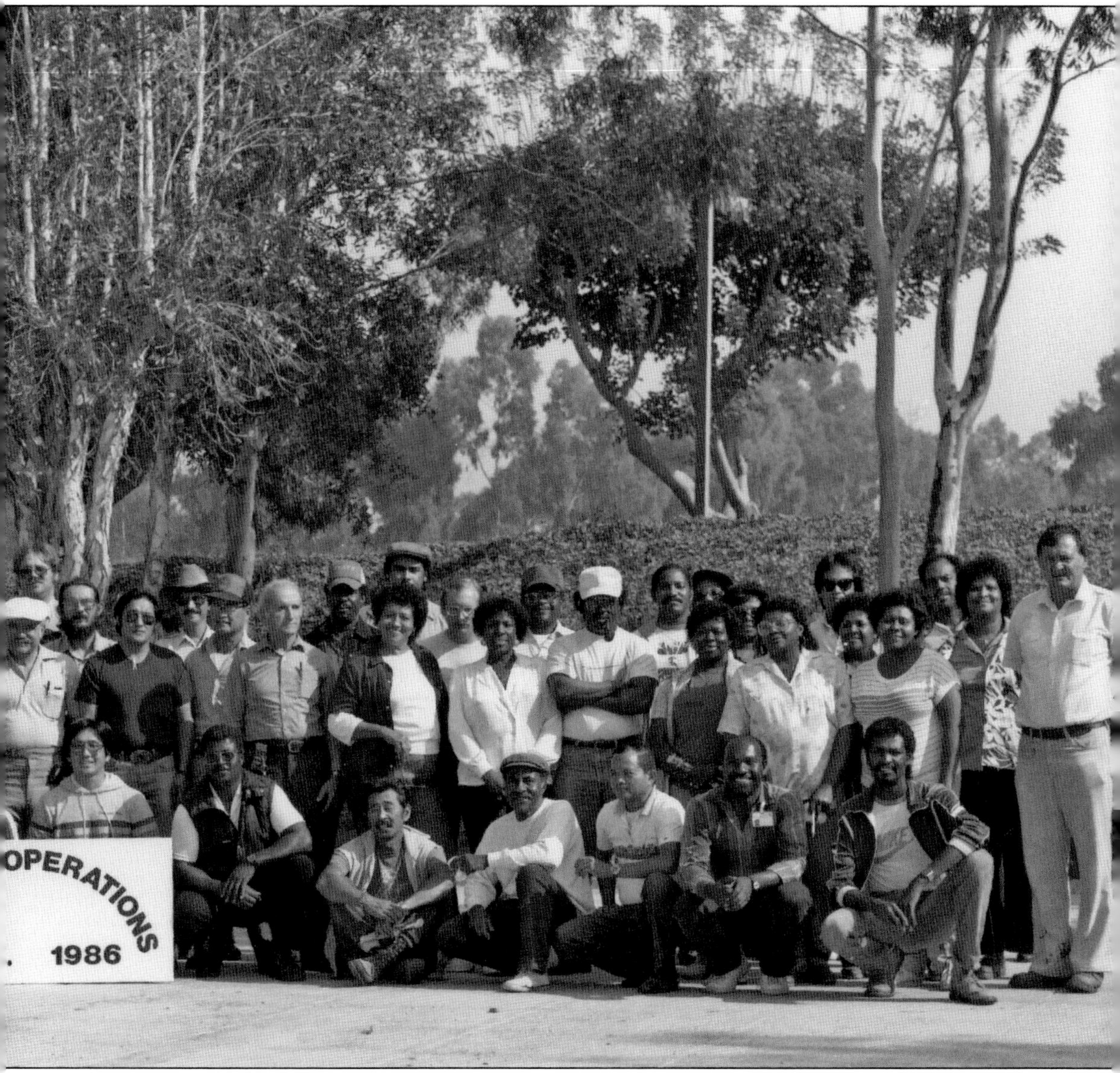

with repairs, gardening, deliveries, custodial work, and a host of other jobs that keep the university functioning.

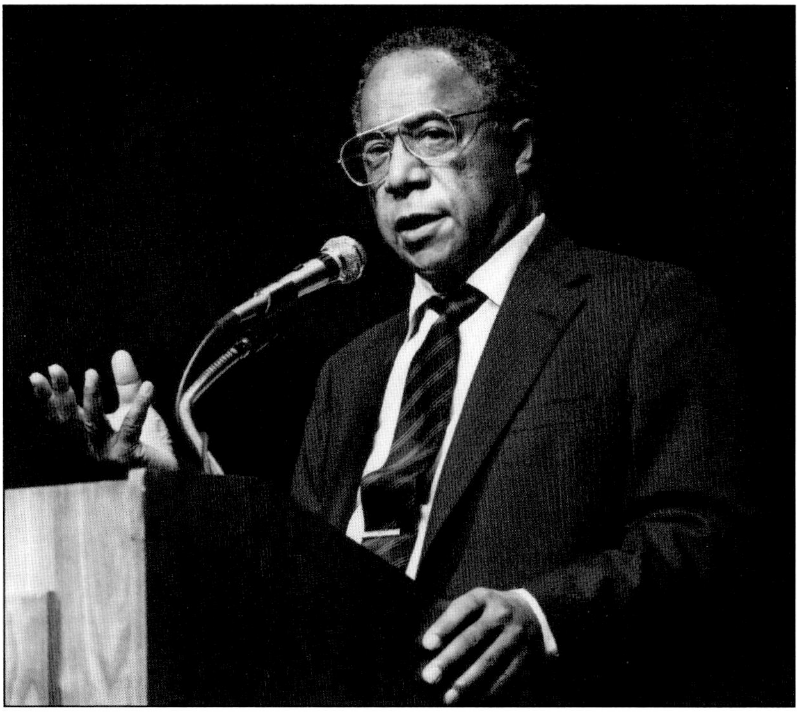

Brought to campus by the Intellectual Life Committee for the university's 25th anniversary, Alex Haley, author of *Roots* and the *Autobiography of Malcolm X*, spoke on "The Future of the Family" in October 1985.

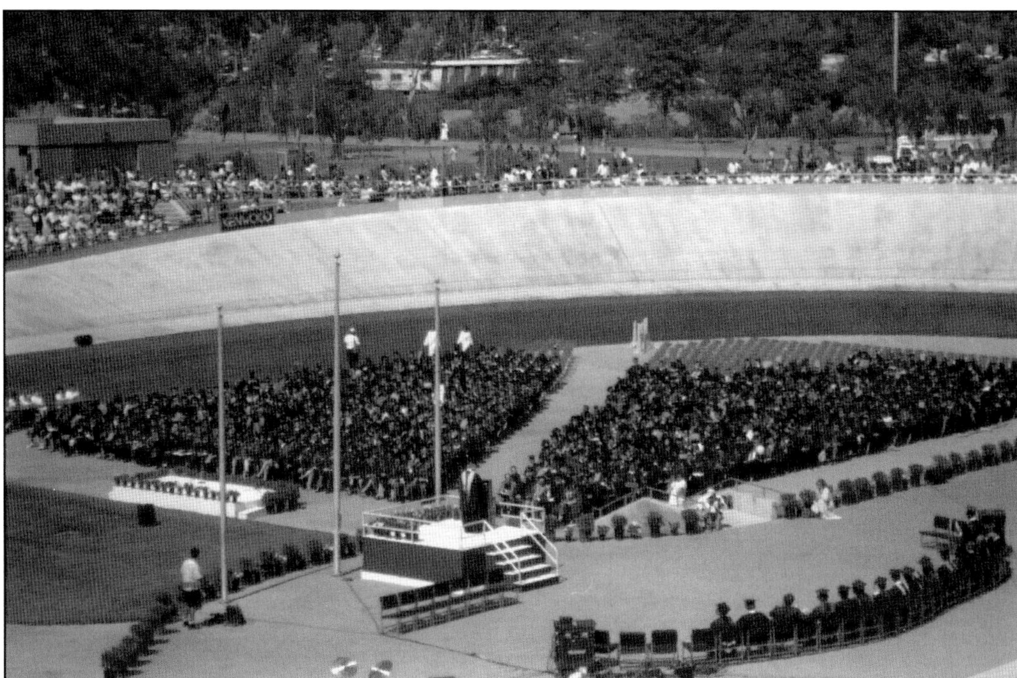

President Butwell addresses the 2,100 graduates of the class of 1985. It was the first graduation ceremony held in the 7-Eleven Olympic Velodrome. Paul Conrad, editorial cartoonist for the *Los Angeles Times*, spoke to the graduates.

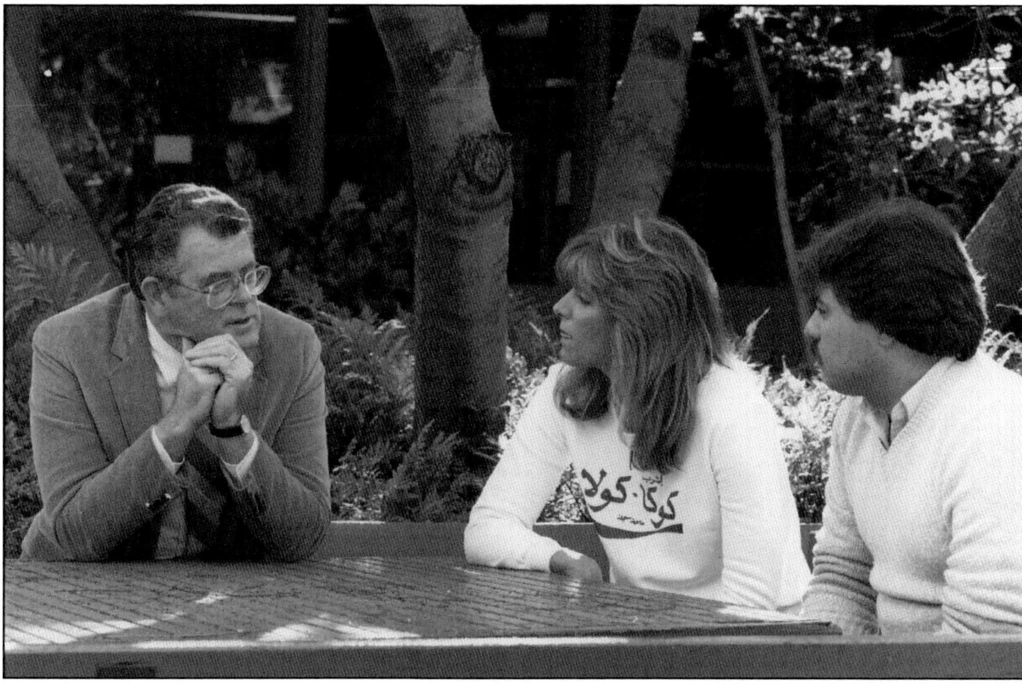

President Butwell speaks with two students in 1986. In early 1987, Butwell died of a heart attack at the age of 57. According to *Dominguez Hills Magazine*, although his administration faced enrollment difficulties and fiscal restraint, Butwell was determined to see the university thrive along with the community it served.

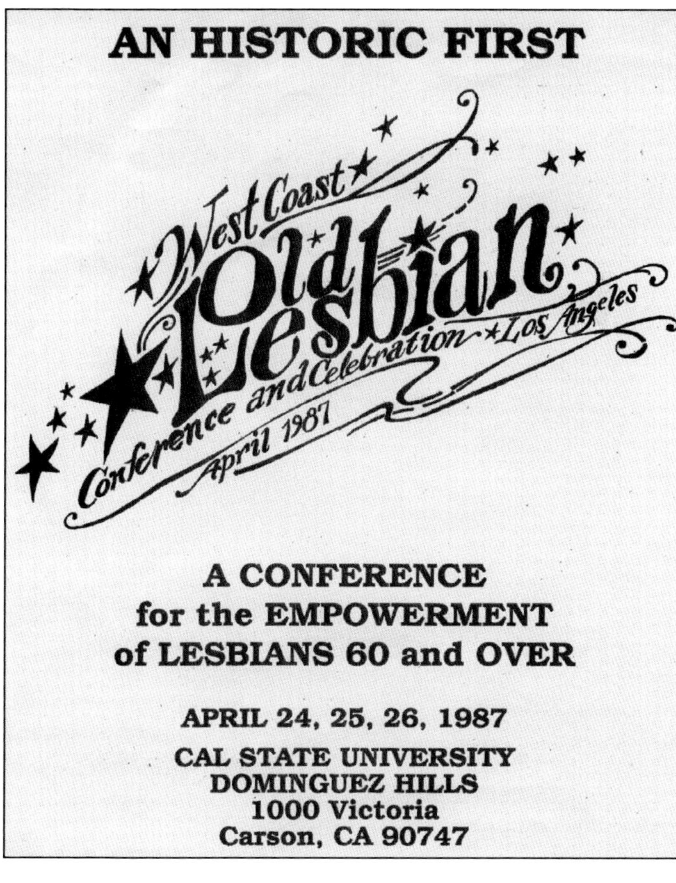

The West Coast Old Lesbian Conference and Celebration was held at CSU Dominguez Hills in April 1987. Sociology professor Sharon Raphael, whose gerontology research has focused on the lives of aging lesbians and gay men, coordinated the program. (Courtesy of ONE Archives.)

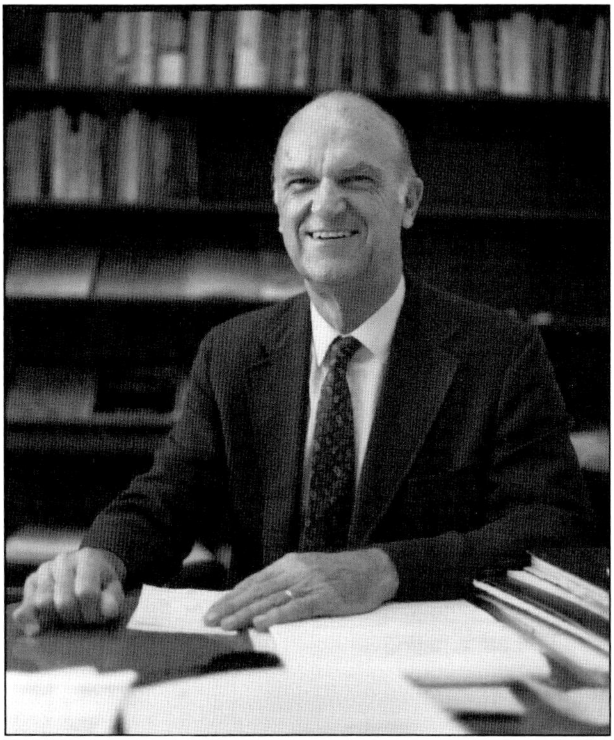

Upon the death of President Butwell, Dr. John Brownell, the university's academic vice president, was named acting president of the university and given a two-year contract. He served between 1987 and 1989 and focused on faculty review procedures, establishing the statewide nursing program, and funding the student union.

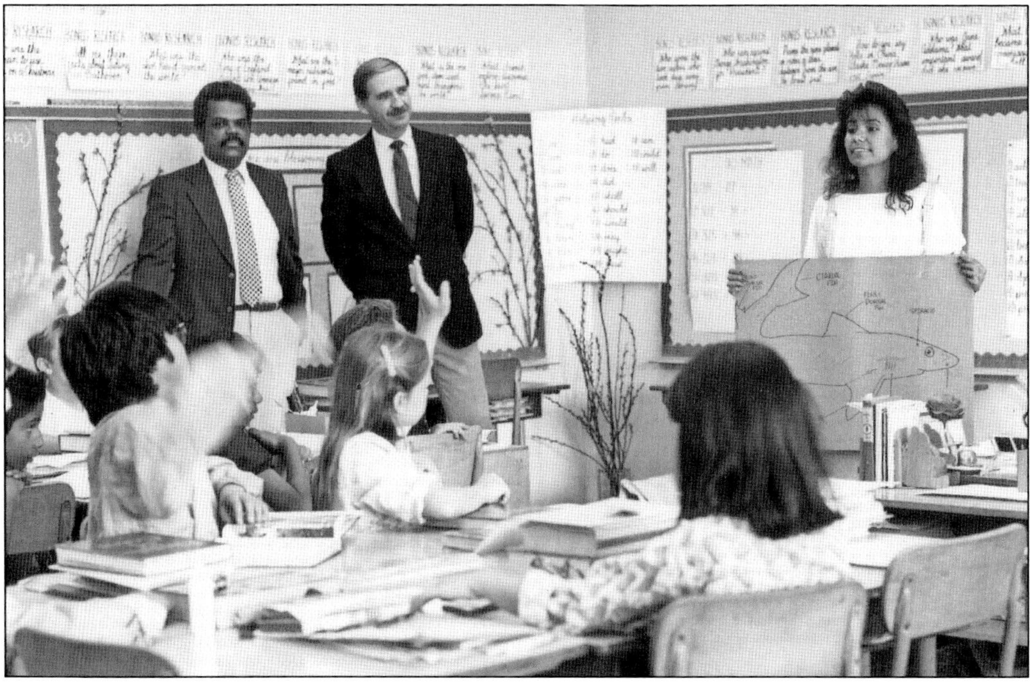

The Minority Teacher Recruitment Program, funded by the Carnegie Corporation, assisted the university with teacher recruitment. In this photograph, Gardena High School counselor Walter Wooden, left, stands next to Judson Taylor, dean of education, as they observe high school student Ruby De La Rosa teaching at the 186th Street Elementary School.

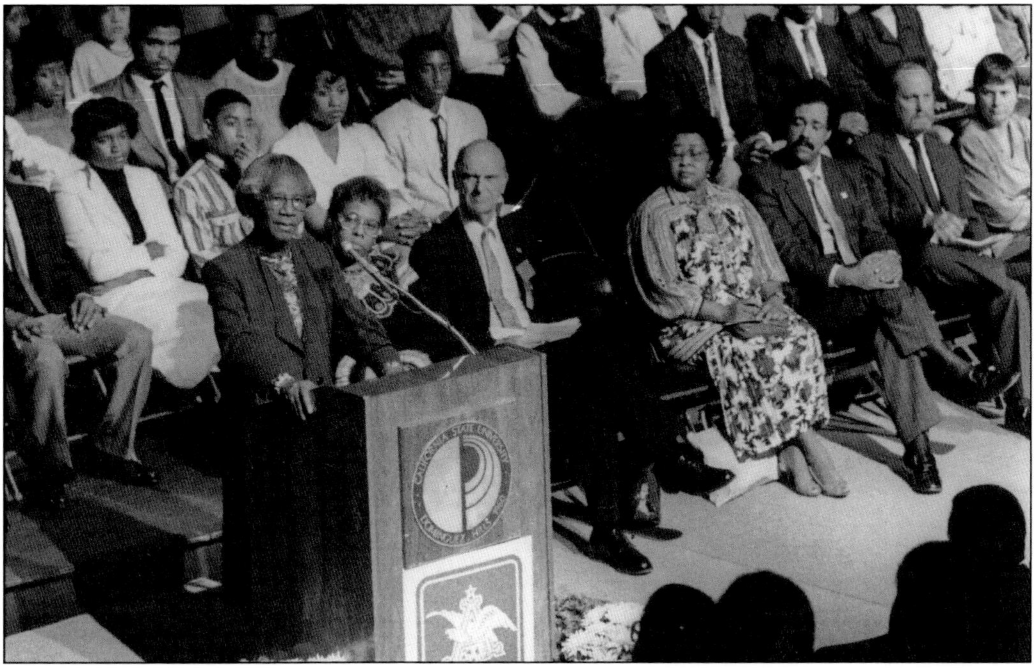

Former congresswoman Shirley Chisholm speaks at the University Theatre during a two-day residency in 1988 that was part of the "Afro-American Renaissance Series." Chisholm also spoke on a panel titled "Constitutional Law and the Political Process" as well as on "A Commitment to Public Service" at the Young, Gifted, and Black Honors Program.

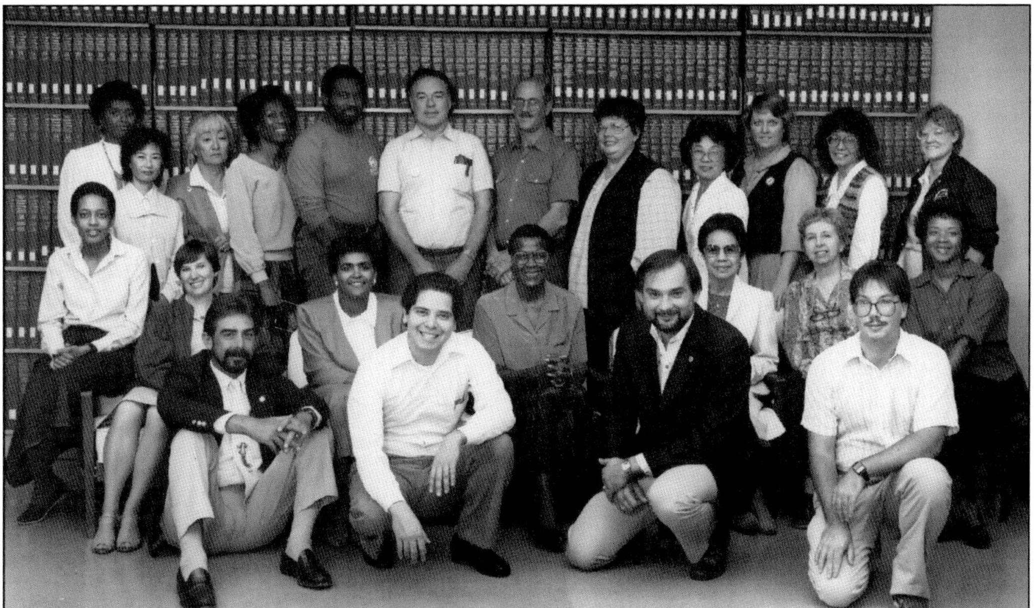

The University Library staff and faculty pose with the instructional media staff in the Victoria Room of the Educational Resources Center in 1986. Betty Blackman, library dean, is seated in the center. Those on the floor in the front are, from left to right, Frank Paine, David Quant, Prof. James Sudalnik, and Mario Congreve.

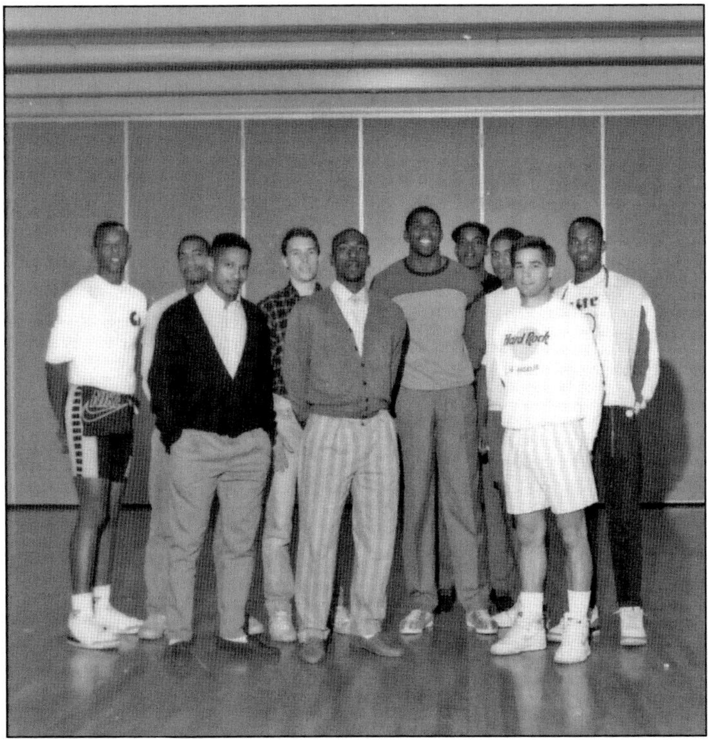

Michigan State University and Los Angeles Lakers basketball star Earvin "Magic" Johnson visits the Toros basketball team in December 1988. Johnson also spoke in the University Theatre.

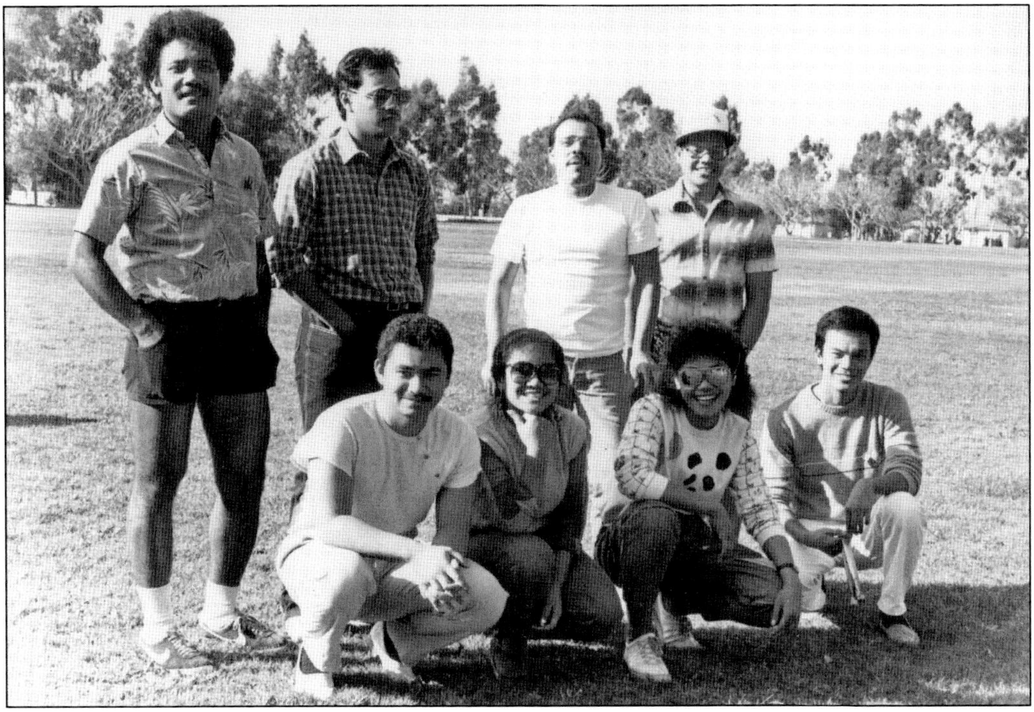

Members of the Polynesian Club pose on the campus mall. The club was created in 1980 and included many students of Samoan, Tongan, Hawaiian, and other Pacific island ethnicities living in surrounding communities. In 1991, the campus held a Pacific Islander Awareness Week.

Four

COMMITMENT TO DIVERSITY
THE 1990S

The university can only meet its mission by serving students and we need to serve more of them in order to have our fullest impact on the region. Enrollment growth is critical, too, if the campus is to earn the additional resources needed to enhance the quality and breadth of academic programs. We must engage in an aggressive outreach effort in schools and colleges, expand scholarship programs to attract qualified students, inform adult learners about our programs, seek additional graduate students, and identify other audiences of students to serve.

—Pres. Robert C. Detweiler, September 1990.

After a year in office, Pres. Robert Detweiler saw enrollment rise seven percent over the previous year, reaching a record 12,000 students. Of those students, 9,200 attended classes on campus. Another 2,800 were enrolled in the new Statewide Nursing Program.

Immediately after this enrollment increase, more than $6 million was cut from university programs during budget crises between 1991 and 1993. Several programs were dropped, and longtime professors took a "golden handshake" retirement.

Regardless, throughout the 1990s, the university focused on expanding the campus, obtaining grants, funding scholarships, and participating in community partnerships. These achievements included the establishment of the California Academy of Mathematics and Science High School (1990), the opening of the Donald P. and Katherine B. Loker Student Union after years of effort (1992), the first University Merit Scholarships being awarded (1993), nearly $2 million in gifts being raised from alumni and others (1993), a $1.3-million grant for a nursing education program (1994), 60 chief executive officers from South Bay companies meeting on campus to discuss job opportunities for students (1995), and the inaugural Presidential Scholarship and Awards Dinner (1999).

The campus began its distance-learning program in 1991, and by 1997, it was recognized in *Forbes* as one of the top 20 cyber-universities in the country. Also in 1997, *U.S. News and World Report* ranked the university the most diverse among Western universities.

Longtime faculty members continued to be recognized as the CSU's Outstanding Professor. Historian Donald Hata (1990) and sociologist Hal Charnofsky (1992) joined biologist Lois Chi (1979) and musician Richard Bunger (1982) as honorees.

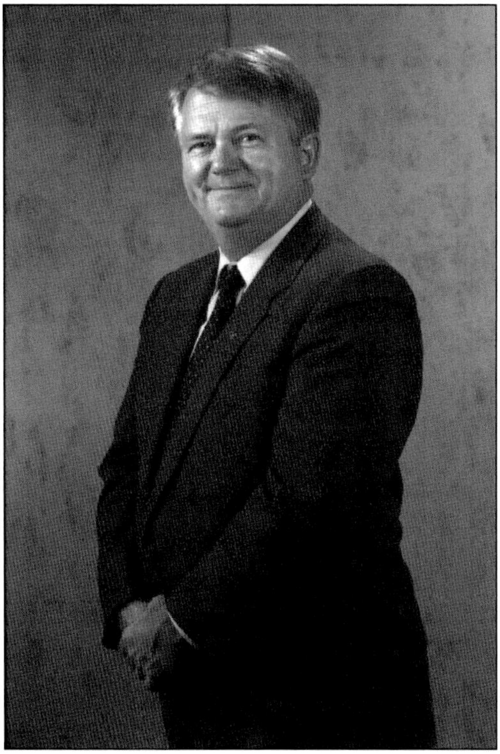

In 1989, Robert C. Detweiler was named university president. Formerly vice president of academic affairs at CSU San Bernardino and a dean at San Diego State University, Detweiler said at the time of his hiring that "We must make special efforts to ensure that our student body reflects the community. . . . We must find ways to relate our teaching and research to the needs of a dynamic, new society in California."

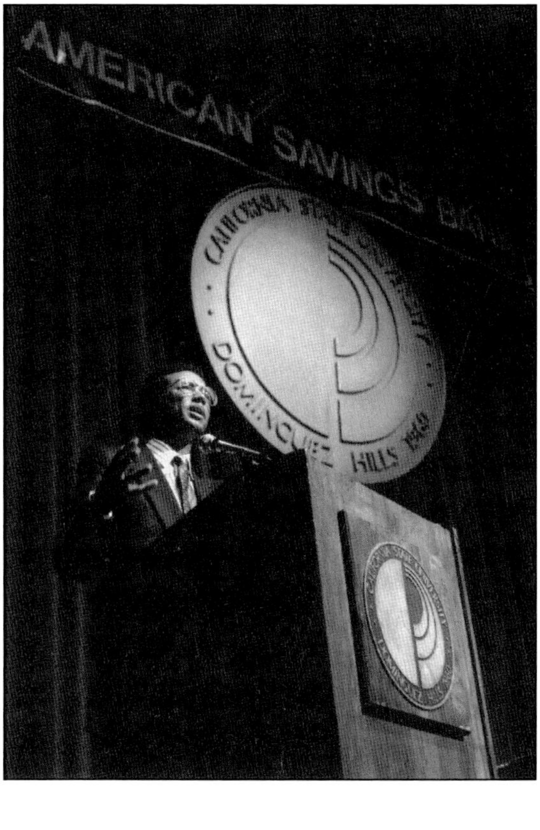

Tennis star Arthur Ashe encourages academic preparation and educational achievement for African American athletes during his Young, Gifted, and Black Honors Program residency at CSU Dominguez Hills in 1990.

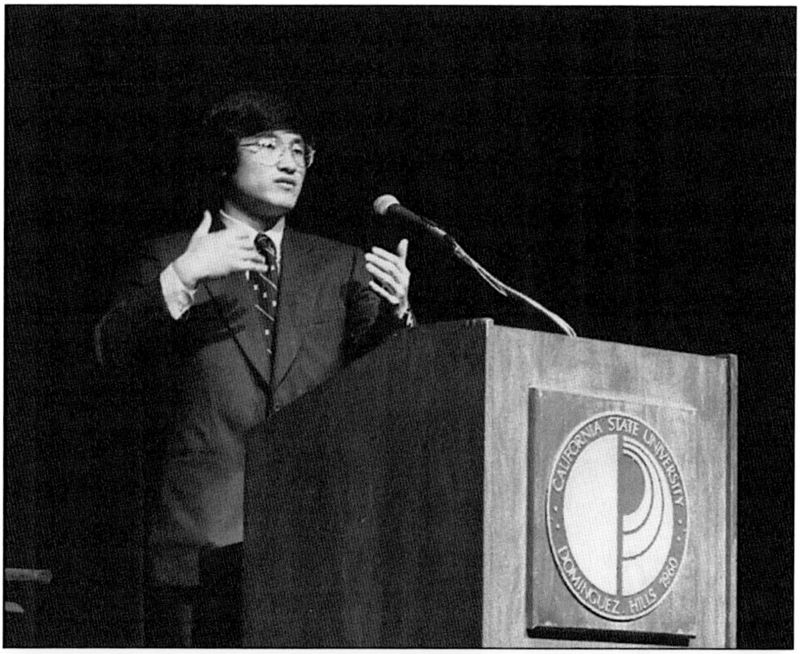

Li Lu, organizer and leader of the Chinese student dissent group that took part in the Tiananmen Square protest of 1989, speaks at the university in 1990.

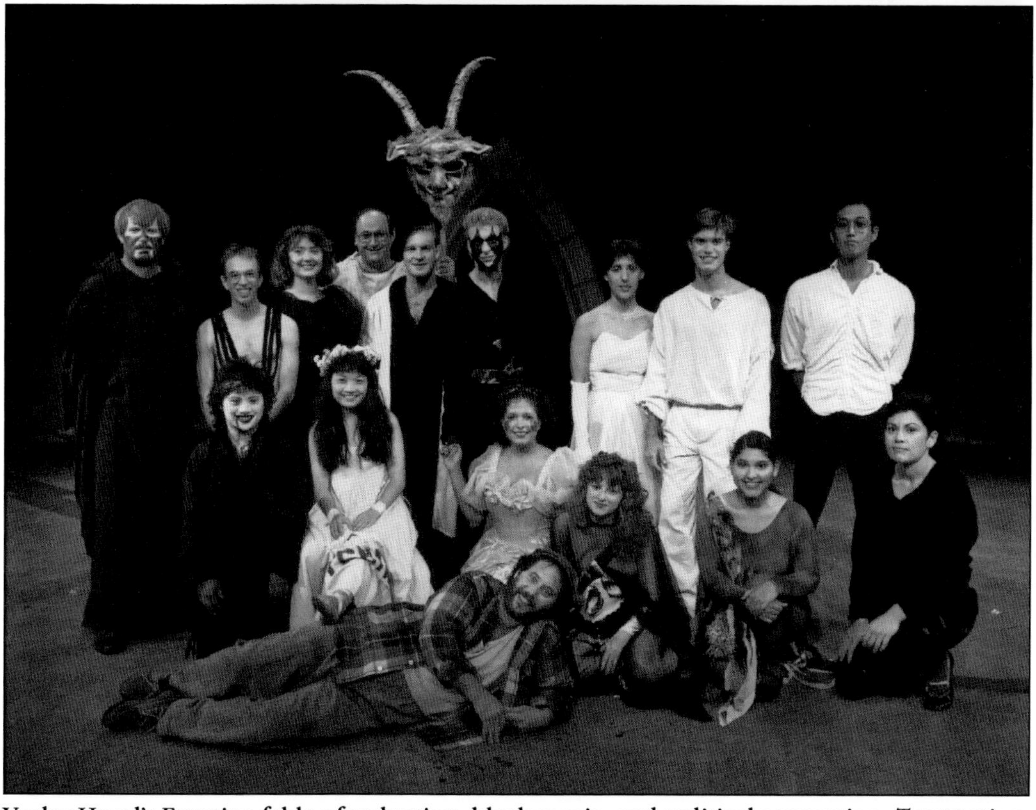

Vaclav Havel's Faustian fable of seduction, black magic, and political corruption, *Temptation*, opened the 1990–1991 university theater season. At the time of the production, Havel, a former political prisoner, was the president of Czechoslovakia.

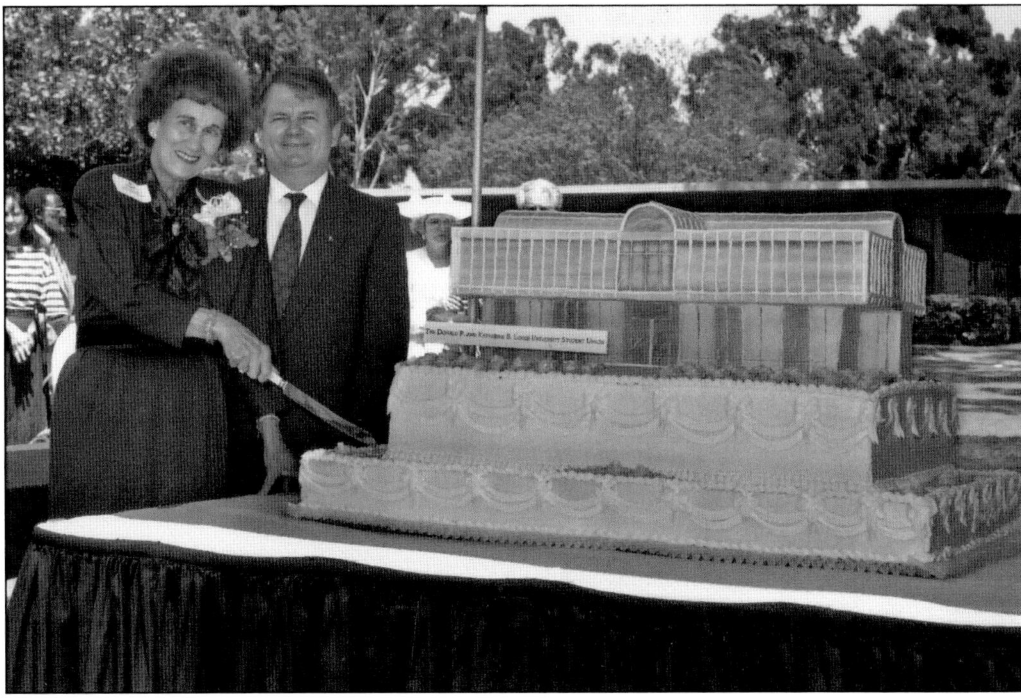

Katherine B. Loker cuts a cake shaped like the future Donald P. and Katherine B. Loker Student Union as President Detweiler looks on during the 1990 ground-breaking.

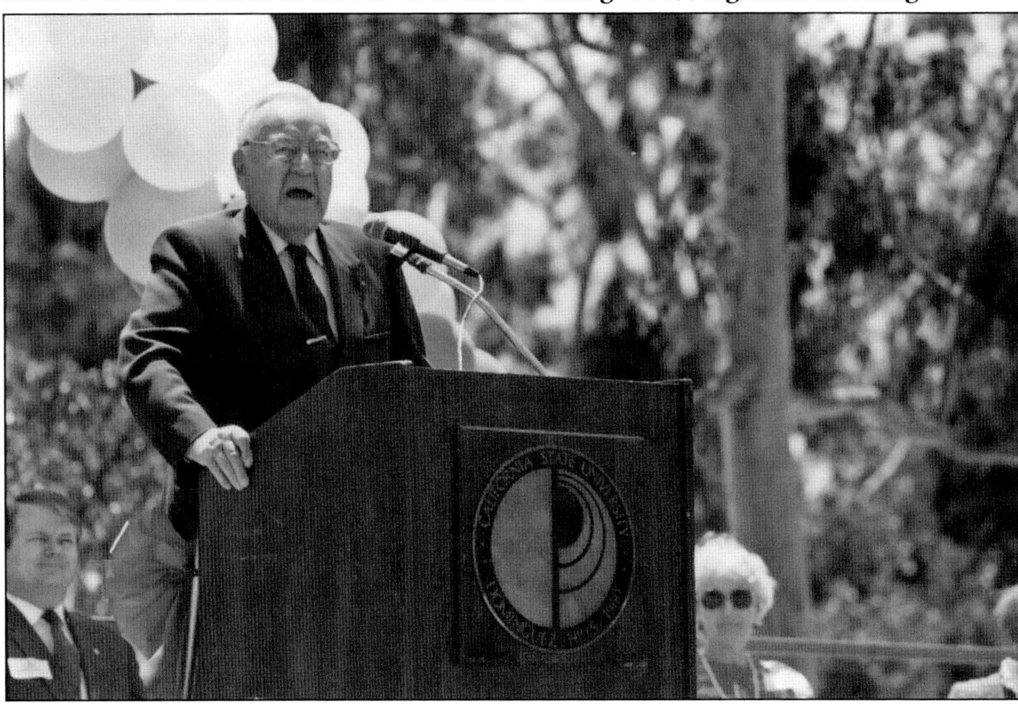

Longtime friend of the university and former California governor Edmund "Pat" Brown speaks in 1990 at the ground-breaking ceremony for the Donald P. and Katherine B. Loker Student Union.

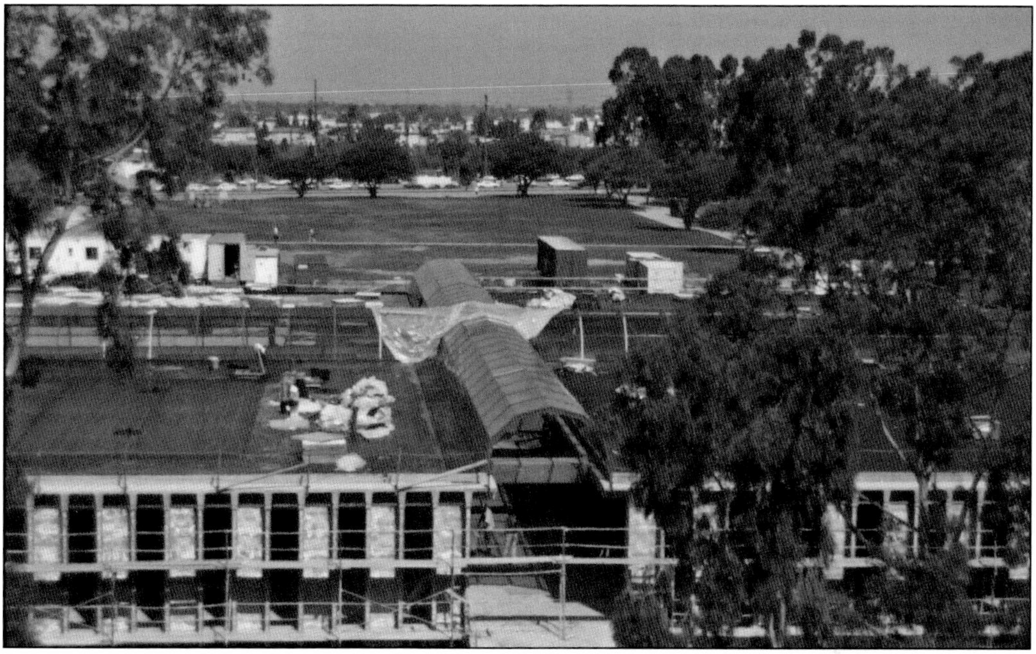

After students approved a fee increase in 1985 to raise funds for a student union, the university held a capital campaign, and Donald P. and Katherine B. Loker pledged $500,000. Construction finally began in 1990, and in 1992, the Donald P. and Katherine B. Loker Student Union was completed.

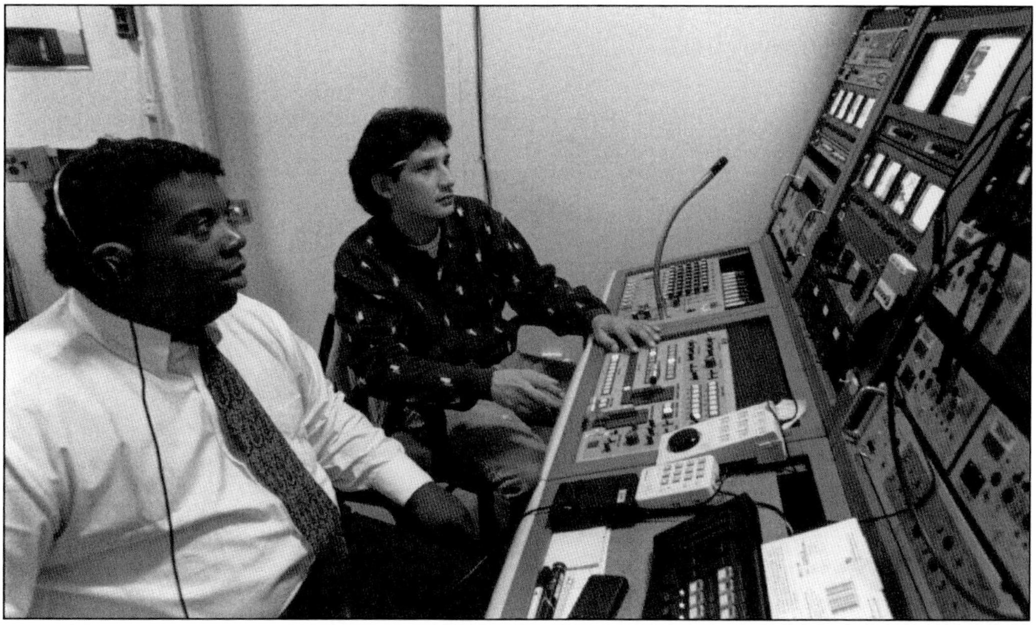

Assistant director Van L. Bridgeman (left) and student Jose Reano operate the control board for one of the many live and interactive courses taught through the Mediated Instruction and Distance Learning program in 1994. Courses are broadcast via the campus cable television (DHTV) and the Internet, enabling viewers to call instructors during classes. The campus has the largest distance-learning program in the CSU system.

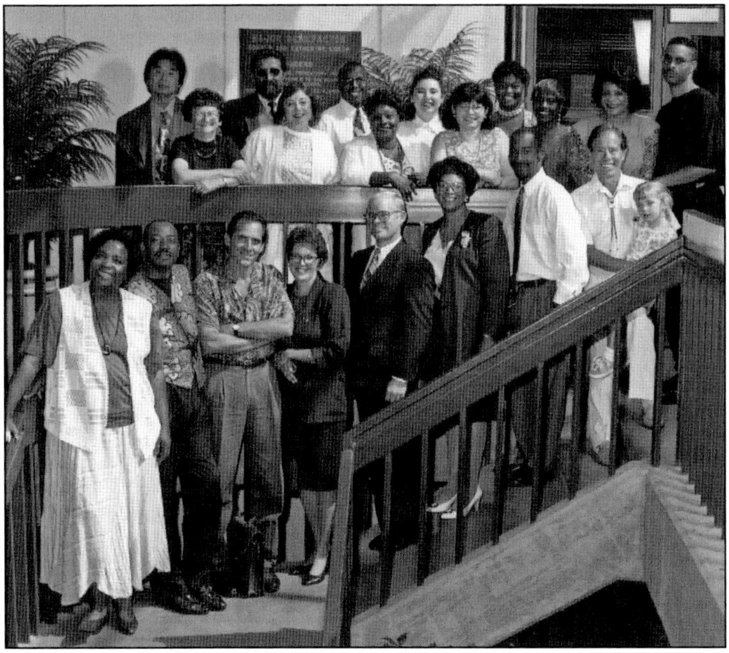

The Summer Bridge Program, designed to ease the transition of high school and transfer students to university life, celebrated its 10th year in 1994. Pictured are teachers, tutors, resident advisers, and Educational Opportunity Program (EOP) staff.

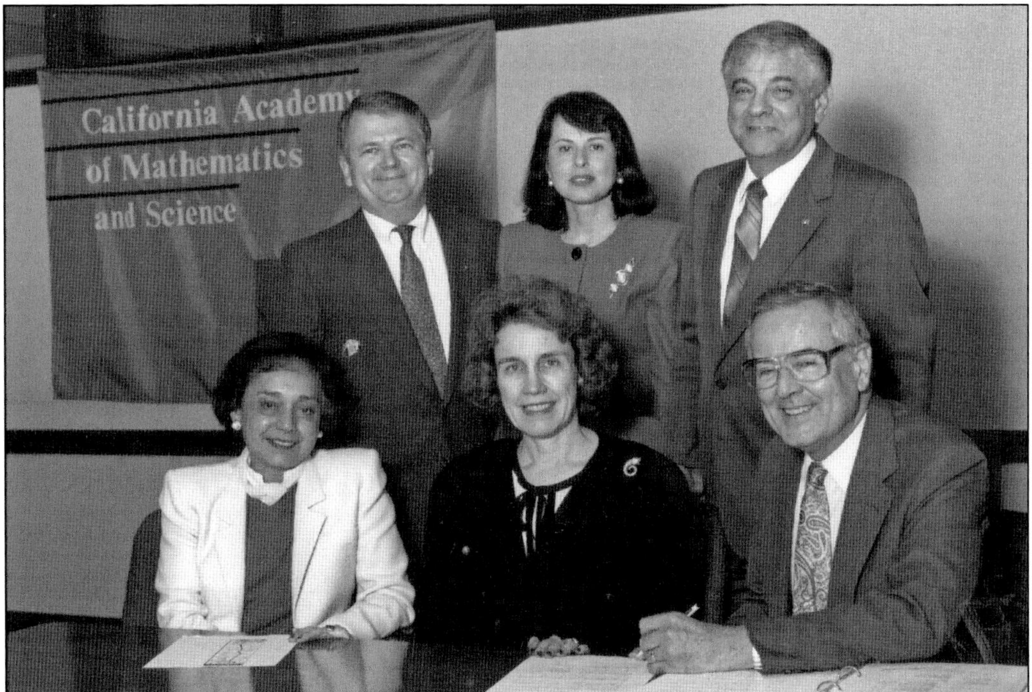

President Detweiler (standing at left), with dignitaries and CSU chancellor Ann Reynolds (seated at center), celebrate the agreement to open the California Academy of Mathematics and Science (CAMS) high school on the CSU Dominguez Hills campus. The school was designed to prepare students for careers in science, math, and engineering. It opened in 1994 with 120 students from schools throughout Los Angeles.

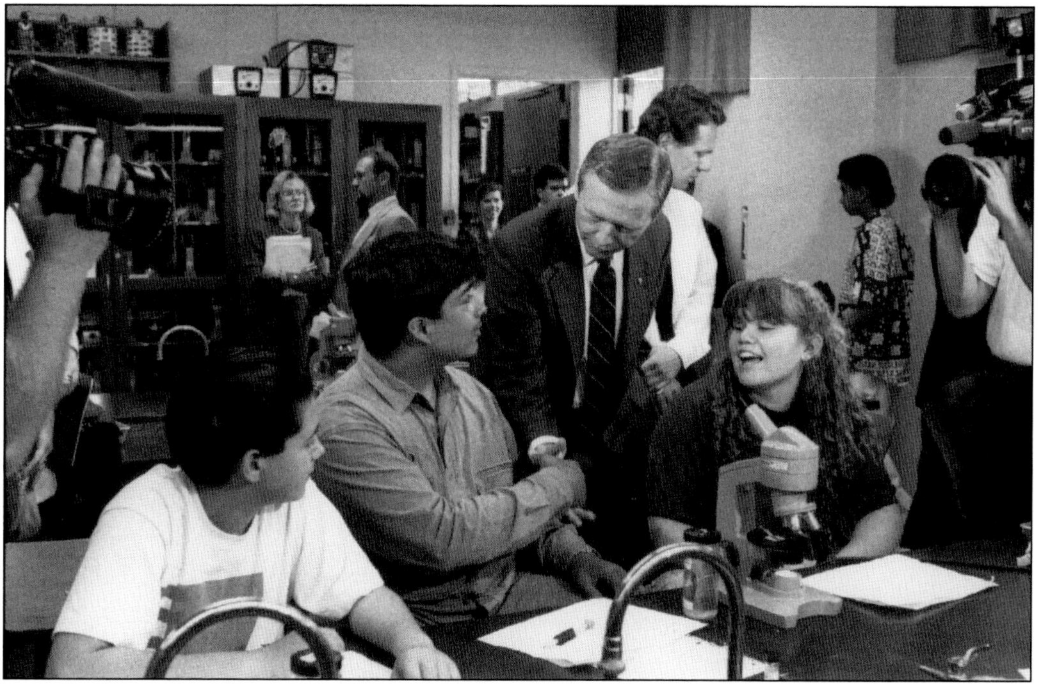

Senator Pete Wilson, then campaigning for the office of California governor, visits the university and the California Academy of Mathematics and Science on September 26, 1990. Wilson returned to CAMS in 1994 to address the first graduating class. CAMS has consistently been ranked in several surveys as one of the top high schools in the nation.

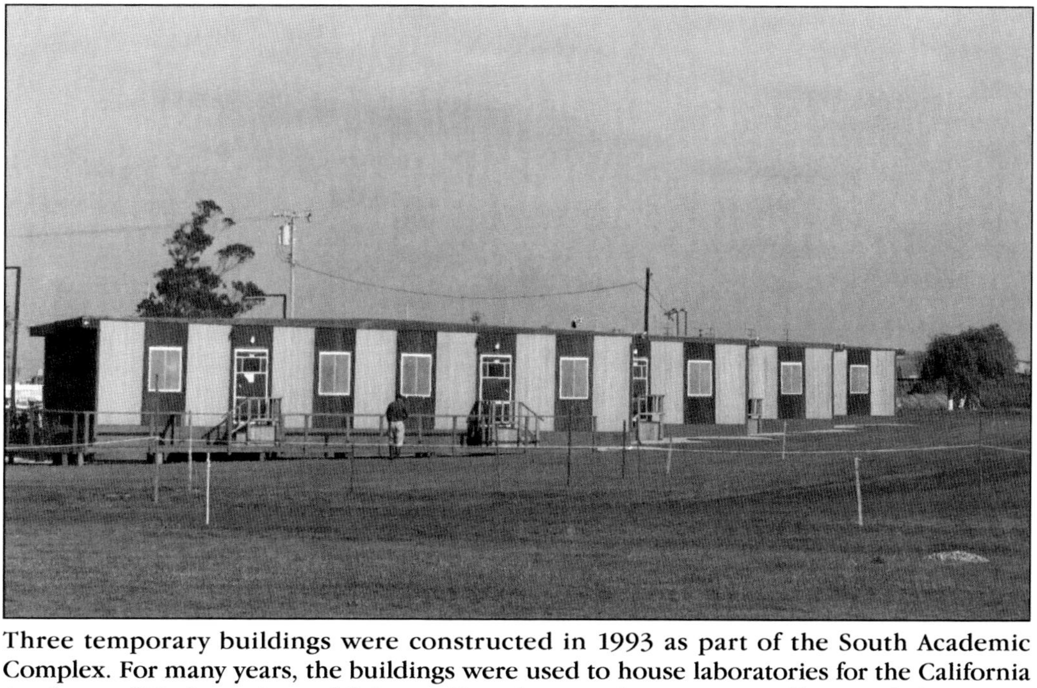

Three temporary buildings were constructed in 1993 as part of the South Academic Complex. For many years, the buildings were used to house laboratories for the California Academy of Mathematics and Science. Now the complex serves as offices and classrooms for the university.

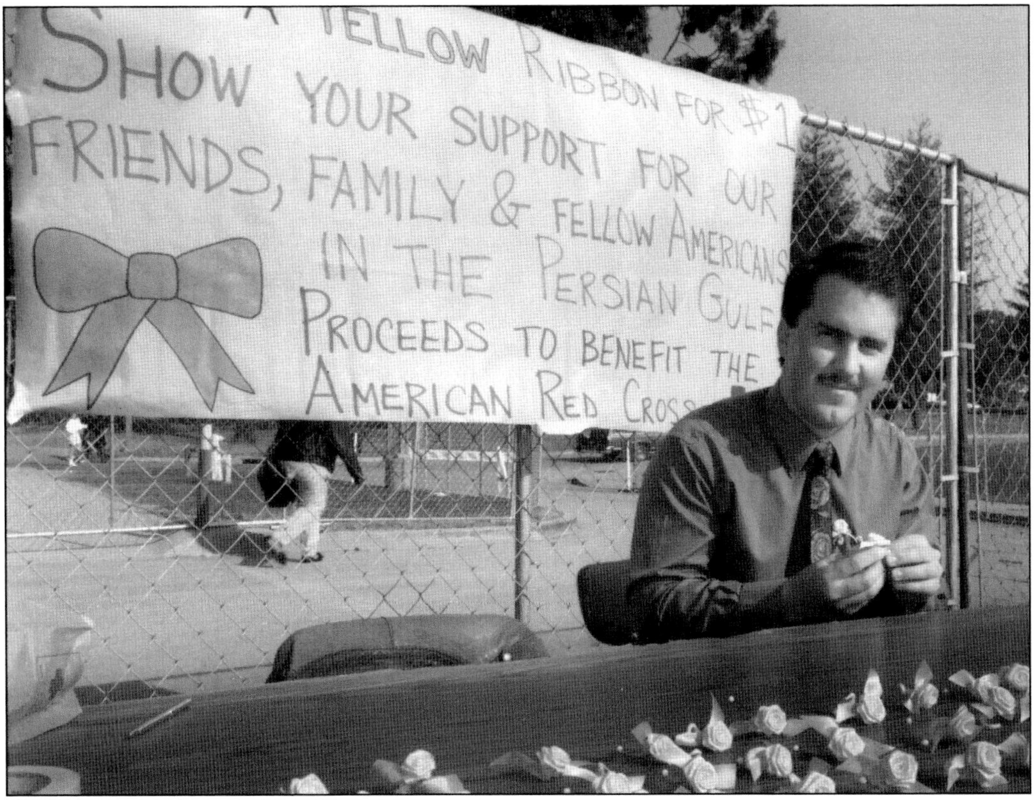

Glen Hamilton, student and Sigma Pi fraternity member, makes yellow ribbons in 1991 to support troops in the Desert Storm campaign in Iraq and Kuwait.

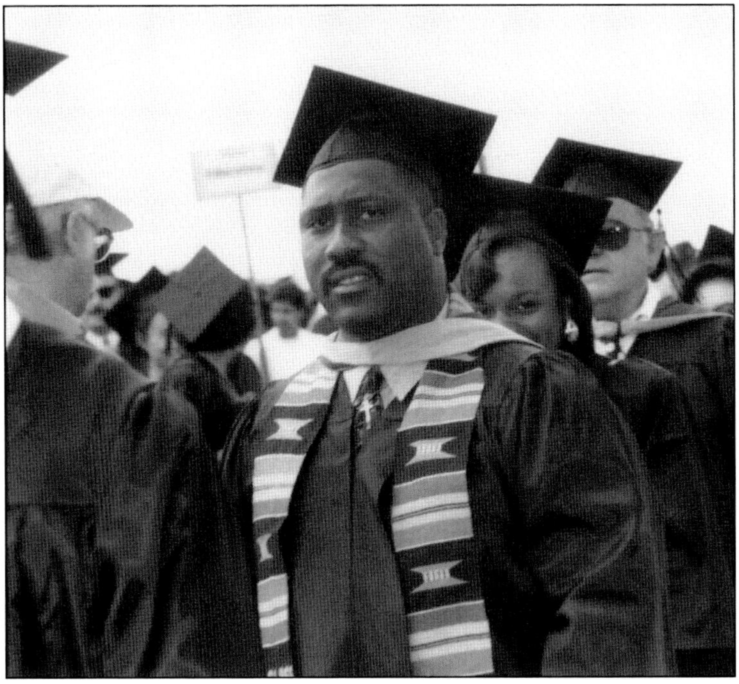

Guy Witherspoon, former student government president and Desert Storm veteran, is shown with fellow graduates during commencement in 1993. Witherspoon, who graduated with a degree in computer systems, later became executive director of Associated Students, Inc., at CSU Dominguez Hills.

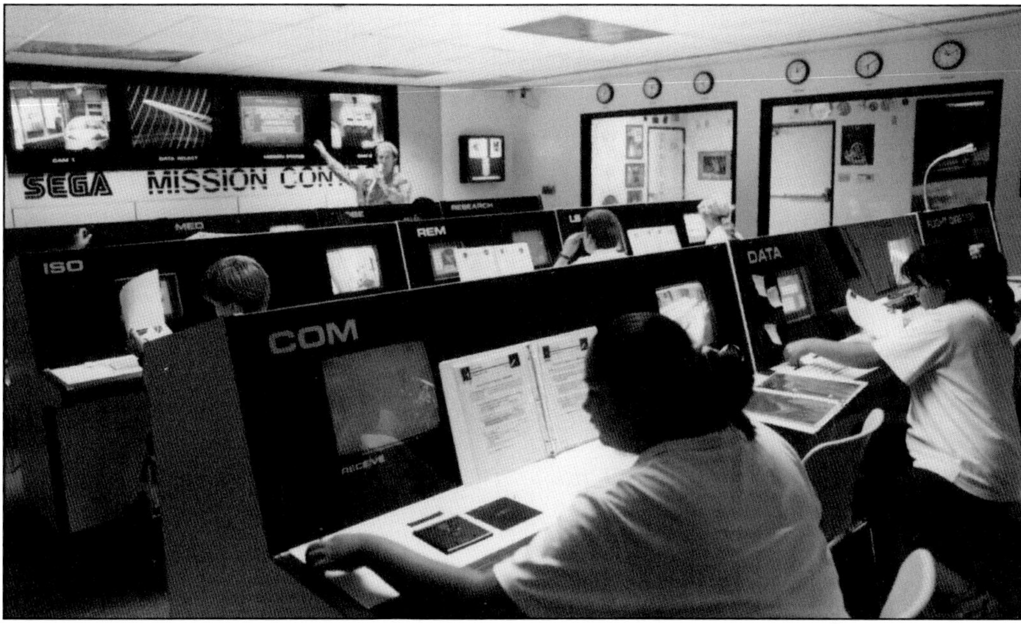

In 1994, CSU Dominguez Hills launched the Challenger Learning Center, which functioned as a futuristic space station where students learned to fly simulated space shuttle missions. The on-campus program was introduced mainly to build math and science skills among students in grades five through eight.

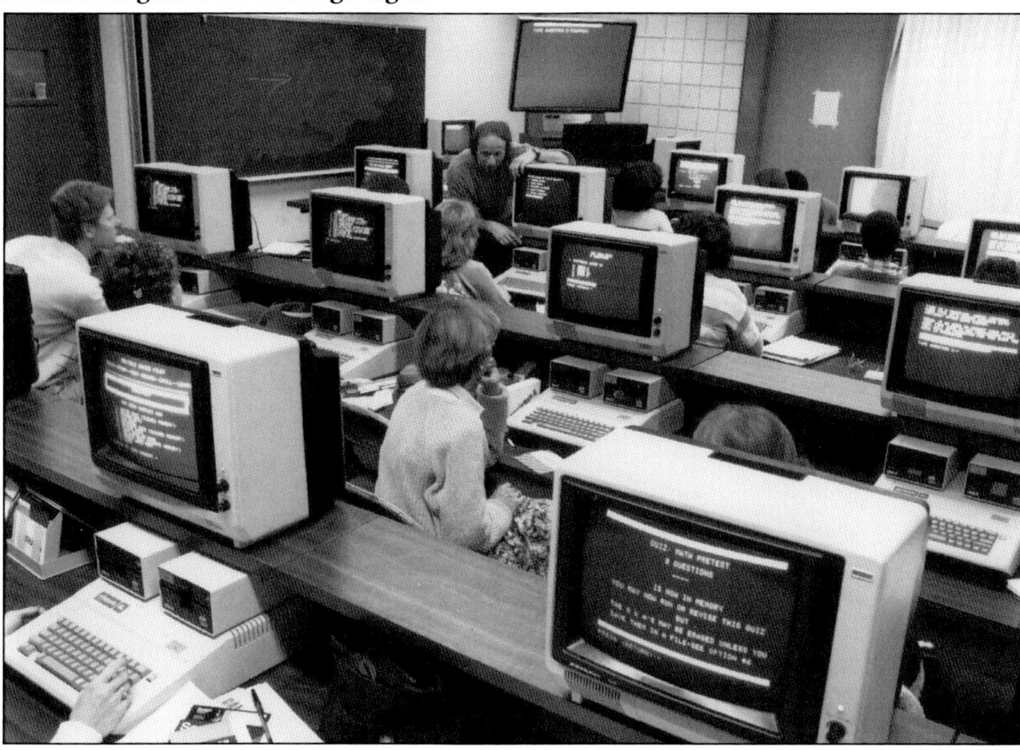

Students in a classroom at the Small College work at computers as Peter Desberg, professor of graduate education, directs them in the 1990s.

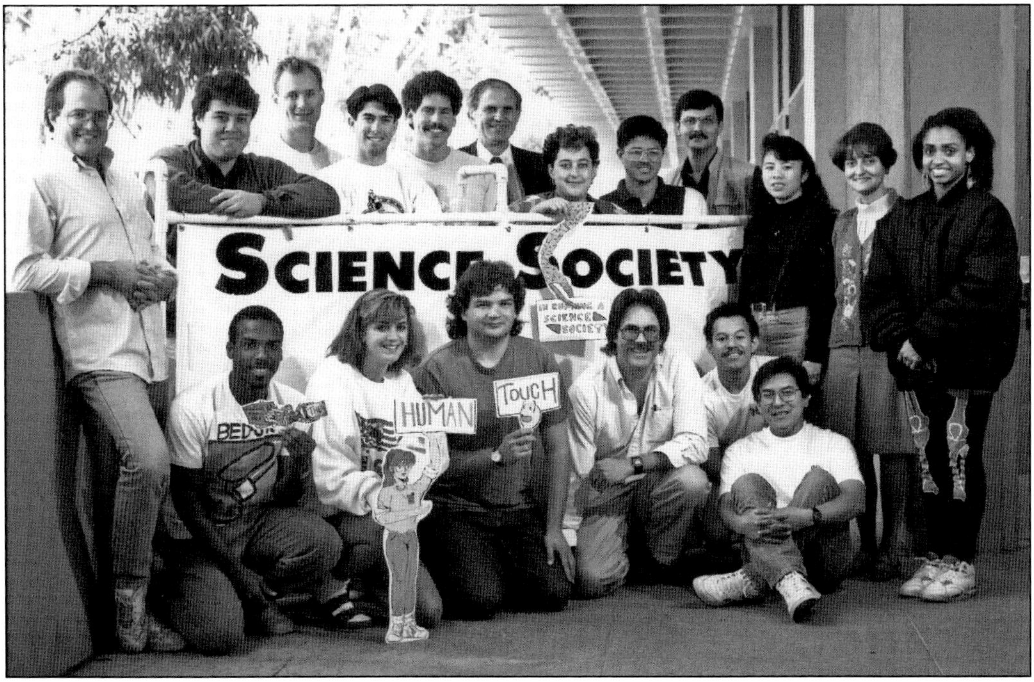

The Science Society Club with their adviser, Sofia Pappatheodorou (standing second from right), are pictured here. A 1990 *Los Angeles Times* article wrote about Professor Pappatheodorou's approach to teaching science and described a class where the guest lecturer was a magician who mixed chemicals and produced minor explosions.

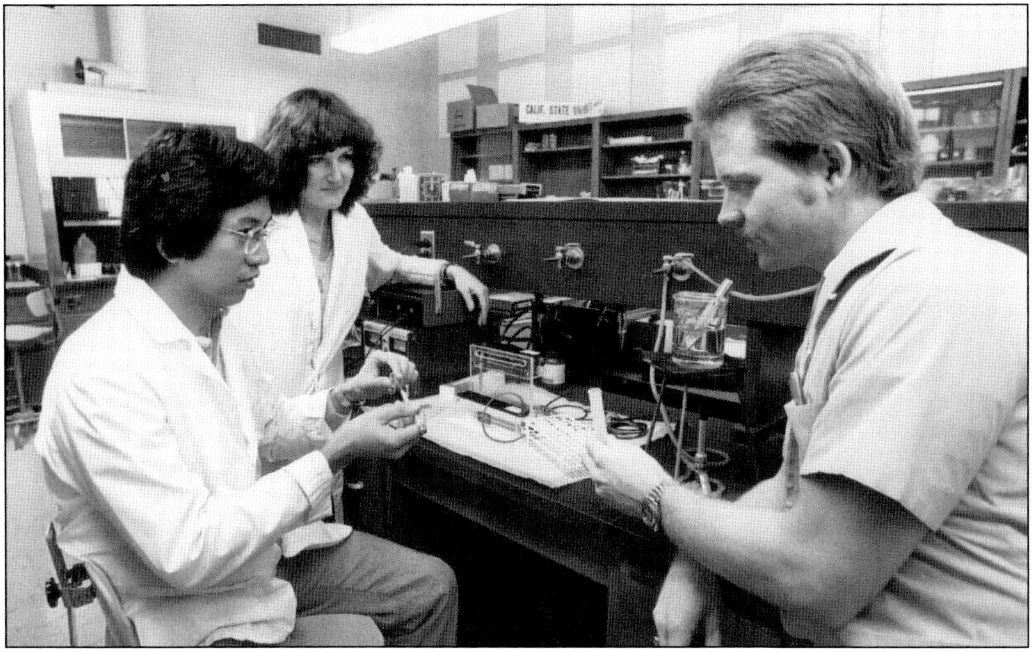

Laura Robles directs biology students in laboratory work during the early 1990s. A professor and administrator at CSU Dominguez Hills since 1975, Robles has conducted research focused on the retinal photoreceptor proteins that power vision in the octopus.

The Orthotics and Prosthetics Program, offered through the School of Health since 1983, trains students in the manufacture and fitting of artificial limbs and the design and bracing of such products. In this 1990s image, a student and faculty member work on the construction of a prosthetic leg. In 2009, the program moved its operations to the Long Beach Veteran's Administration Medical Center to better serve veterans as well as the general public.

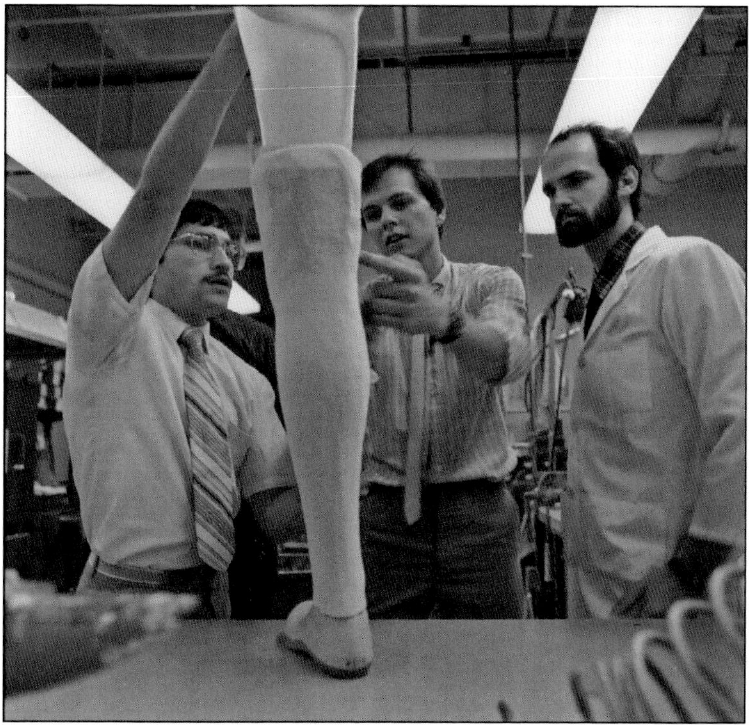

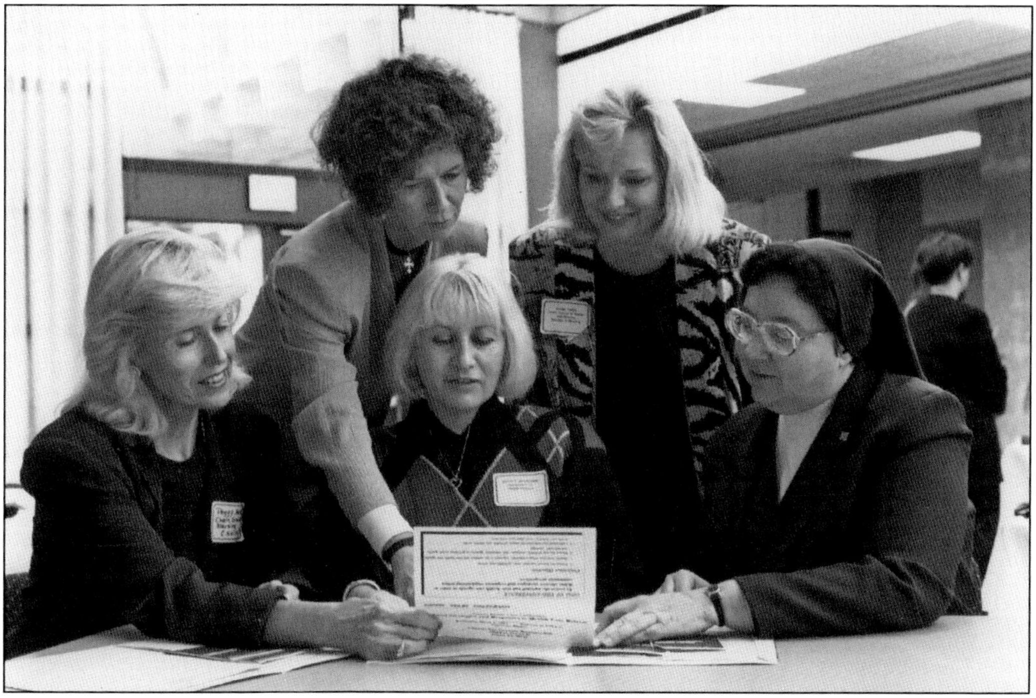

Nurses gather to focus on the Targeting Healthy Communities project in 1994. CSU Dominguez Hills began administering the Statewide Nursing Program, in which registered nurses can obtain master's and bachelor's degrees, in 1987.

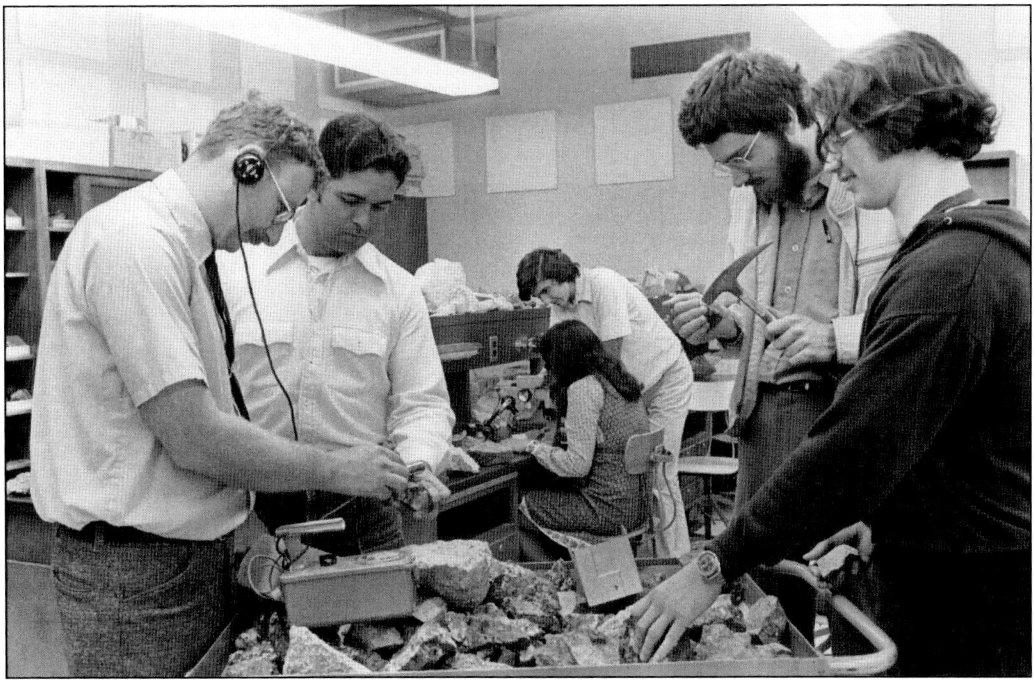

David Sigurdson, professor of earth sciences (at left), holds a Geiger counter to rock samples as students in his earth science class examine the rocks.

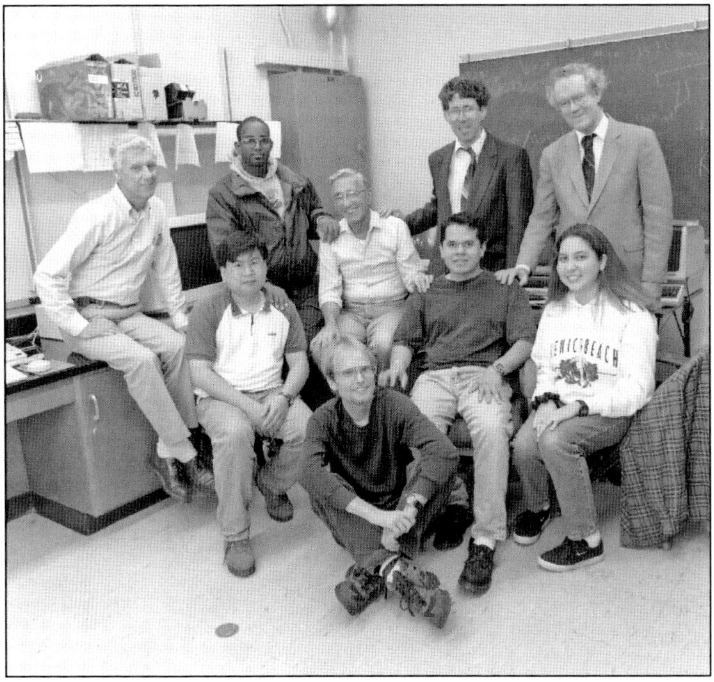

Kenneth Ganezer (standing at center), William Keig (standing at right), Ulrich de la Camp (far left), and their students pose here in 1996 to celebrate a National Science Foundation award that included university students in research on the Super Kamiokande nucleon decay experiment in Japan. The project's findings have changed the theories of particle physics by proving that neutrinos have mass. The Physics Department has been engaged in research on solar neutrinos for over 15 years.

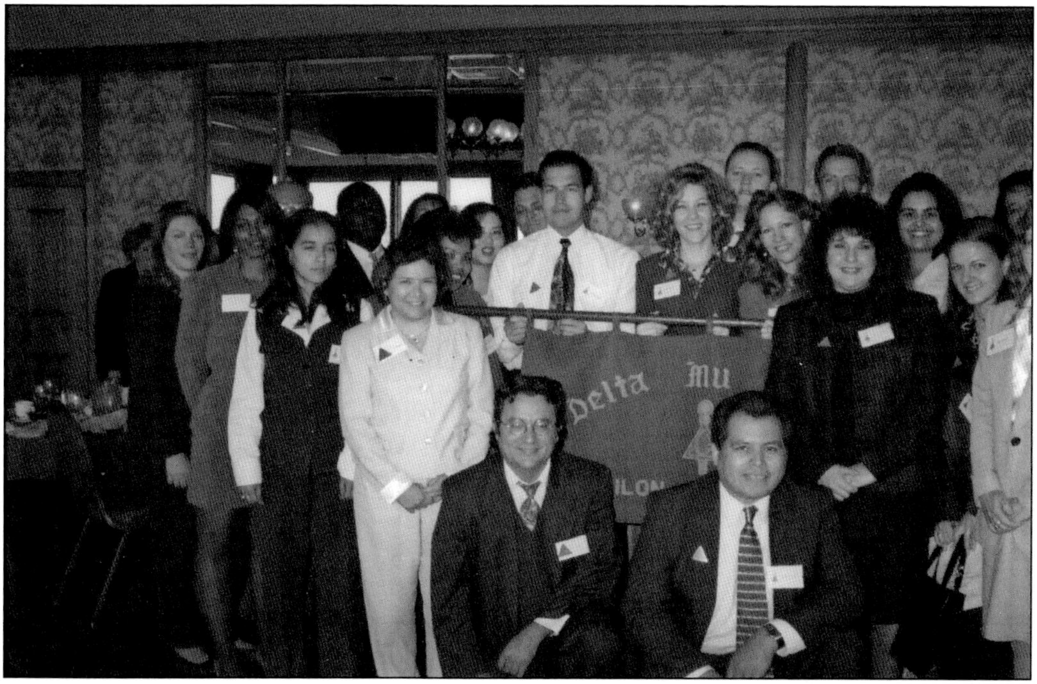

Members of Delta Mu Delta Epsilon Mu, the School of Management honors society, pose at their annual awards dinner in 1998. The School of Management was founded in 1972. Under its current name, the College of Business Administration and Public Policy encompasses an MBA program, information systems, management and marketing, political science, and other departments.

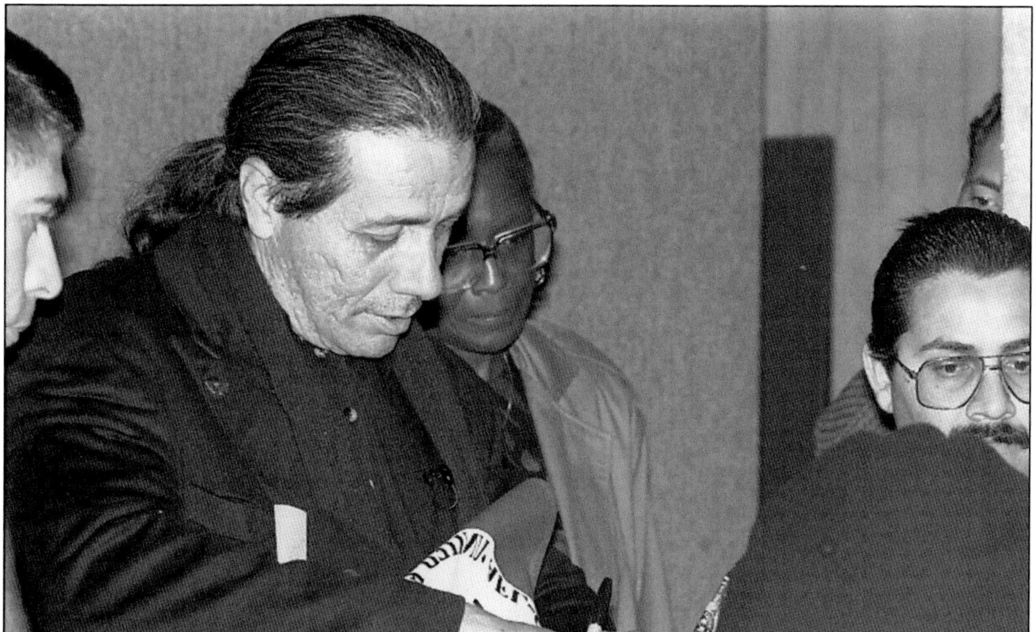

Actor and activist Edward James Olmos visited the University Theatre in March 1994 for a presentation titled "We're All in the Same Gang."

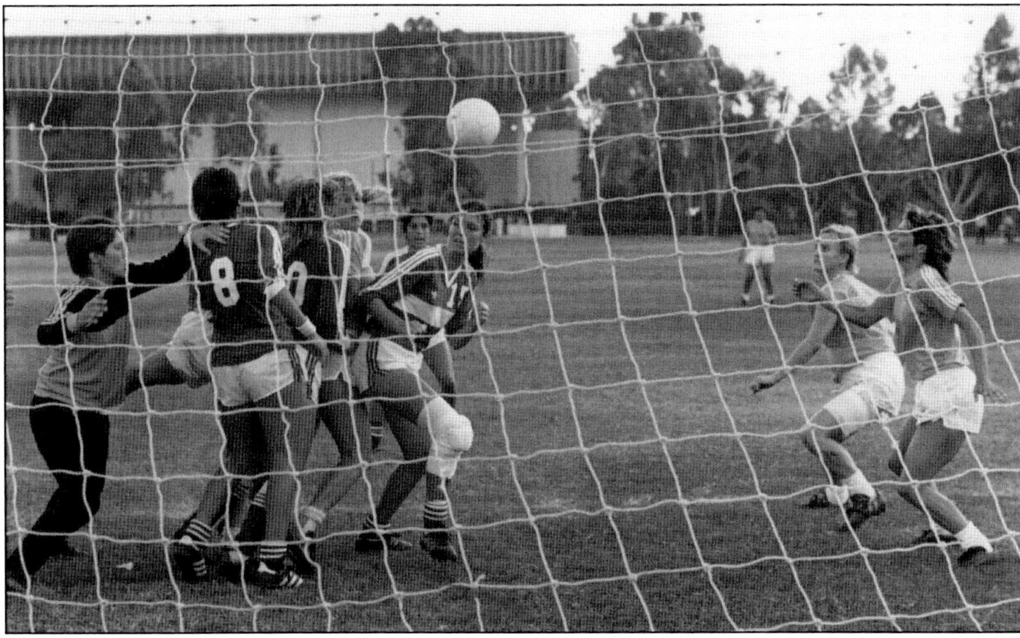

The Toro women's soccer team and their opponents race for the ball in front of goal on a field near the University Library.

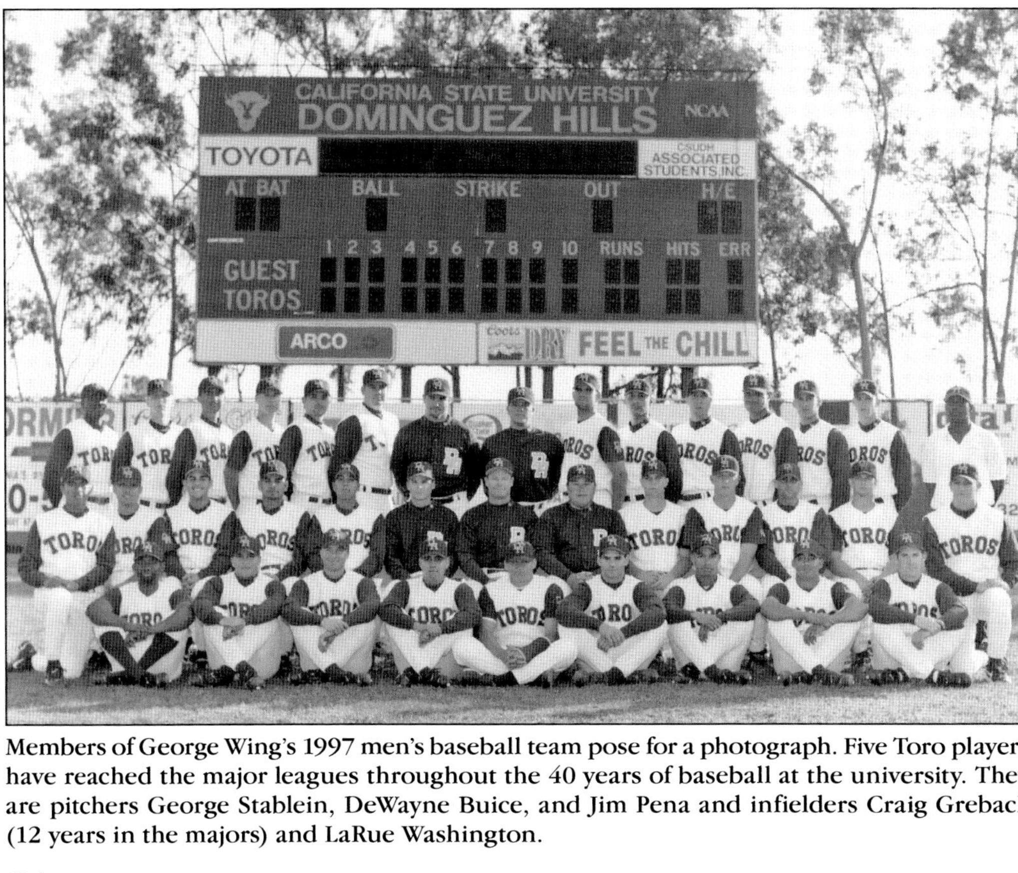

Members of George Wing's 1997 men's baseball team pose for a photograph. Five Toro players have reached the major leagues throughout the 40 years of baseball at the university. They are pitchers George Stablein, DeWayne Buice, and Jim Pena and infielders Craig Greback (12 years in the majors) and LaRue Washington.

A painting of a large bull representing the CSU Dominguez Hills Toro lurks behind the 1991–1992 women's basketball team in the gymnasium. Head coach Van Girard (right) and assistant coach Pam Paulson (left) are on opposite ends of the back row.

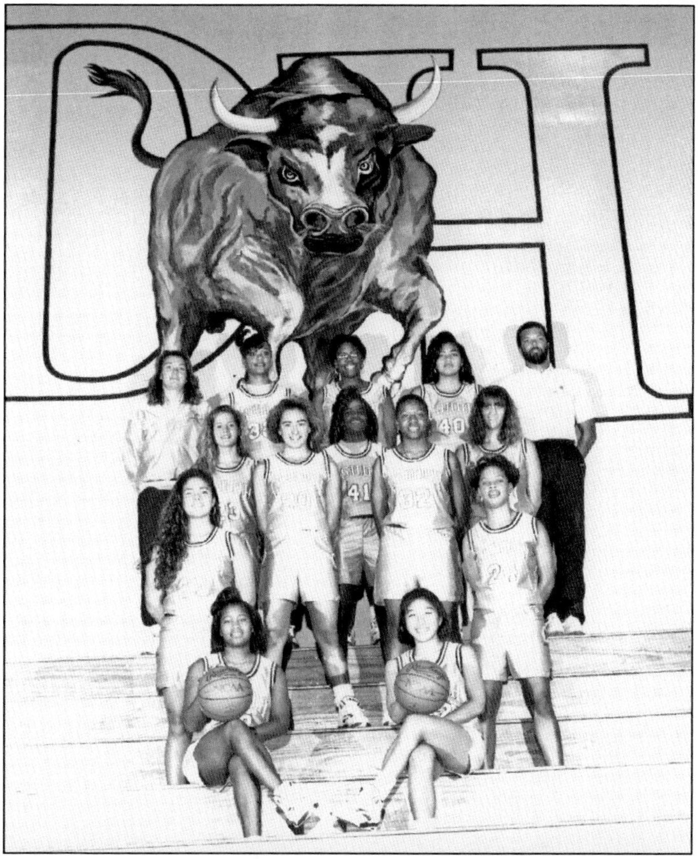

Toro cheerleaders prepare for a basketball game in the 1990s.

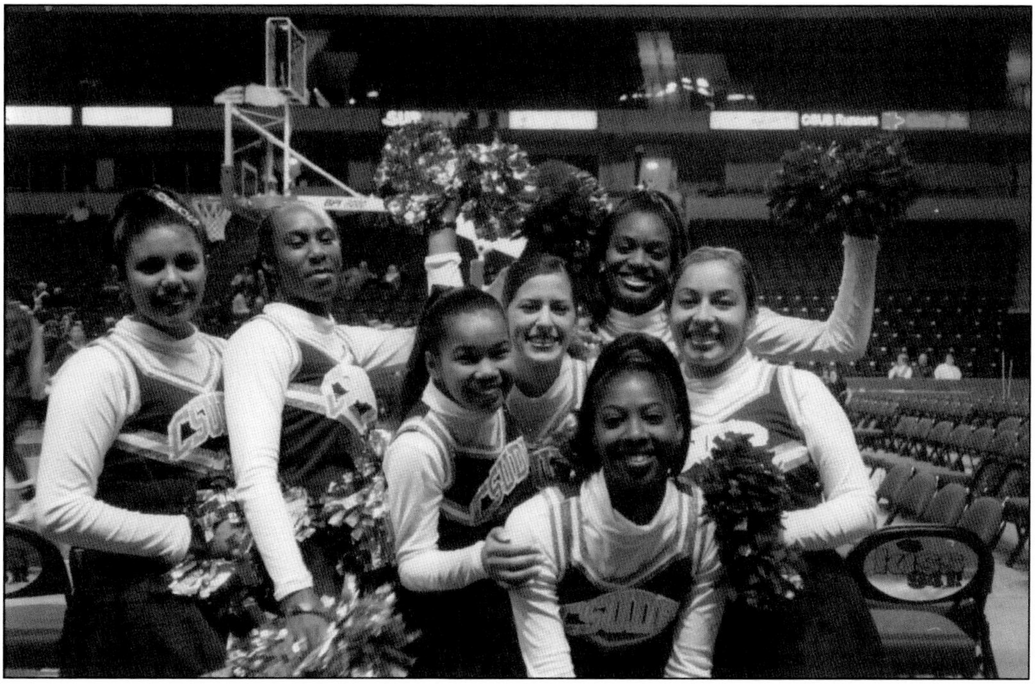

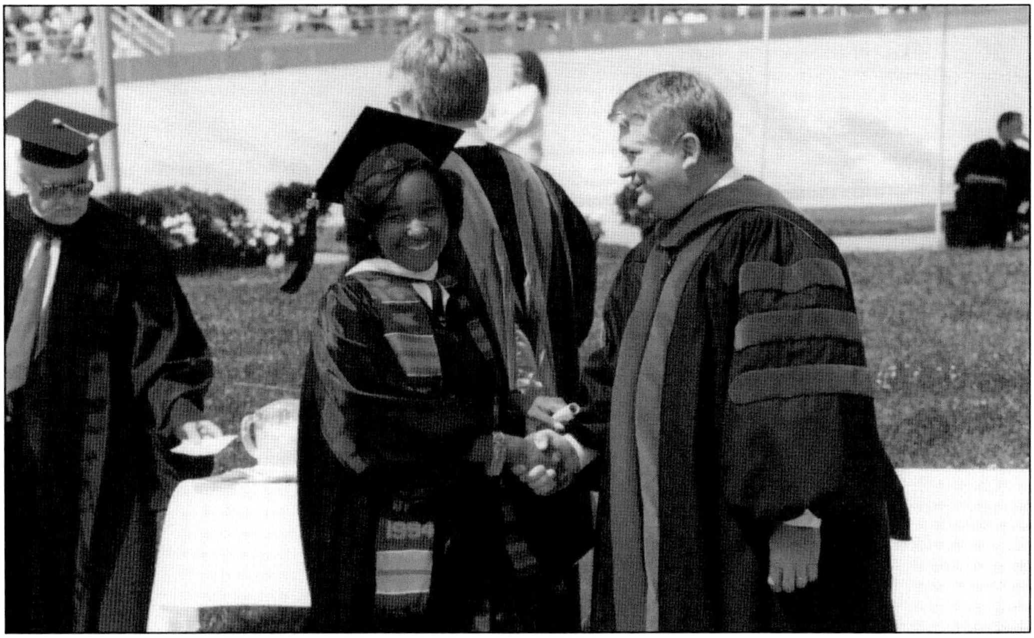

President Detweiler shakes hands with a graduate after she receives her diploma during the 1994 commencement ceremony in the velodrome.

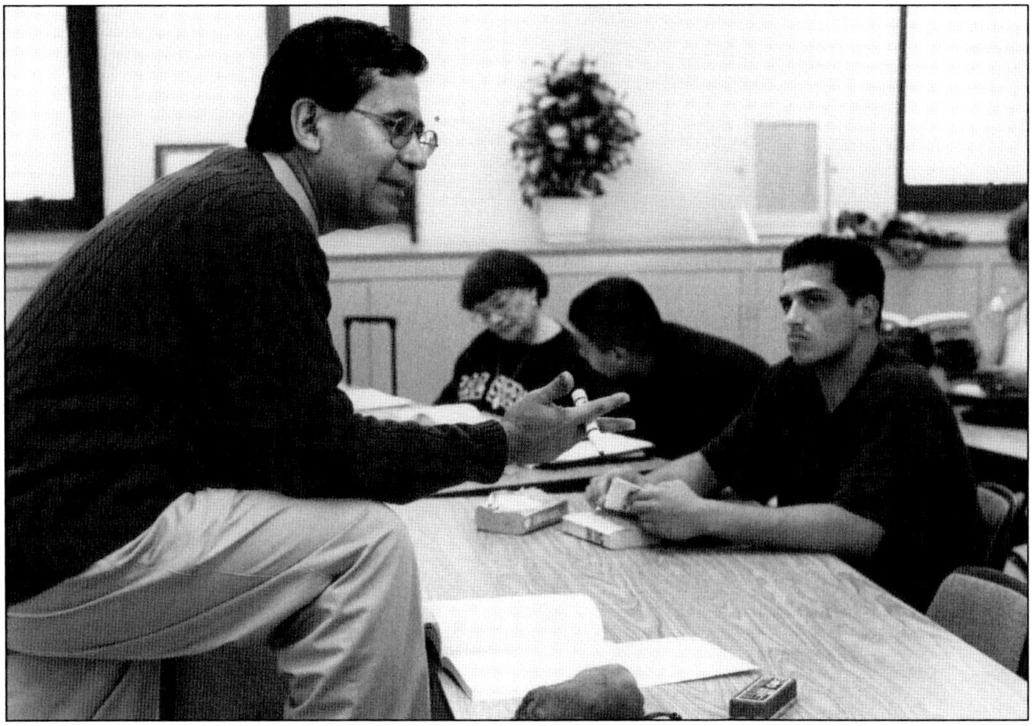

Miguel Dominguez, chair and professor of the Modern Languages Department, is pictured in the classroom. Dominguez is a founding member of the Chicana/o Studies Department. He is pictured in 1993 at the time he was awarded the Lyle E. Gibson Dominguez Hills Distinguished Teacher Award.

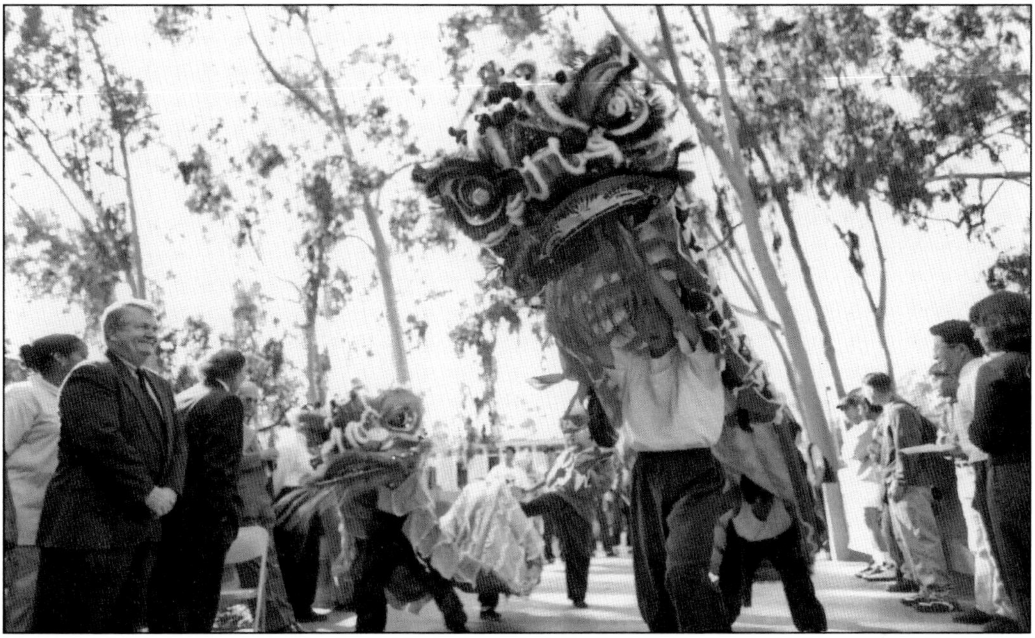

President Detweiler looks on during the university's Chinese New Year celebration in March 1997. The parade was sponsored by the Chinese Student Association.

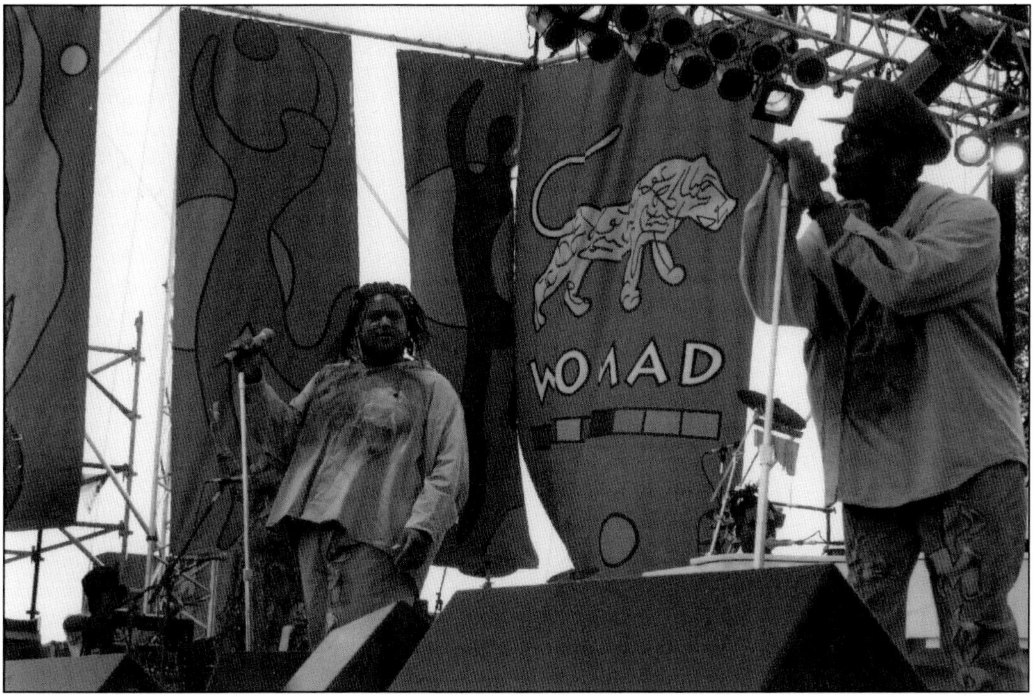

The velodrome continued to host bicycling events after the 1984 Olympics, but it was also used for concerts. The campus has hosted the Grateful Dead (banned after a show in 1990), the Beastie Boys, Metallica, the Reggae Splash Jam, and the Lollapalooza Festival. Pictured here is the World of Music and Dance (WOMAD) Festival, held in 1993. The daylong festival featured Peter Gabriel, Ziggy Marley, and others.

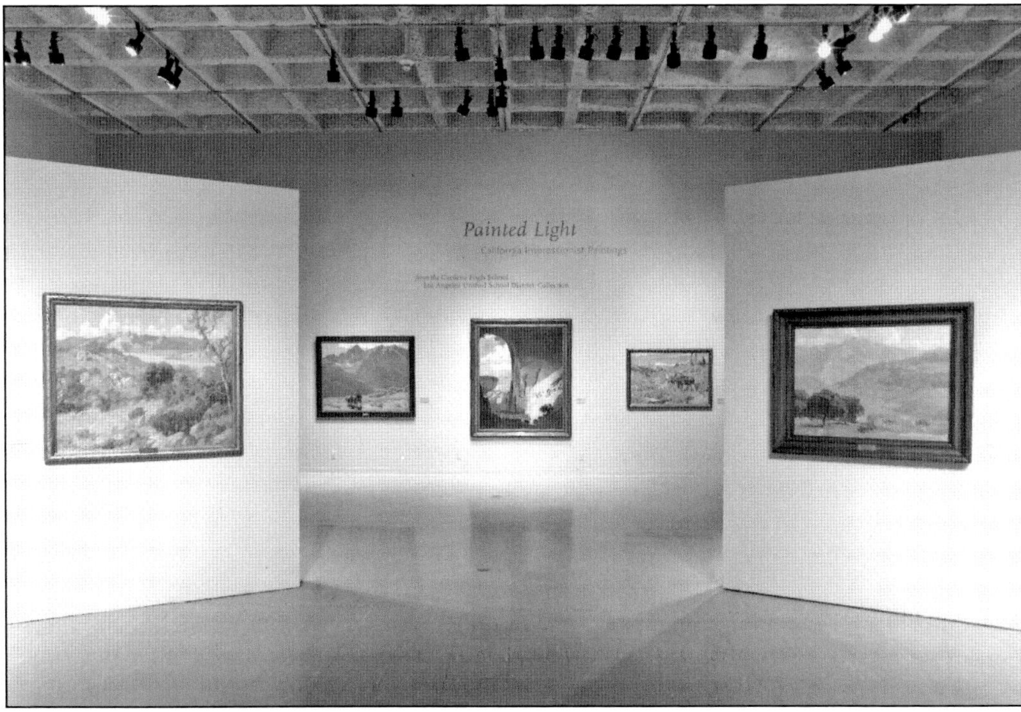

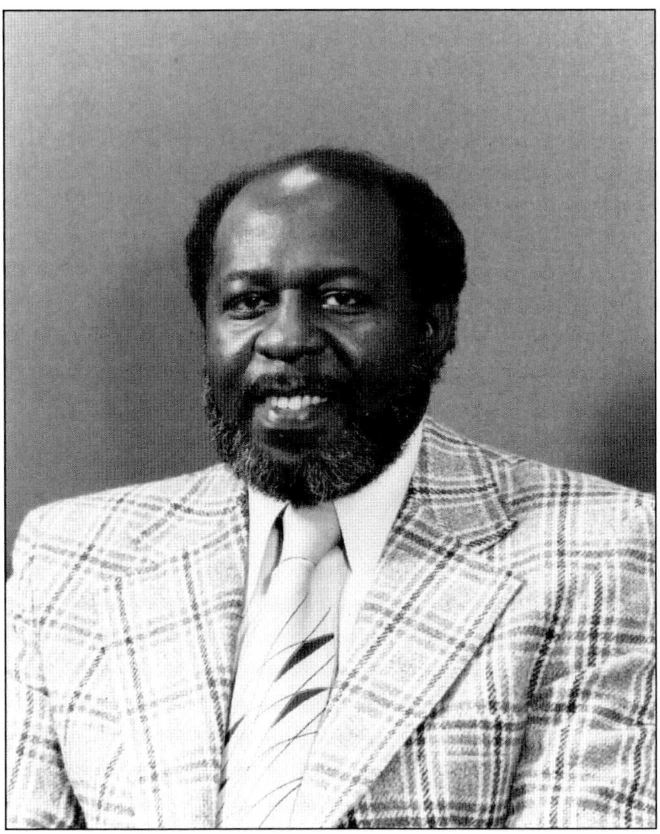

"Painted Light: California Impressionist Paintings" from the Gardena High School Collection was displayed at the University Art Gallery in 1999. Aided by grants and partnerships, the gallery was able to arrange, restore, display, and prepare curriculum materials on 31 examples of plein air paintings from the first half of the 20th century.

Herbert L. Carter served as interim president of the university in 1998 and 1999. The longtime CSU administrator has served as executive vice-chancellor and is the current chair of the CSU Board of Trustees. During his term as university president, he focused on campus beautification and land use.

Five

EXPANDING OPPORTUNITY
THE 2000S

It is here [CSU Dominguez Hills] where I saw a public, urban institution doing the work that all in higher education should be doing—serving students who are hungry to learn and who are seizing the opportunity for intellectual empowerment and economic independence. As the demographics in this country continue to change, where we become more multicultural, multiracial, international, and where everyone will need a higher education regardless of race, class, gender, or orientation, it will be Dominguez Hills who will be the role model, for it was founded on this very reality.

—Pres. Mildred García, May 2, 2008.

The new century brought about an expansion that many could not have foreseen 20 years earlier. CSU Dominguez Hills remained one of the most diverse campuses in the United States, with enrollment averaging 12,000 full- and part-time students. The 2000s have also seen successful accreditation reviews, hard-fought-for enrollment increases, and an in-depth round of strategic planning. By fall 2009, enrollment grew to 14,400 students. The decade also brought enormous growth and far-reaching budget cuts. This expansion included the construction of Welch Hall (originally known as the technology center), the Extended Education building, the 2007 Loker Student Union expansion, a new California Academy of Mathematics and Science building, a new library addition, and the Home Depot Center.

While university leaders had long discussed plans for the western side of the campus, it wasn't until 2003 that the land was developed. Initially the master plan for the campus called for student housing and parking lots to fill the area. In 1984, the Olympic Velodrome took some of the land, but a large chunk remained. A portion of the land, enhanced by occasional flooding, became a nature preserve and is now used for instruction.

In the mid-1990s, plans were drawn up to develop the Arnold Palmer Golf Academy with a nine-hole golf course and a conference center; however, this plan was abandoned. Finally the Anschutz Entertainment Group proposed the National Training Center. It was renamed the Home Depot Center and now includes soccer and tennis stadiums, a track and field area, and an indoor velodrome.

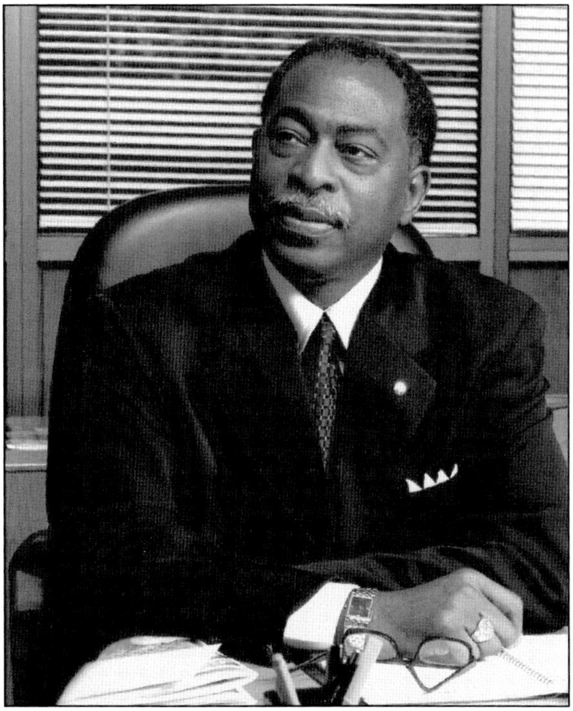

Dr. James E. Lyons Sr. became president of CSU Dominguez Hills on July 1, 1999. Previously Lyons had served as president of Bowie State University and Jackson State University. A Peace Corps veteran, he received his doctorate from the University of Connecticut. During his administration, Lyons focused on expanding the physical campus, accreditation, and the concept of "communiversity," or the connection between the university and community.

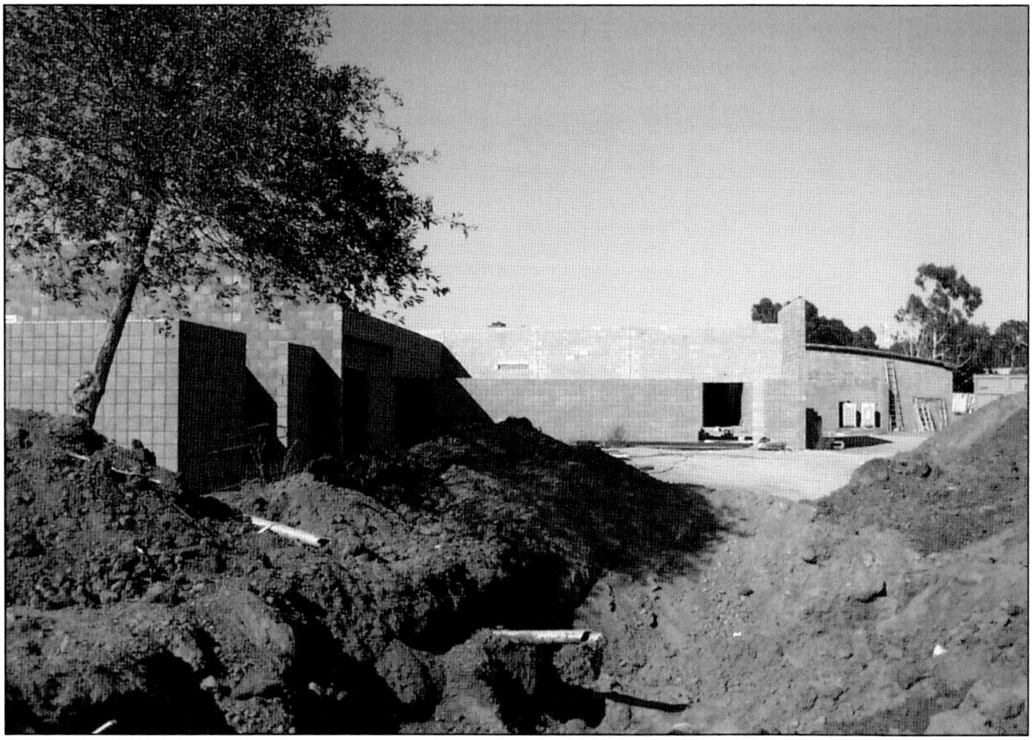

The Extended Education building was completed in 2000. The building houses most of the College of Extended and International Education's operations, which include credit and non-credit instructional programs as well as distance and online programs.

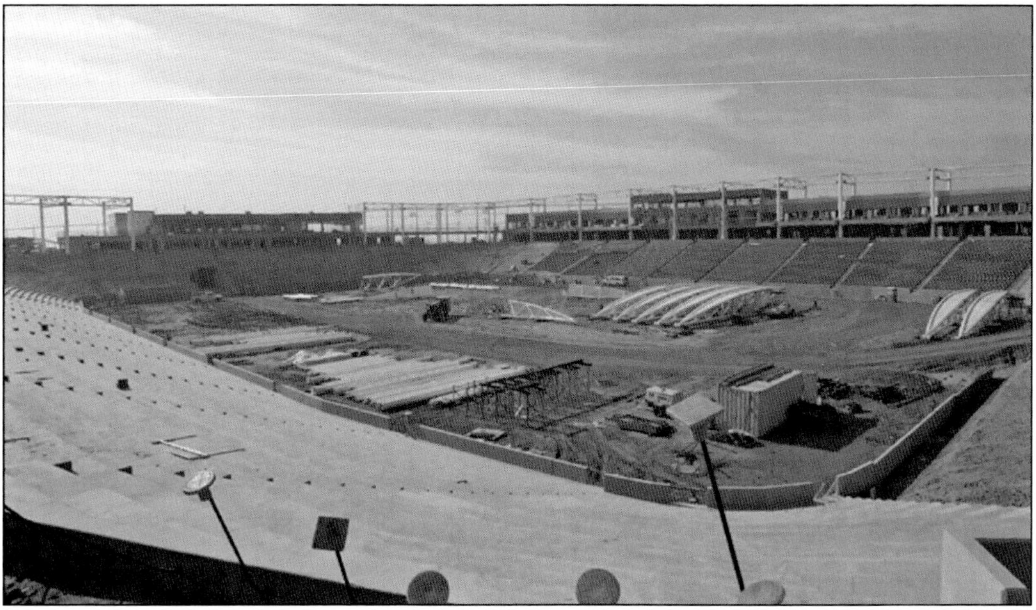

The issue of what to do with a good deal of campus acreage came to a conclusion in June 2001, when the CSU Board of Trustees approved a deal to bring the 85-acre National Training Center to the campus. The $130-million project was developed by Anschutz Entertainment Group (AEG). Ground-breaking for the project took place in February 2002.

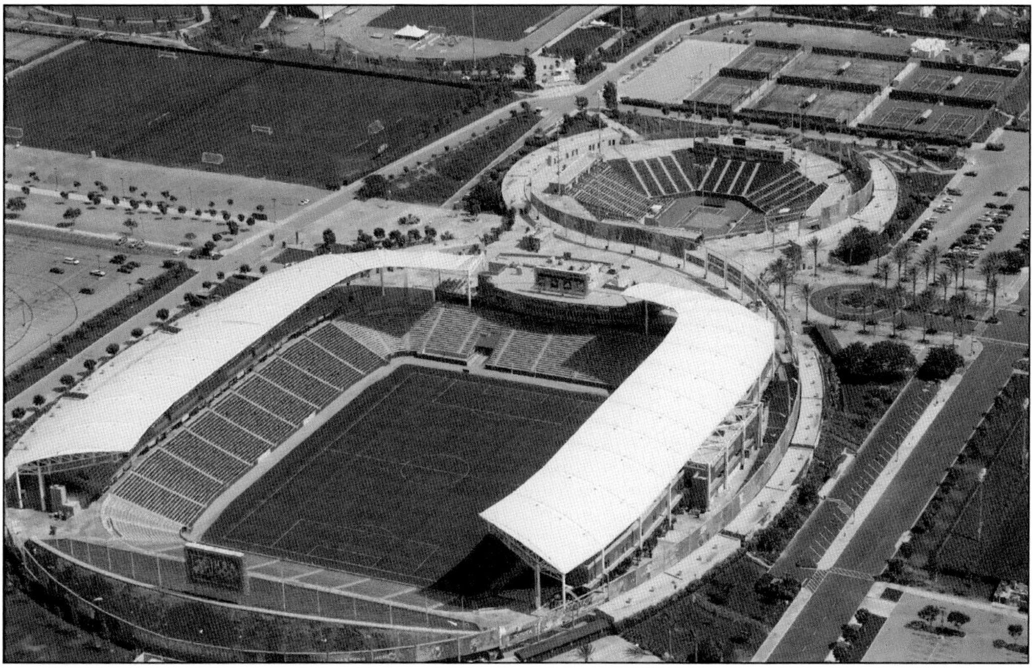

To make way for the Home Depot Center's soccer and tennis stadiums, practice fields, track and field area, and an indoor velodrome, the Olympic Velodrome was demolished. The first events at the Home Depot Center took place in June 2003. It has been the site of professional soccer events, concerts, boxing matches, commencement ceremonies, tennis events, track and field competition, cycling races, the X-Games, and many other events.

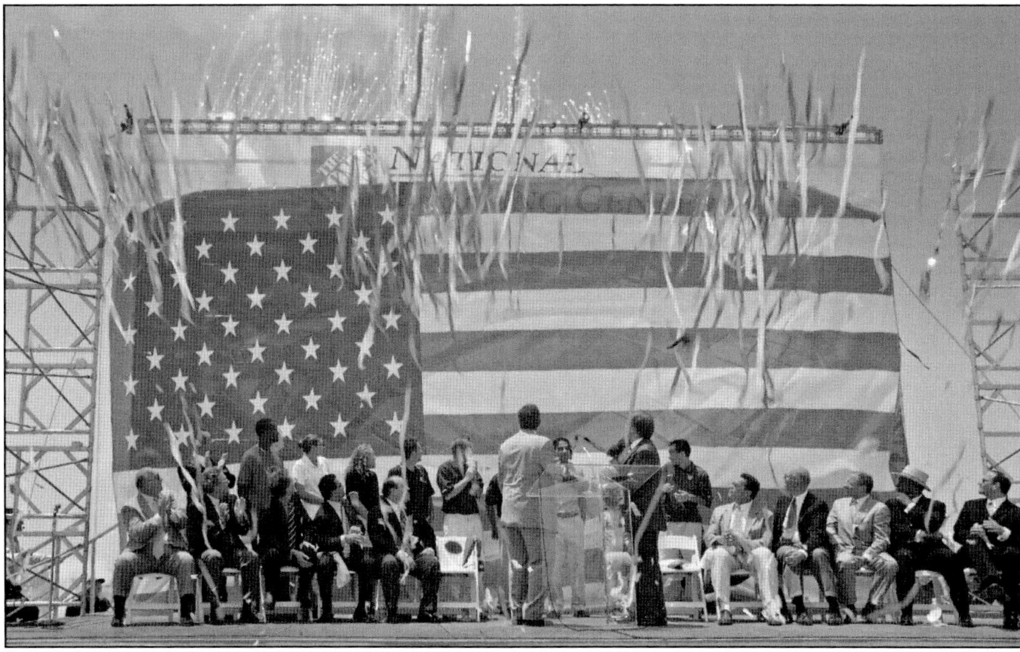

Prior to its opening, the naming rights for the National Training Center were sold by AEG to the Home Depot. In attendance at the unveiling of the name change on July 8, 2002, were CSU chancellor Charles Reed, President Lyons, Lt. Gov. Cruz Bustamante, and his rival in the gubernatorial election a few months away, Arnold Schwarzenegger.

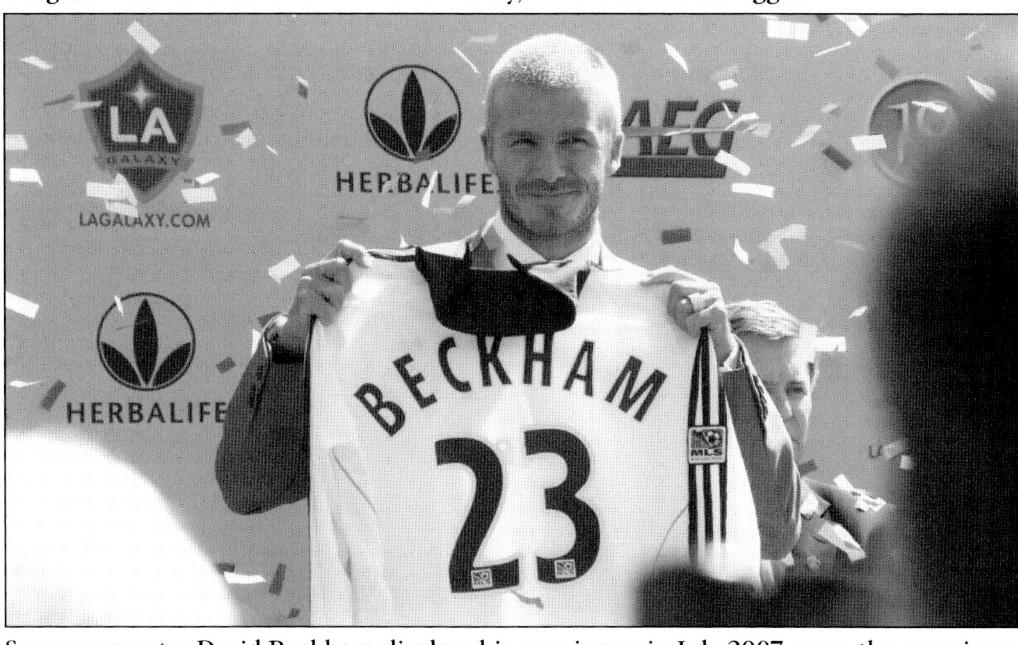

Soccer superstar David Beckham displays his new jersey in July 2007 upon the occasion of his recruitment to the Los Angeles Galaxy soccer team. The Galaxy plays its Major League Soccer home games at the Home Depot Center. The complex is also home to Chivas USA, the American franchise of Mexico's Club Deportivo Guadalajara. The David Beckham Academy, also located in the complex, holds camps for young soccer players.

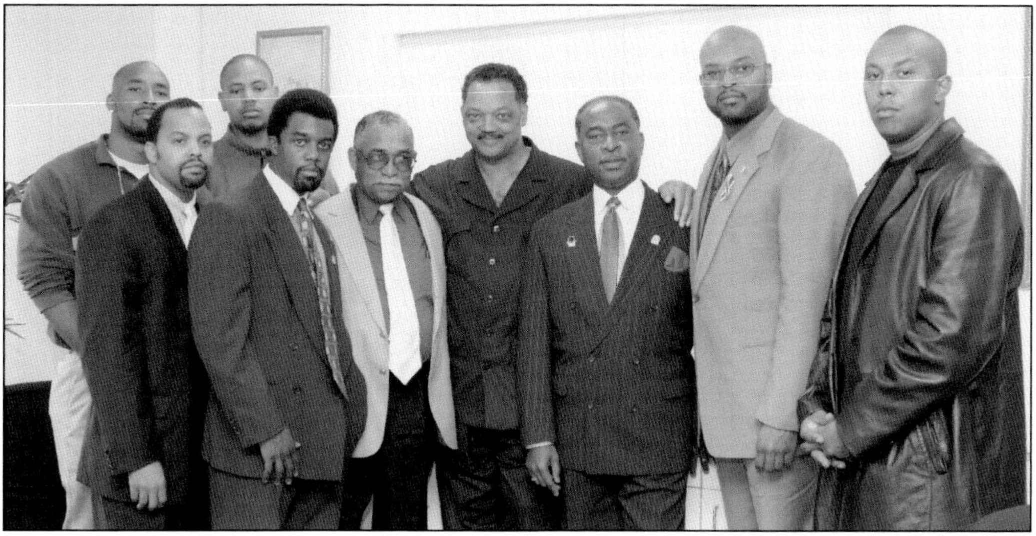

Civil rights leader Rev. Jesse Jackson, pictured here with President Lyons and members of the Omega Psi Phi fraternity, spoke to students in the University Theatre in 2003. Speaking on life choices, Jackson asked the student audience: "Mediocrity or excellence. . . . Which side are you on?"

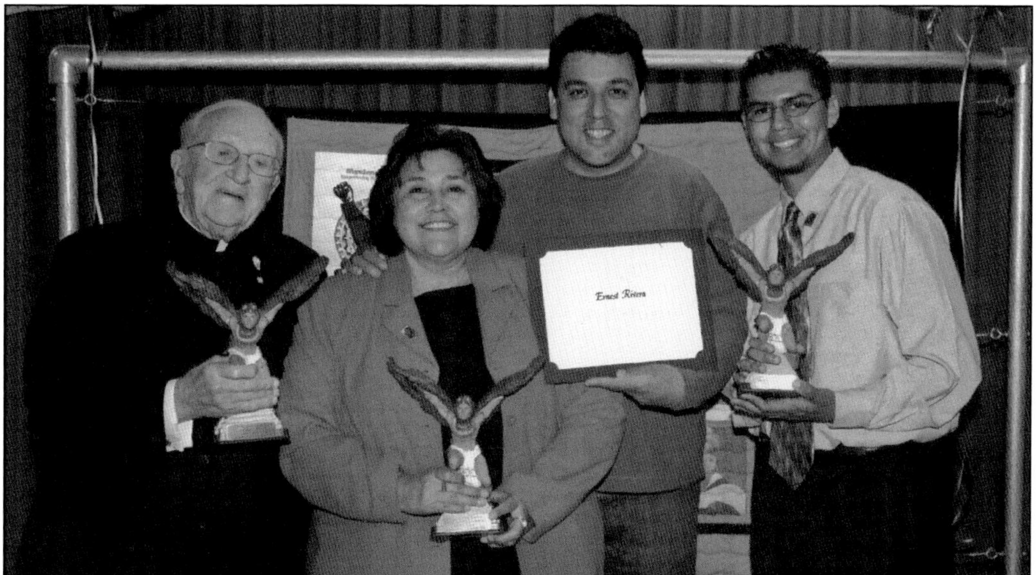

At the 2003 Cesar Chavez Tardeada celebration, sponsored by the Latino Faculty and Staff Association, Father Pat McPolin, longtime university supporter and founder of the Rancho Dominguez Museum, is given an award, along with Jennie Jurado-Rodriguez (next to Father Pat) and students Ernest Rivera (holding certificate) and David Gamboa.

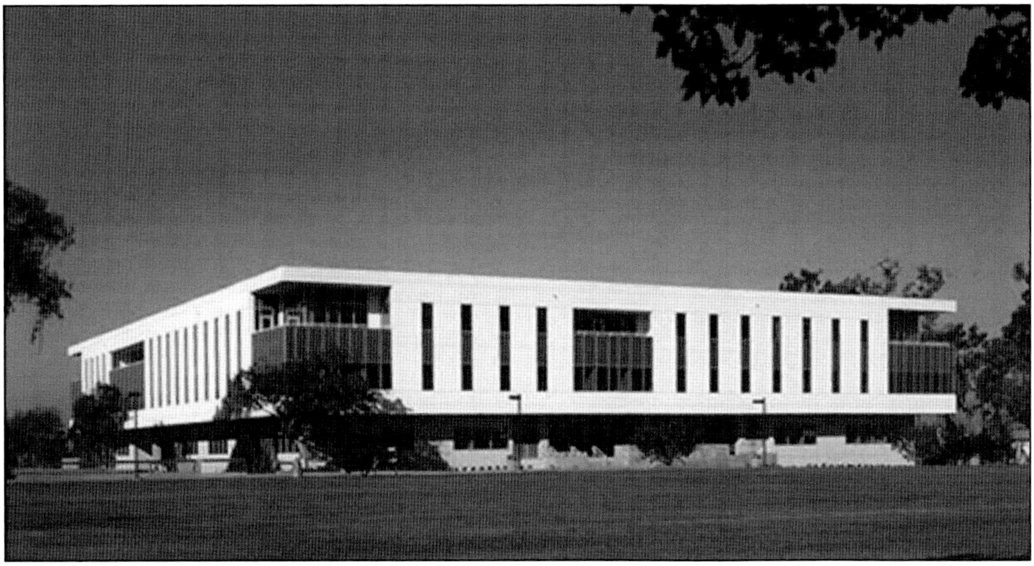

James L. Welch Hall, named for the founding faculty member of the Clinical Science Department and founder of the Occupational Therapy Department, was the first state-funded building constructed on campus in over 20 years. Originally planned as an information technology building, Welch Hall houses the School of Health, the Computer Center, and university administration. The building's large lecture hall is named for Claudia Hampton, longtime CSU trustee and university supporter.

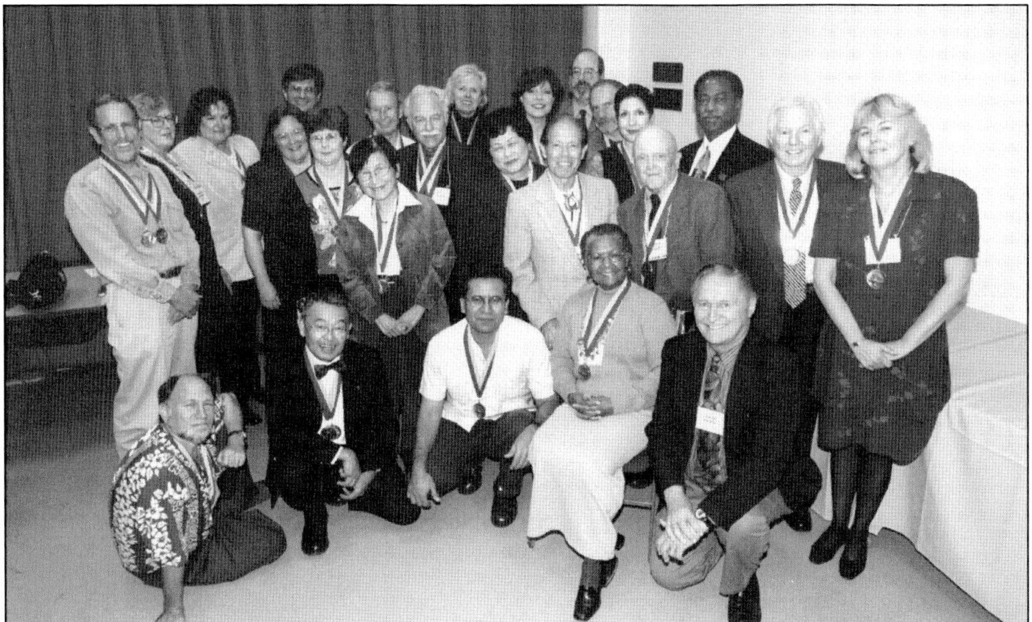

At the 2000 Academic Affairs Awards reception, past recipients of the Lyle E. Gibson Distinguished Teaching Award gather for a photograph. Also at the reception were recipients of the Outstanding Professor Award. Many of the awardees are members of the Emeritus Faculty Association. EFA members raise funds for a variety of student and faculty causes and volunteer their time to assist junior faculty, administrators, and staff.

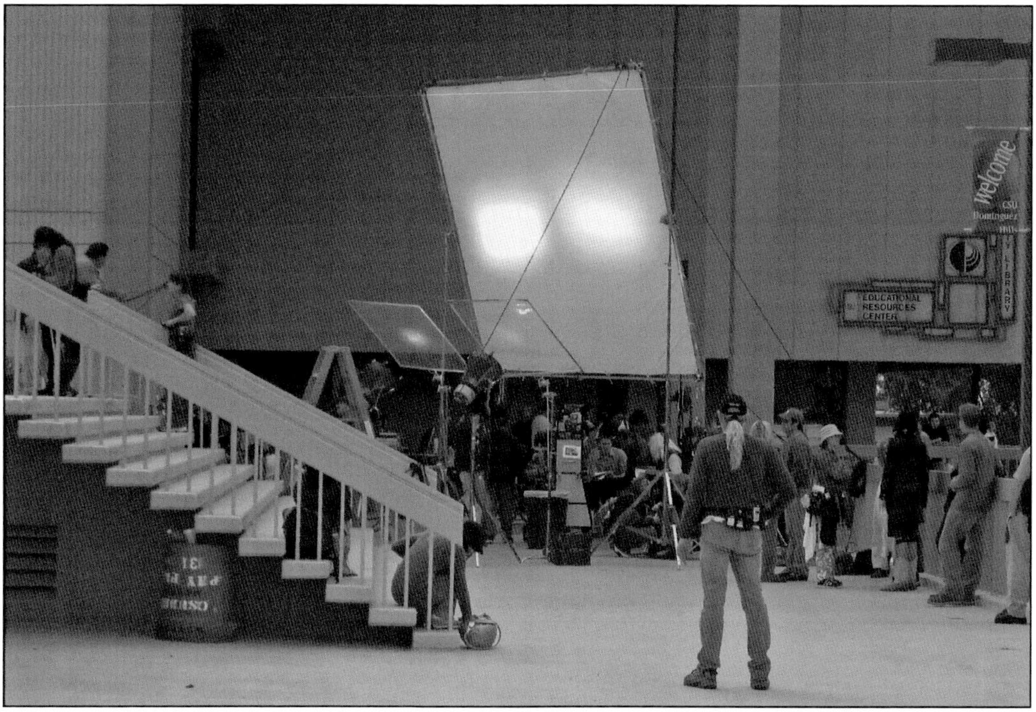

A production crew from the television series *24* film an episode of the show at the Cain Library in 2004. The campus also has served as the location for other television shows, such as *Six Feet Under* and *Knots Landing*, as well as for numerous commercials and other film events.

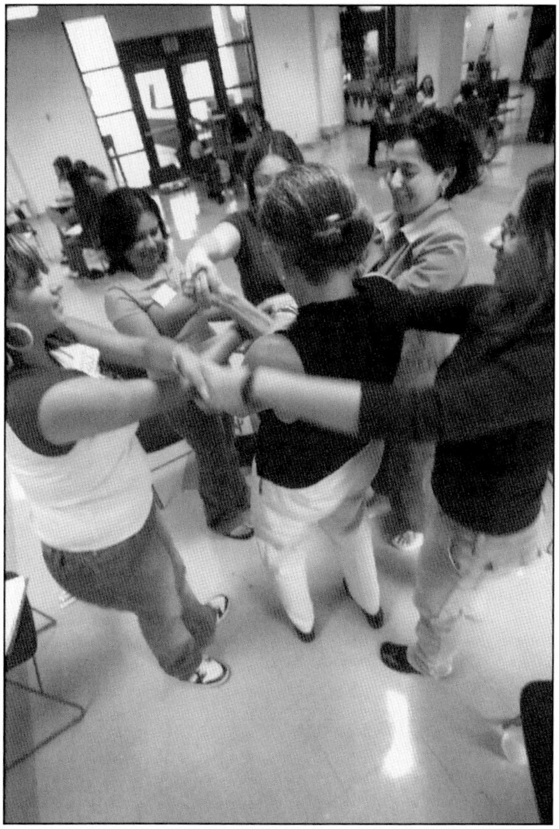

Pictured here are members of the Latinas Juntas (Latin Women Together) program in 2004. The program was designed to promote networking between Latina students, faculty, and staff and to explore the role of culture and family in academic careers.

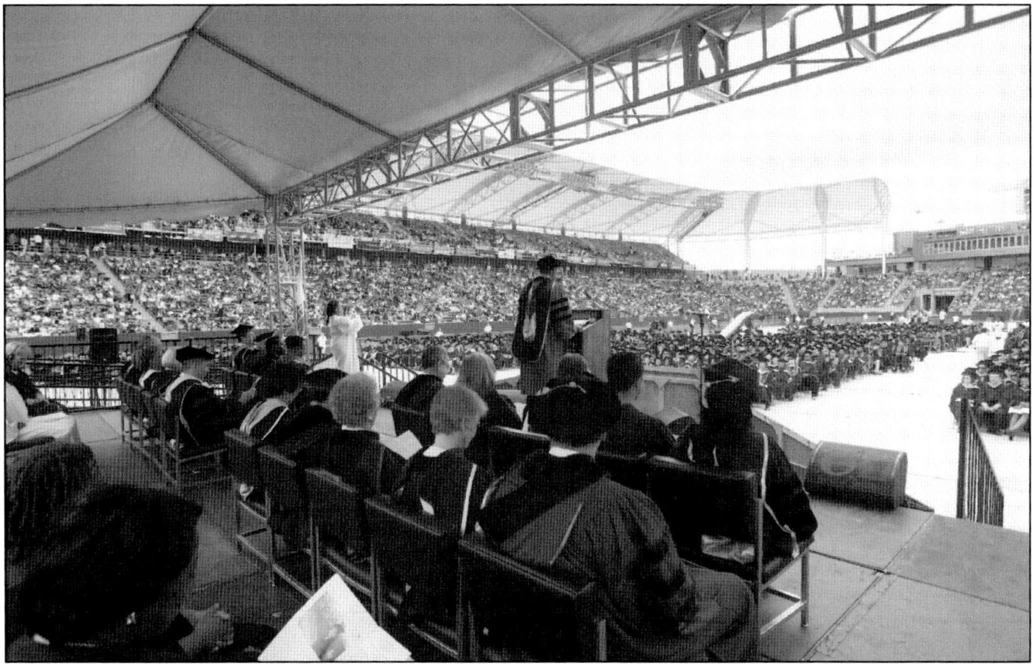

The first commencement in the Home Depot Center was held in 2004. President Lyons served as keynote speaker. In previous years, the university commencement was held at the Forum in Inglewood because of construction and space concerns on campus.

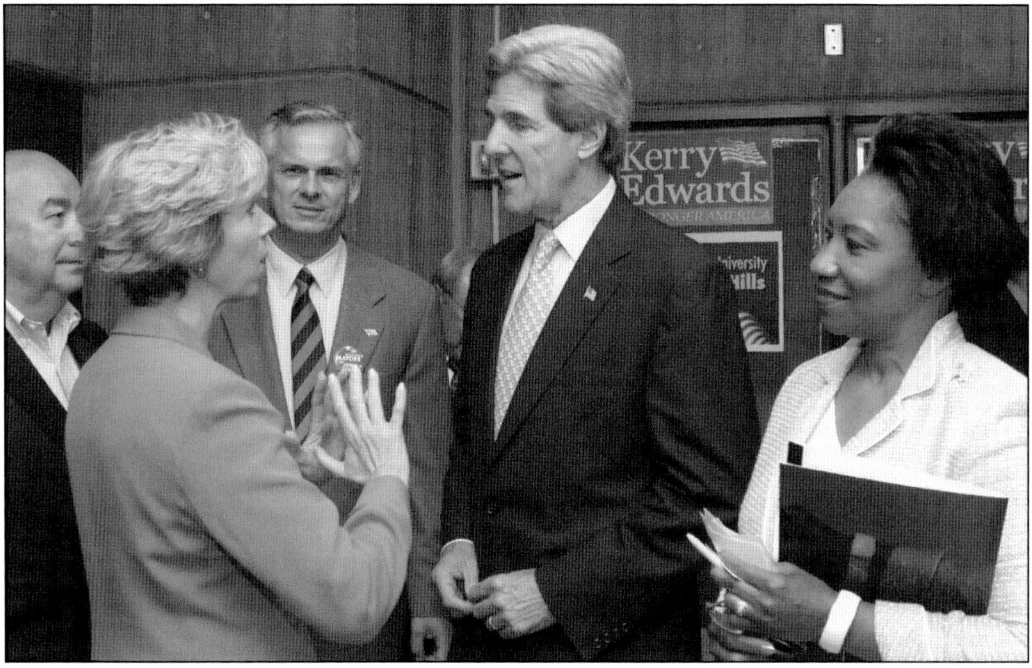

During the 2004 presidential election campaign, Democratic Party candidate Sen. John Kerry visited the university to deliver a speech on his economic proposals. With Senator Kerry are, from left to right, CSU chancellor Charles Reed, Los Angeles councilwoman Janice Hahn, Los Angeles mayor James Hahn, and Congresswoman Juanita Millender-McDonald.

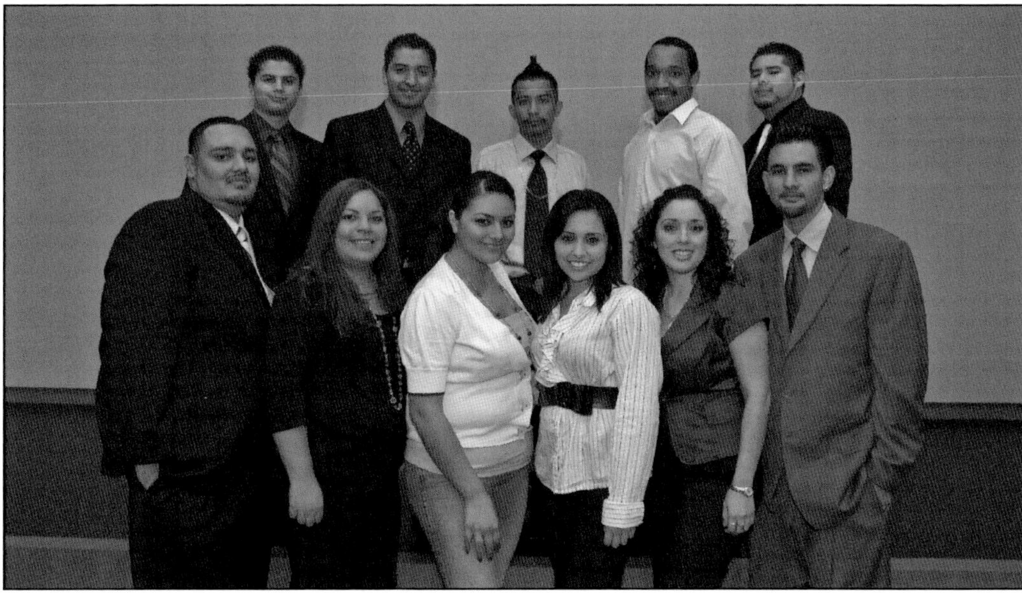

The Latino Student Business Association (LSBA) provides workshops and networking opportunities for students to enhance their business skills. Since 1998, the LSBA has been holding summer retreats, new student orientations, community involvement projects, and a variety of programs in conjunction with the National Hispanic Business Association.

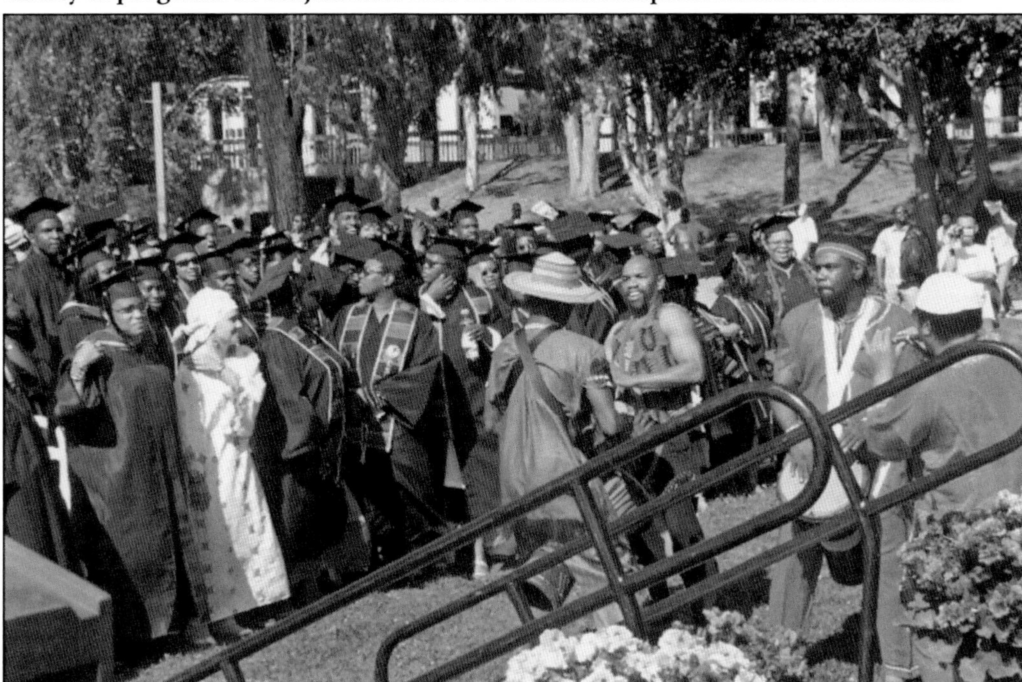

Musicians and speakers arrive at the 2004 Frederick Douglass and Mary McLeod Bethune Graduation Celebration. Celebrated since 1996, the African American–centered program acknowledges the accomplishments of graduates and recognizes the contributions of community elders who exemplify strong leadership.

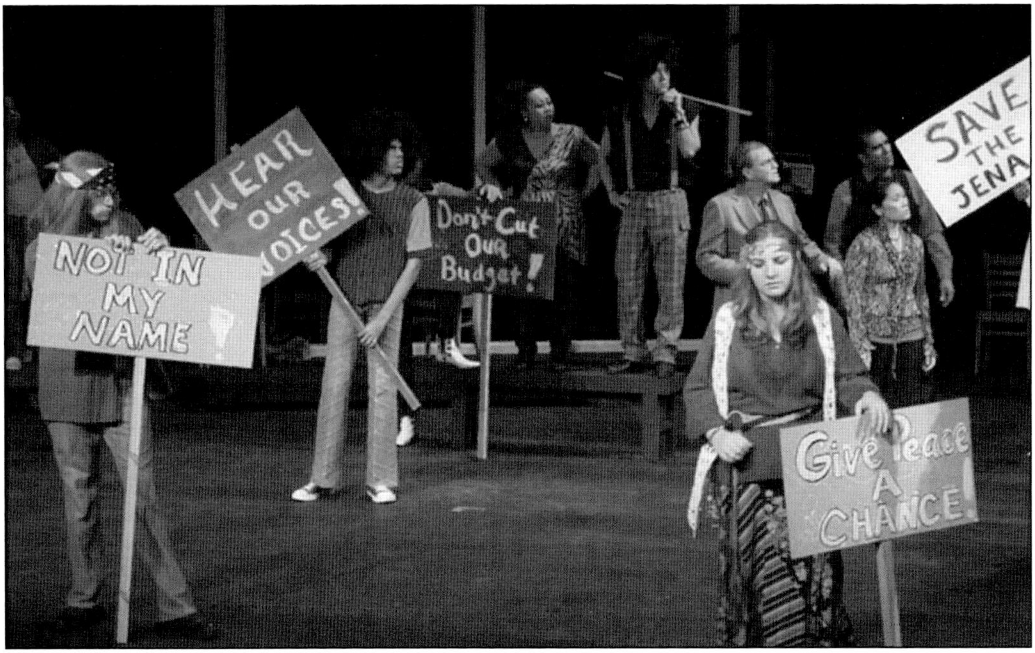

The Little College on a Hill, a play written by Brenda Killian and Naomi Buckley, was directed by Bill DeLuca and produced in 2007. It resulted from interviews with 100 local residents for the "Carson Bridge Project." The story concerns students trying to finish a documentary about the history of the campus. One scene recreates the 1969 Temple of Peace event on the Watt Campus. (Courtesy of Tom Marinello.)

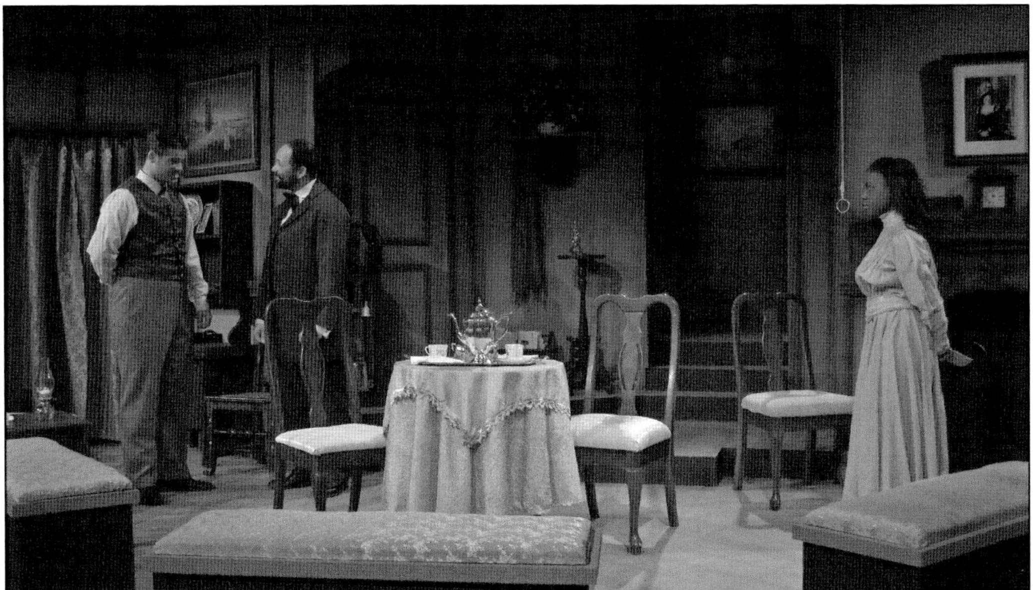

The Heiress, based on Henry James's novel *Washington Square*, was performed at the Edison Studio Theater in 2009. The play, directed by Donis Leonard, was a production of the New African Grove Theater Company at Dominguez Hills. It was selected to participate in the 2009 National Black Theater Festival in North Carolina. (Courtesy of Tom Marinello.)

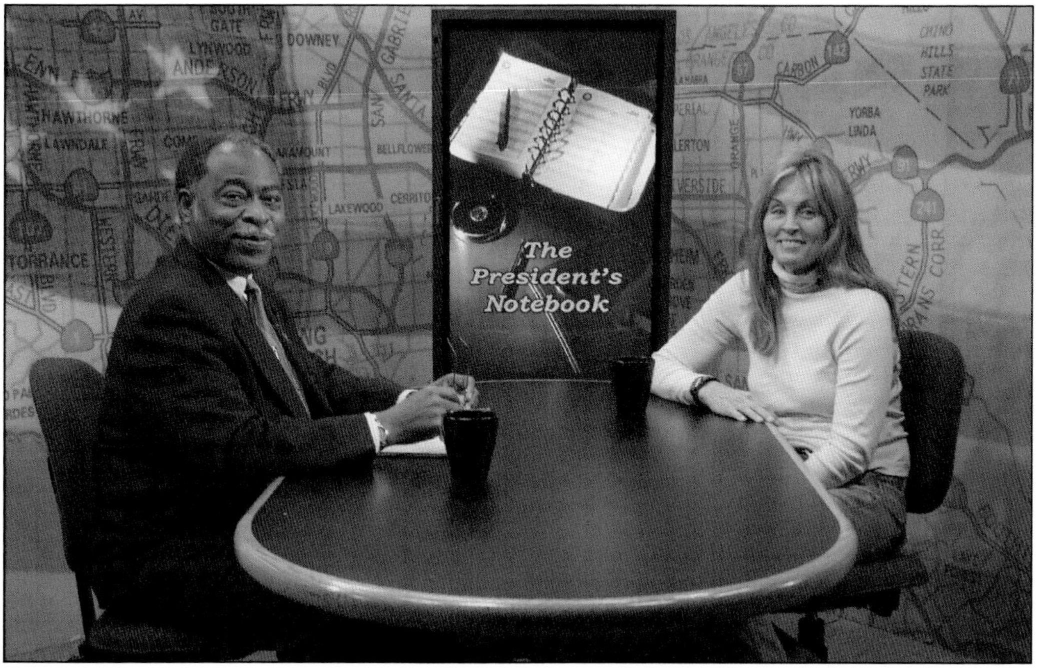

President Lyons speaks to *Brokeback Mountain* screenwriter Diana Ossana on a DHTV episode of *The President's Notebook*. Ossana came to the university to talk about the film's impact on the lives of gay men. The following week, she won the 2006 Oscar for Best Screenplay, along with author Larry McMurtry.

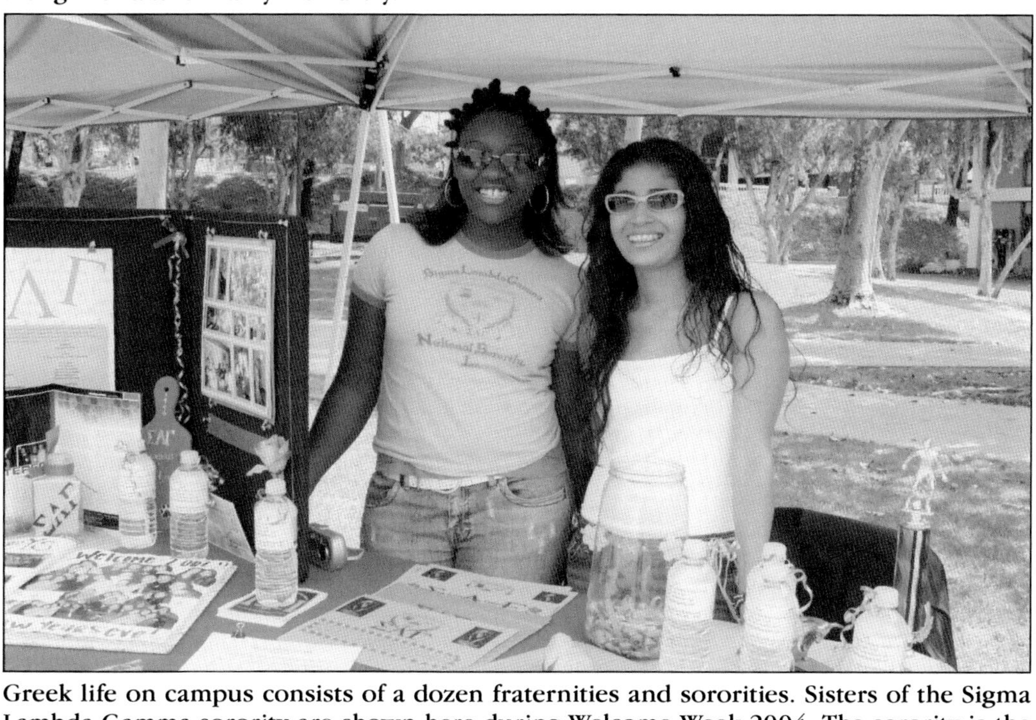

Greek life on campus consists of a dozen fraternities and sororities. Sisters of the Sigma Lambda Gamma sorority are shown here during Welcome Week 2004. The sorority is the largest Latina-based national sorority with a multi-cultural membership.

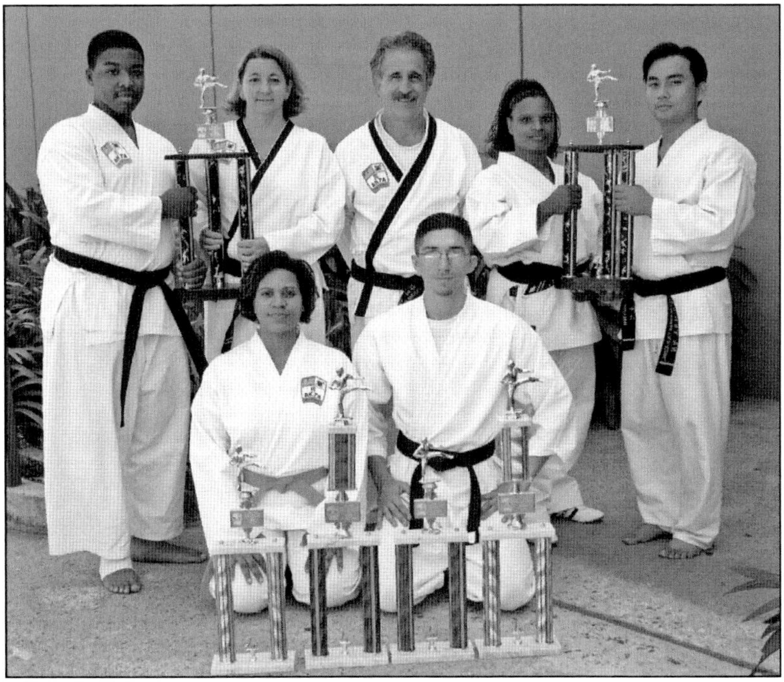

Led by instructor Joel Colbert (center), a professor of teacher education, the CSU Dominguez Hills Tae Kwon Do team participated in a national tournament in 2001 and brought home 10 trophies. In 2002, the team won 15 trophies.

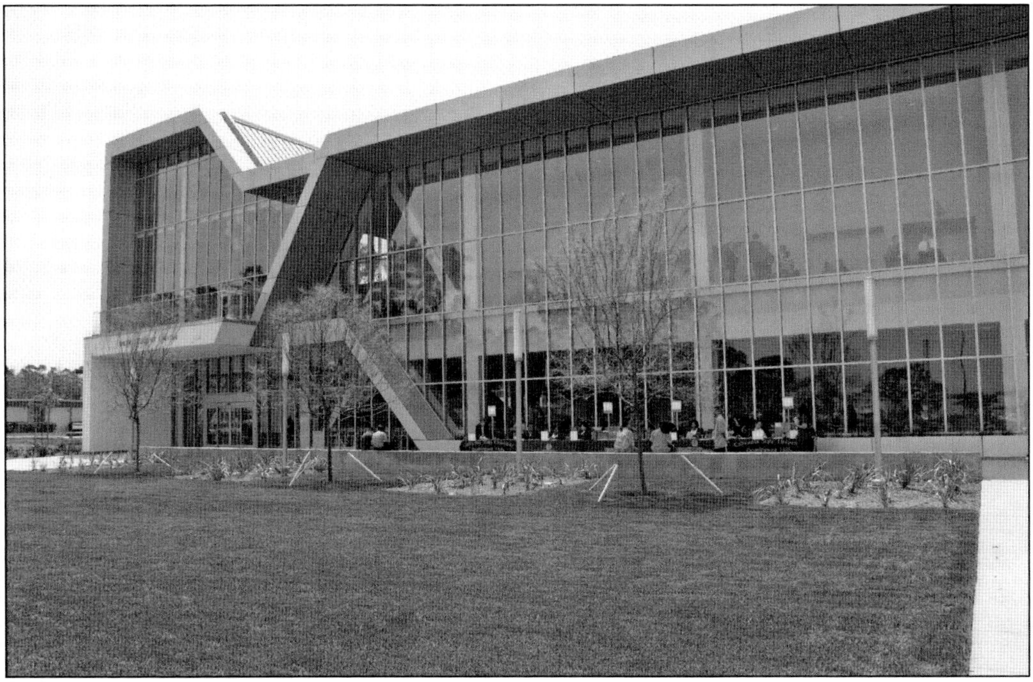

Construction began on the expanded Loker Student Union in 2004. Thanks to an additional gift by Katherine B. Loker, a bond issue, and an increase in student fees, the university was able to expand the student union to 120,000 square feet. The project resulted in a new bookstore, larger dining areas, student association offices, meeting spaces, and a ballroom with seating for up to 1,000 people.

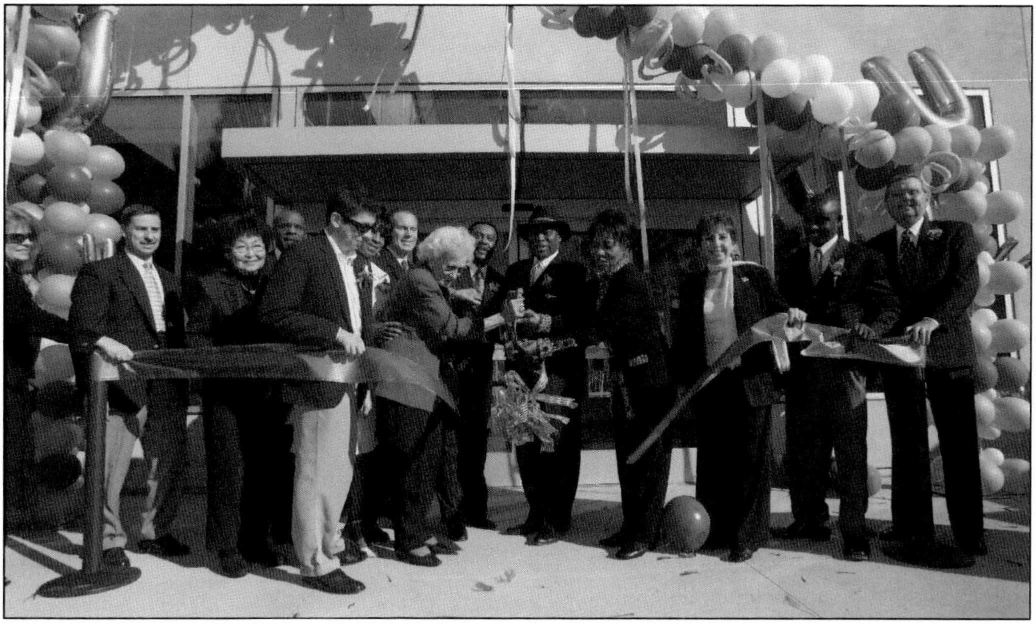

The ribbon-cutting for the expanded Loker Student Union in 2007 was presided over by Katherine B. Loker (center left, holding scissors), Pres. James E. Lyons (center, wearing hat), and Congresswoman Juanita Millender-McDonald (right of Lyons). Loker and her late husband, Donald P. Loker, were involved in enhancing the campus for more than four decades.

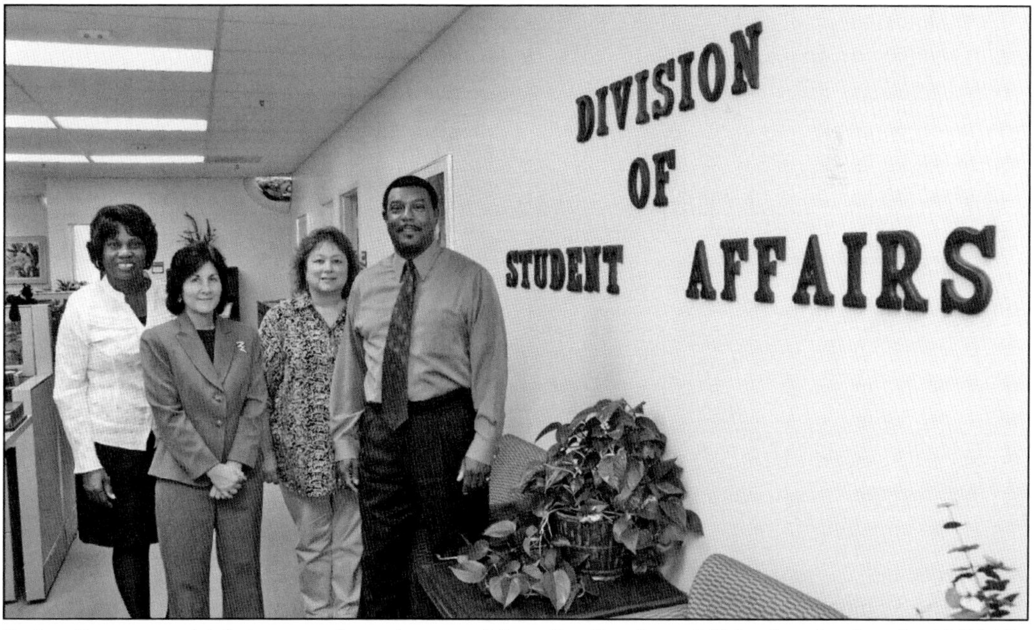

Boice Bowman (right) served as vice president for Student Affairs beginning in 1997. He was named interim university president in 2007, after the retirement of James E. Lyons. Also shown are, from left to right, Martha Alexander, Suzanne Wallace, and Melica Bodnar.

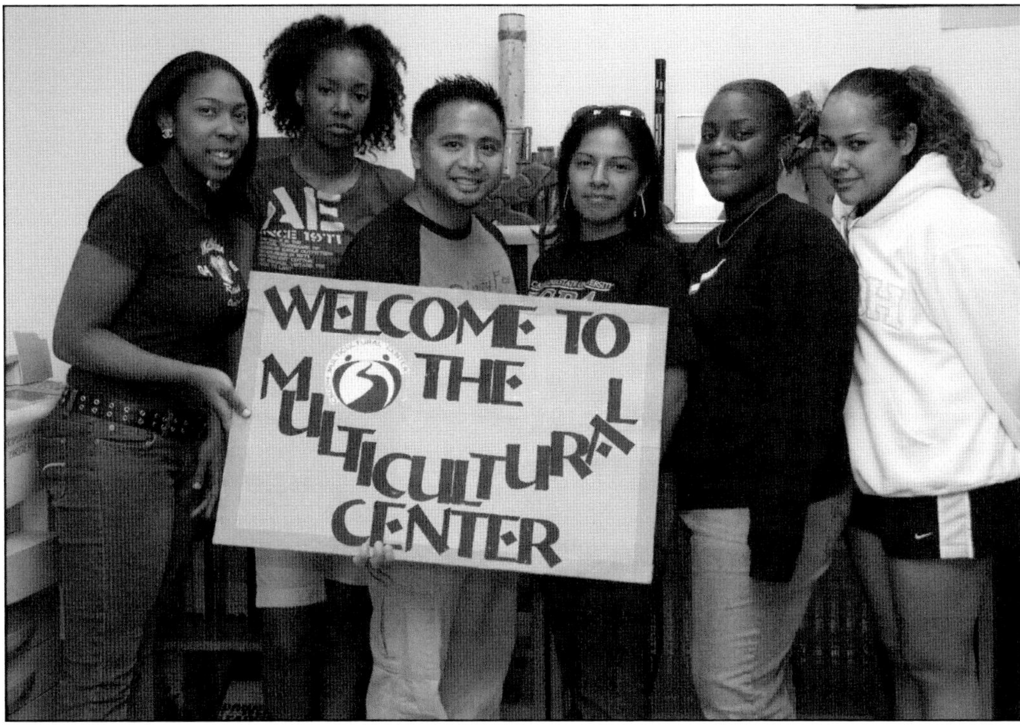

Lui Amador (third from left), coordinator of the Multicultural Center, stands with several students in the mid-2000s. The Multicultural Center was founded in 1994 and is dedicated to empowering students through a variety of activities, including an annual Cross Cultural Retreat, multicultural festivals, poetry performances, lectures, and concerts.

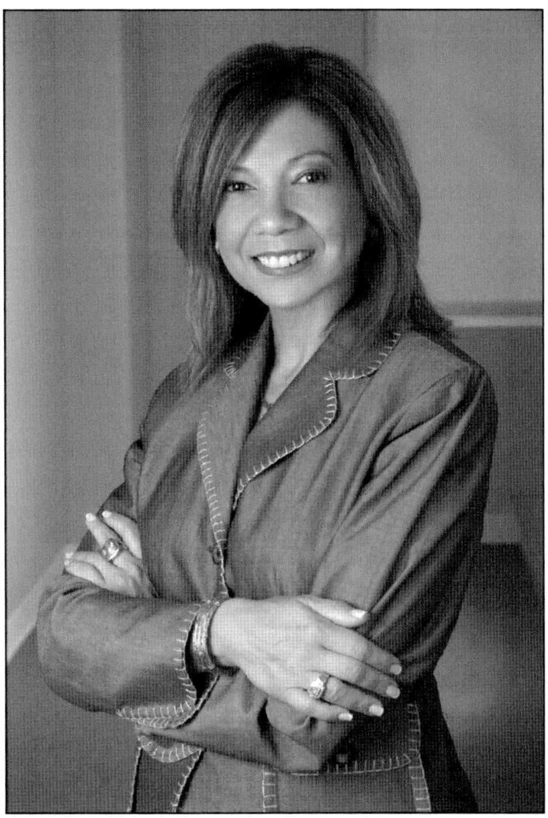

Dr. Mildred García became president of the university in August 2007. She had previously been president of Berkeley College in New York and New Jersey and served in administrative capacities at Arizona State University and Montclair State University. The first Latina to be chosen president of a CSU campus, President García was named to *Hispanic Business Magazine*'s "100 Most Influential Hispanics" list in 2007.

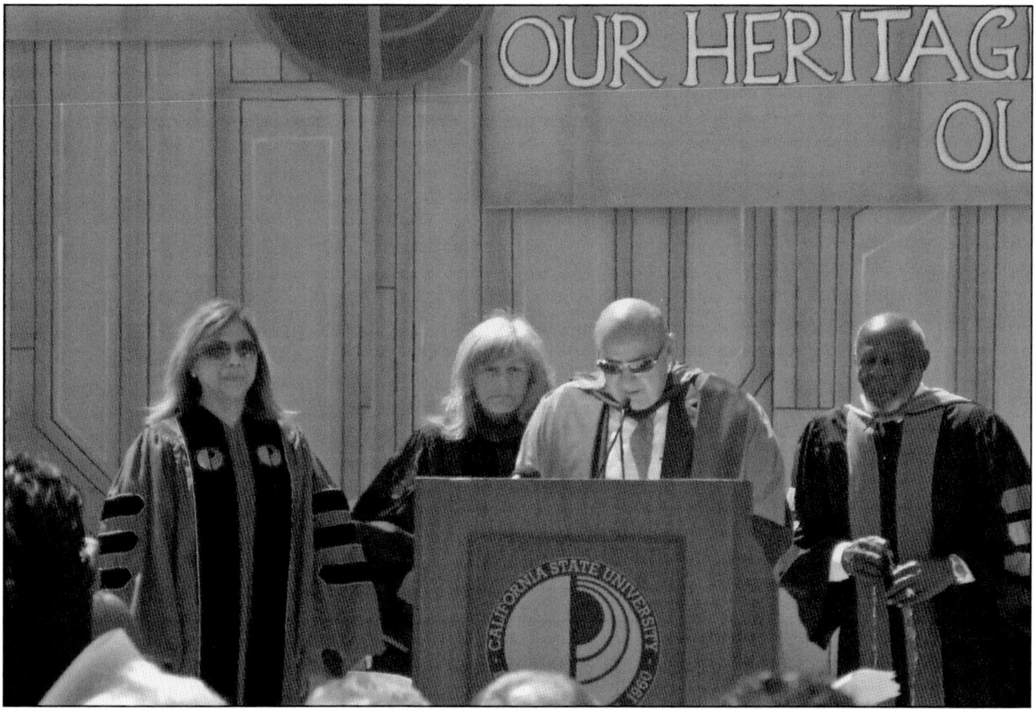

Mildred García was inaugurated as president of the university during ceremonies on the campus mall in May 2008. CSU chancellor Charles Reed speaks while President García (left), CSU Board of Trustees chair Roberta Achtenberg (center), and CSU trustee (and former CSU Dominguez Hills president) Herbert L. Carter listen.

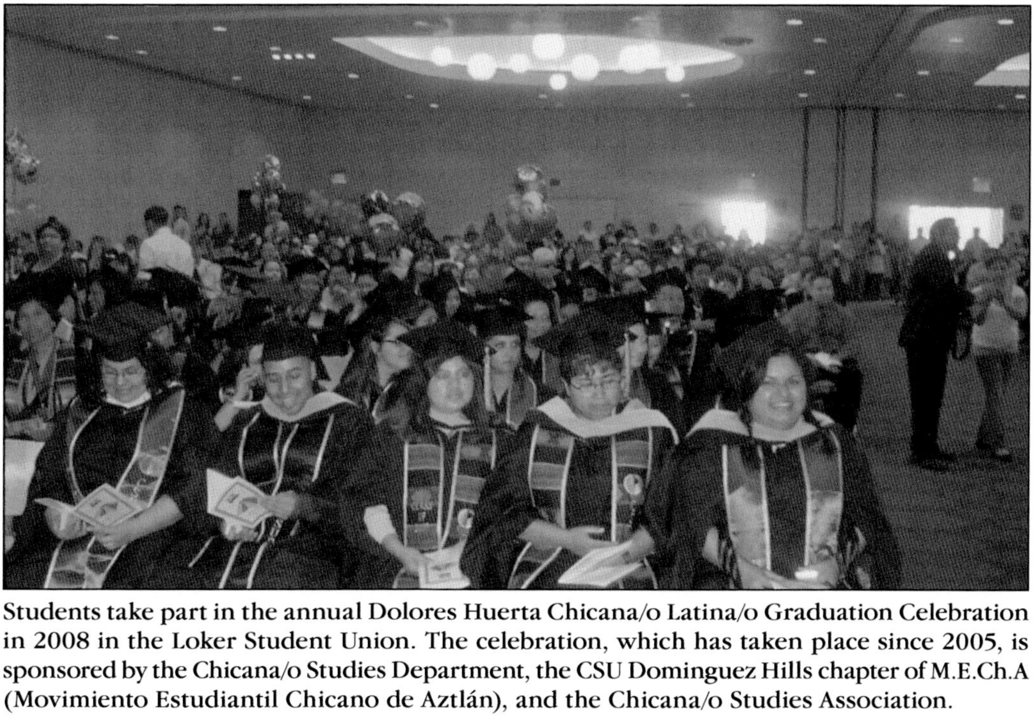

Students take part in the annual Dolores Huerta Chicana/o Latina/o Graduation Celebration in 2008 in the Loker Student Union. The celebration, which has taken place since 2005, is sponsored by the Chicana/o Studies Department, the CSU Dominguez Hills chapter of M.E.Ch.A (Movimiento Estudiantil Chicano de Aztlán), and the Chicana/o Studies Association.

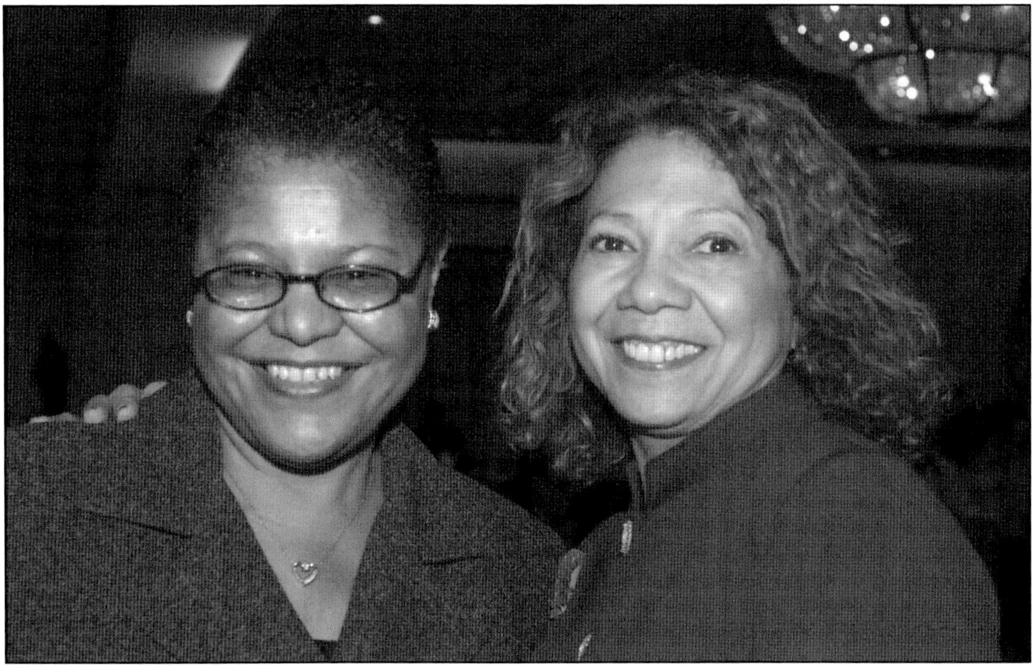

One of CSU Dominguez Hills' distinguished alumnae, California State Assembly Speaker Karen Bass (at left, class of 1990, B.S., health sciences) joins President García after the 2008 Martin Luther King Kingdom Day Parade. President García served as grand marshal of the parade.

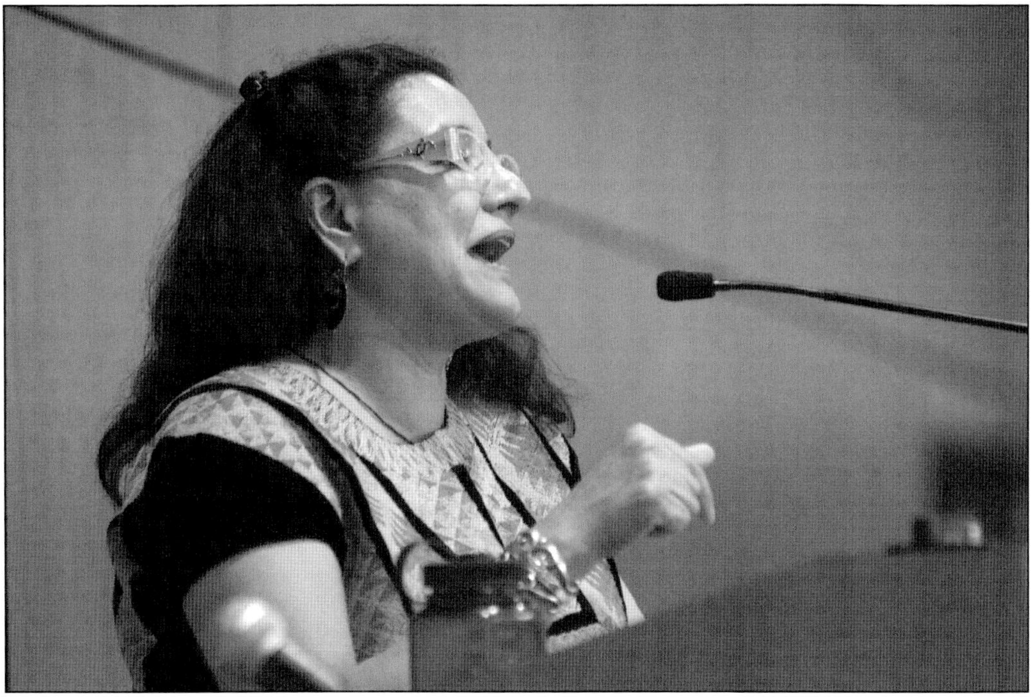

Sandra Cisneros, author of *The House on Mango Street*, spoke to a large crowd of students, faculty, and community members in the Loker Student Union in September 2007 as part of Latino Heritage Month.

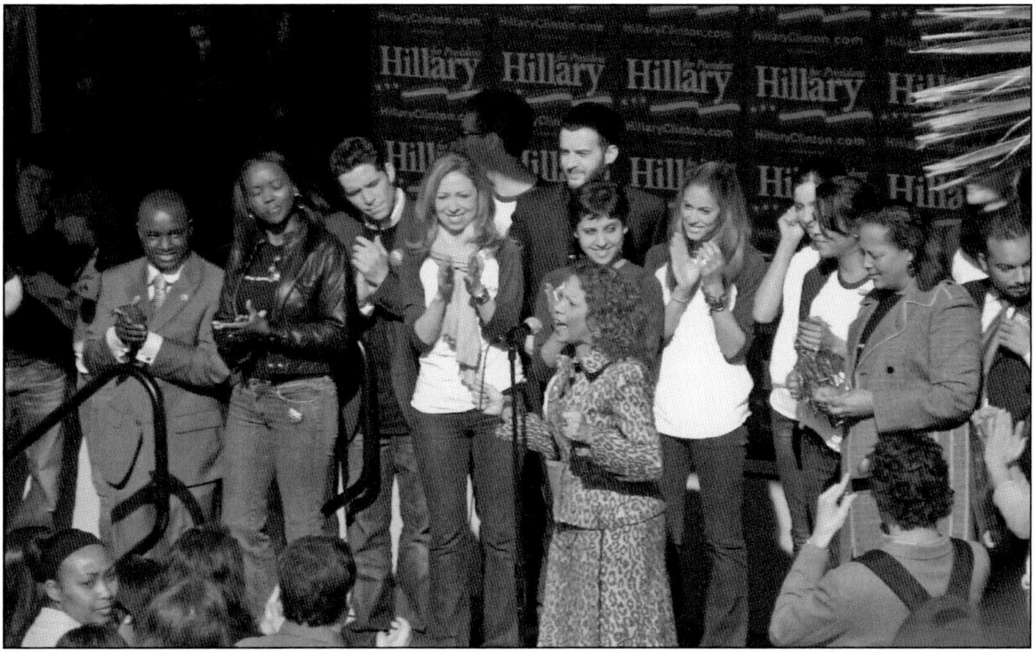

Prior to the 2008 California presidential primary, Chelsea Clinton campaigned at the university for her mother, Sen. Hillary Clinton. In this photograph, President García introduces Clinton (left of García). She was joined by Congresswoman Laura Richardson, actor America Ferrera, and several others in the Loker Student Union's Palm Court.

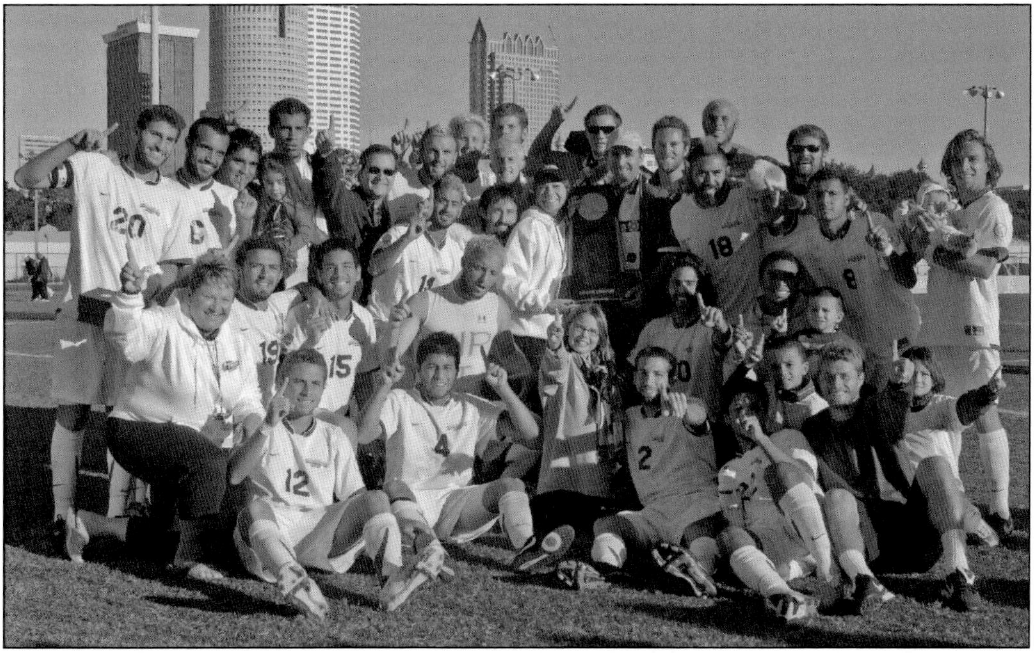

Led by coach Joe Flanagan and National Soccer Coaches Association of America (NSCAA) Player of the Year Kevin Gallaugher, the Toro's men's soccer team won the 2008 NCAA Division II National Championship. President García celebrates with the team in Tampa after their victory. The men's soccer team previously won the national championship in 2001.

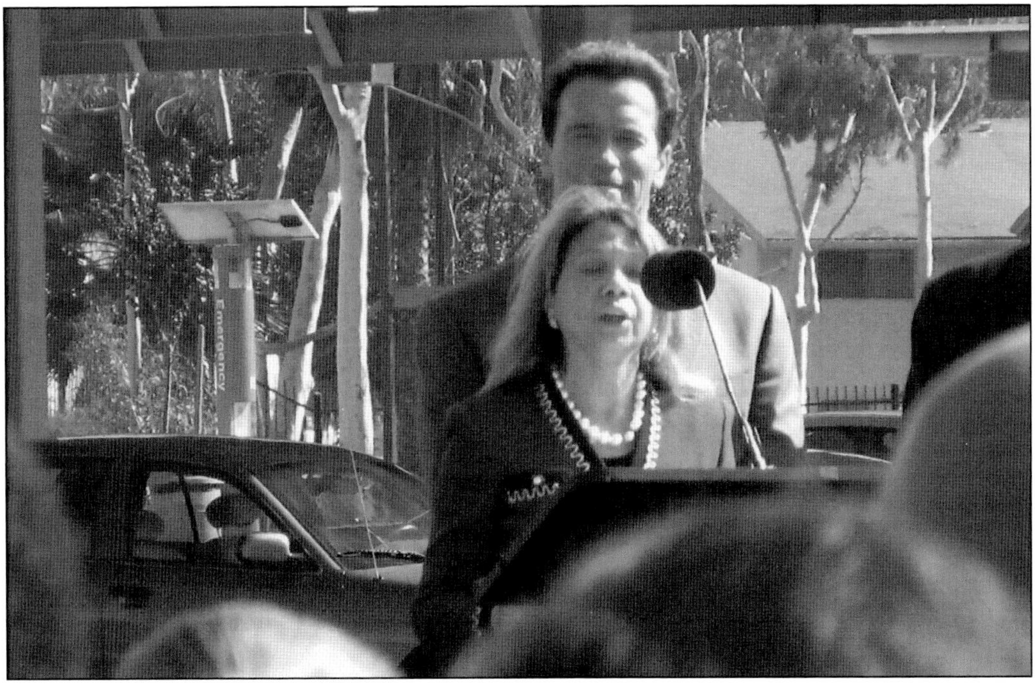

President García welcomed Gov. Arnold Schwarzenegger to the campus in 2008 for a press conference to announce an innovative public-private partnership to generate clean and renewable energy on the campuses within the CSU system. The photovoltaic project in Parking Lot 1 on campus served as an example of the types of projects this partnership would create.

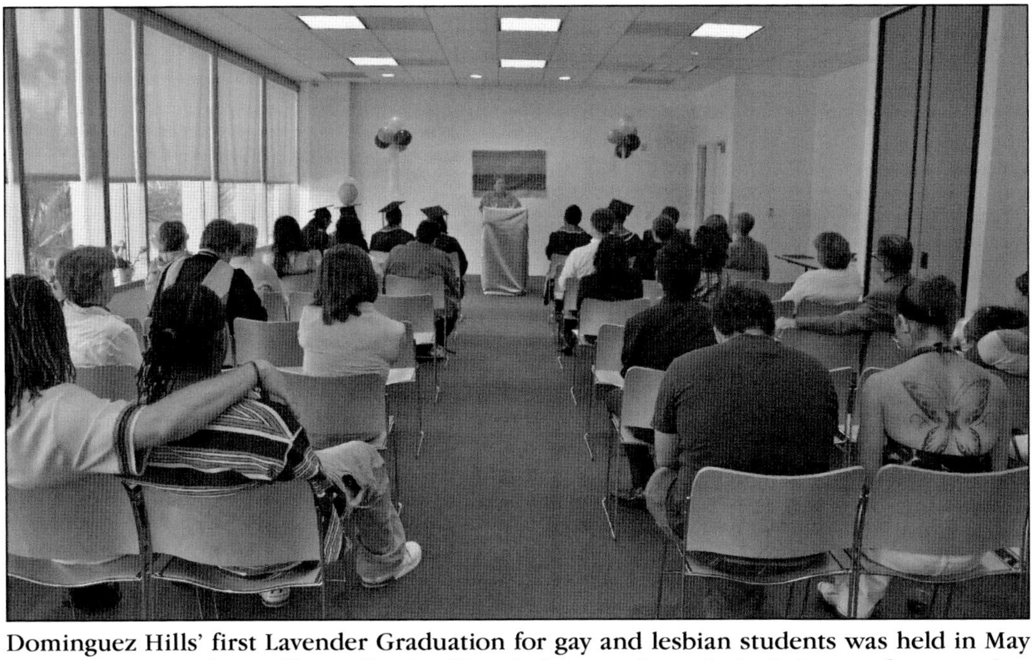

Dominguez Hills' first Lavender Graduation for gay and lesbian students was held in May 2009. Emerita professor Sharon Raphael handed the students their diplomas after speeches by several members of the CSU Dominguez Hills community.

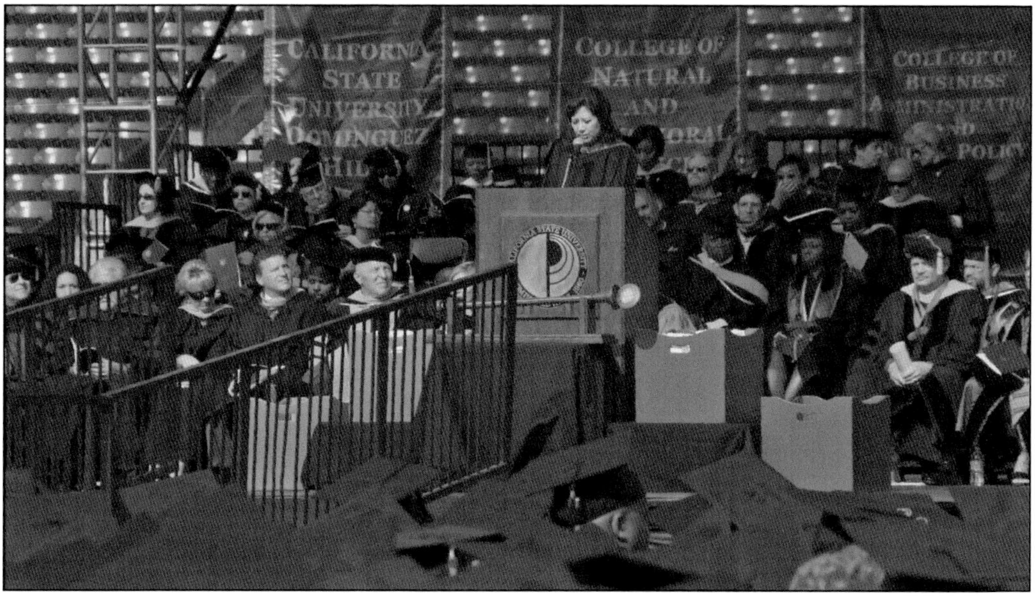

U.S. Secretary of Labor Hilda Solis addresses the 1,525 undergraduates at commencement in 2009. Speaking about her career and educational choices, the first Latina to become a cabinet secretary recalled that she had been initially encouraged to become a secretary, but instead she became the first person in her family to graduate from college. She quipped, "It's okay to be a secretary . . . a cabinet secretary in the Department of Labor."

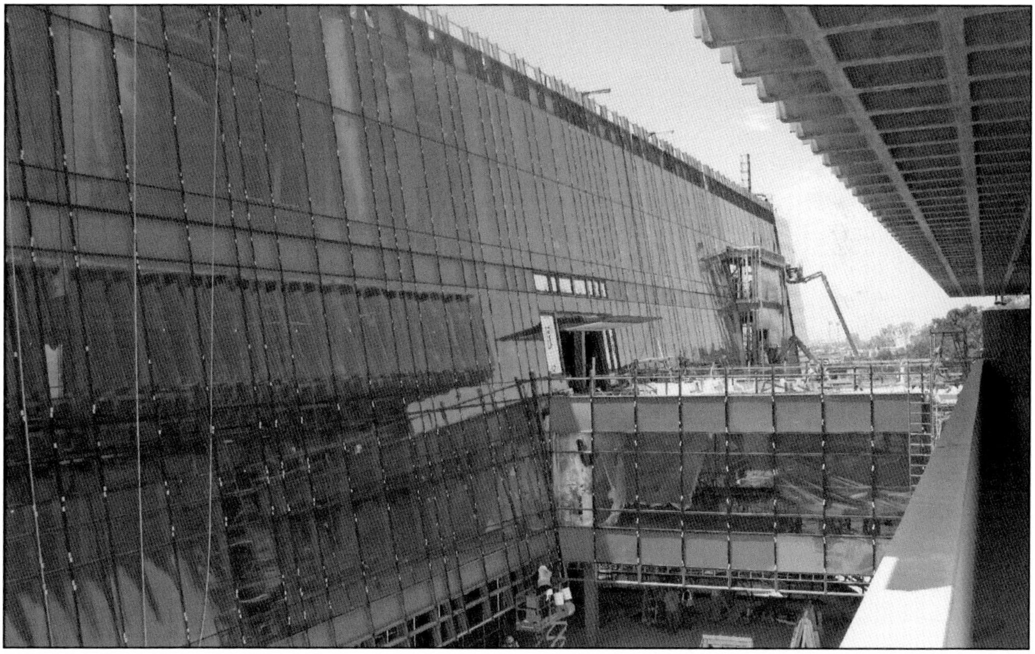

In 2010 the University Library opened a 140,000-square-foot, five-story addition. The expanded library provides 1,600 reader stations, learning labs, archival storage, 250 computer workstations, and double the space for book storage. The building, with a cost of $51 million, was funded by voters as part of two bond measures. In 1966, the state legislature set aside $42 million to build the entire first segment of CSU Dominguez Hills.

www.arcadiapublishing.com

Discover books about the town where you grew up, the cities where your friends and families live, the town where your parents met, or even that retirement spot you've been dreaming about. Our Web site provides history lovers with exclusive deals, advanced notification about new titles, e-mail alerts of author events, and much more.

MADE IN THE USA

Arcadia Publishing, the leading local history publisher in the United States, is committed to making history accessible and meaningful through publishing books that celebrate and preserve the heritage of America's people and places. Consistent with our mission to preserve history on a local level, this book was printed in South Carolina on American-made paper and manufactured entirely in the United States.

This book carries the accredited Forest Stewardship Council (FSC) label and is printed on 100 percent FSC-certified paper. Products carrying the FSC label are independently certified to assure consumers that they come from forests that are managed to meet the social, economic, and ecological needs of present and future generations.

FSC
Mixed Sources
Product group from well-managed forests and other controlled sources
Cert no. SW-COC-001530
www.fsc.org